# Oracle APEX Cookbook

## Second Edition

Create reliable, modern web applications for desktop and mobile devices with Oracle Application Express

**Marcel van der Plas**

**Michel van Zoest**

[PACKT] enterprise
PUBLISHING
professional expertise distilled

BIRMINGHAM - MUMBAI

# Oracle APEX Cookbook
## *Second Edition*

Copyright © 2013 Packt Publishing

First published: December 2010

Second Edition: October 2013

Production Reference: 1221013

Published by Packt Publishing Ltd.
Livery Place
35 Livery Street
Birmingham B3 2PB, UK.

ISBN 978-1-78217-967-2

www.packtpub.com

Cover Image by Artie Ng (artherng@yahoo.com.au)

# Credits

**Authors**

Marcel van der Plas

Michel van Zoest

**Reviewers**

Learco Brizzi

Benjamin Kweku Intsiful

Tony Jedlinski

Surachart Opun

Ronald Rood

Iloon Ellen-Wolff

**Acquisition Editor**

Kunal Parikh

**Lead Technical Editor**

Susmita Panda

**Technical Editors**

Dennis John

Adrian Raposo

Gaurav Thingalaya

**Project Coordinator**

Shiksha Chaturvedi

**Proofreader**

Elinor Perry-Smith

**Indexer**

Hemangini Bari

**Graphics**

Ronak Dhruv

**Production Coordinator**

Arvindkumar Gupta

**Cover Work**

Arvindkumar Gupta

# About the Authors

**Marcel van der Plas** was born in 1969 in Eindhoven and still lives there. He has been an Oracle Consultant for over 15 years. Marcel has worked on many projects with Oracle Designer, Oracle Forms, and Oracle Reports. Later on, he became interested in APEX and did some projects with APEX. Marcel has been working on an APEX project for an electronics company for over 2 years.

Marcel currently works for Ciber. Other companies he worked for are Atos Origin and Whitehorses. For Whitehorses, he wrote some articles (White books) about Oracle.

Marcel wrote the *Oracle APEX 4.0 Cookbook, Packt Publishing,* with Michel van Zoest. You can find APEX blogposts from Marcel at `http://orclapex.blogspot.com`. Besides that, you can follow Marcel on Twitter (`@whmvdp`).

**Michel van Zoest** is a consultant with years of experience in building web applications using Oracle technologies such as Oracle Web Forms, Oracle Designer, MOD_PLSQL, ADF, SOA Suite, and of course, APEX.

He is one of the first Oracle Application Express Developer Certified Experts in the world. He has used his APEX knowledge in projects for companies ranging in size from a single employee to large multinationals. His experience in these projects has been used in the realization of this book.

Michel currently works at Whitehorses in the Netherlands and runs his own blog at `http://www.aboutapex.com`. He also blogs at the company website on `http://blog.whitehorses.nl` and he regularly writes White book articles (in Dutch) for Whitehorses.

You can reach Michel on Twitter at `@mvzoest` or e-mail him at `michel@aboutapex.com`.

First of all, I would like to thank my co-author, Marcel van der Plas. Thanks to the easy way that we could work together, the writing of this book has gone as smooth as possible.

I would like to thank the people at Packt Publishing for offering me the chance to write this book. It has been a long process with a lot of hard work, but I'm very happy with the result. I also would like to thank Douwe Pieter van den Bos for introducing me and Marcel to Packt Publishing and his invaluable help in the early stages of the book.

Furthermore, I would like to thank all reviewers for their hard work in reviewing our drafts. This book has become so much better; thanks to you guys.

I would also like to thank my employer, Whitehorses, for the support that I have been given.

And last but not the least, I would like to thank my family for their love and support. Without the help of my wife Jamila and the "dikke kroelen" from my daughters Naomi and Aniek and my son Kris, this result would not have been possible.

# About the Reviewers

**Learco Brizzi** started working with the early versions of Oracle Forms (3.0), Reports (1.1), and Designer (1.2.1), after he received his Master of Science degree in Information Technology in 1993. When WebDB was launched, Learco took the first steps in building Internet applications. When APEX (HTML DB) hit the market, he saw the potential of this tool and built a complete music download store with it in 2004, including integration with reports and payment service providers. This was one of the very first serious applications ever built with APEX. Nowadays, Learco is dedicated to APEX and PL/SQL development.

He is a very enthusiastic technologist, trainer of advanced APEX courses, organizer of seminars, board member of the OGh (the Oracle user group in the Netherlands), and member of the editorial committee for Oracle magazine *OGh Visie*. For *OGh Visie*, he's responsible for the yearly *APEX World* event that had about 300 attendees in 2013. Since 2013, he's also a member of the APEX Feature Advisory Board.

In 1999, Learco started his own company, Itium, that specializes in Oracle technology and launched the APEX plug-in website for community APEX plug-ins: `http://www.apex-plugin.com`. He is the co-author of the book *Oracle APEX Best Practices*, published by *Packt Publishing*.

In May 2010, Learco was awarded the Oracle ACE membership.

You can contact Learco by e-mail `Lbrizzi@itium.nl` or Twitter (@LBrizzi).

**Benjamin Kweku Intsiful** is a Ghanaian-born technologist who has been working with Oracle products since the turn of the century. During his years working with the retail, government, finance, and construction sectors, Intsiful has actively researched and applied cutting-edge technologies from the Oracle product range and Microsoft paradigms.

His current tool of choice is Application Express (APEX) involved with projects, creating applications pushing the growing limits of this ever-maturing product in Africa.

He is a certified Oracle Application Express expert, which he proudly highlights in his portfolio.

Past experiences are heavy with PL/SQL, Microsoft C#, and Active Server Pages. Notable projects include Voters Management System (VMS) for the Electoral Commission of Ghana. He has participated in a core team of developers for a complex forms project at  the Nation Health Insurance Authority (NHIA) of Ghana.

He is keenly interested in researching and sharing product knowledge on new and sometimes under-utilized but useful functionality at user group events.

Occasionally you'll find him in the OTN forums, PL/SQL Challenge, and Top Coders, exhibiting his skillsets or blogging at `www.bkintsiful.blogspot.com`.

I would like to thank the Almighty God, who made this possible. I would also like to thank my mum and family for supporting me through thick nights when I was stressed, but kept me company to review this awesome book.

**Tony Jedlinski** is an accomplished professional with over 30 years' experience in database development including over 20 years' experience in designing and developing custom Oracle-based applications.

He is a recognized expert in Oracle Application Express and is Oracle Application Express Developer certified (September, 2010).

Tony is the President of Konoso LLC (www.konoso.com) and has presented technical papers on Oracle Application Express at national and international conferences, including Oracle World (2004, 2006), IOUG Live! (2004, 2005), and Collaborate 2006 - 2011, 2013. He was named HTML DB (Oracle Application Express) Developer of the Year in 2005 by Oracle Magazine.

As the Executive Vice President and Director of Web Initiatives—Independent Oracle User Group (IOUG), he led a volunteer effort to design and develop a flexible website hosting system for over 40 Regional User Groups and Special Interest Groups.

**Surachart Opun** has over 10 years' experience in Information Technology. He is a computer engineer and lives in Thailand. His interests include learning about Oracle Technology and other new technologies. He worked with Internet Service Provider Business for over 8 years. He is an Oracle ACE, Oracle 10g RAC Certified Expert, Oracle 11g Performance Tuning Certified Expert, Oracle EM12c Certified Implementation Specialist, and an Oracle 10g/11g Certified Professional.

He also has experience in implementation, migration, and management of Oracle Database in telecommunication business. He has spent time to help people who are interested in Oracle Products. He's currently planning and developing an Oracle APEX group in Thailand.

He was also the technical reviewer of the following books:

- *Oracle APEX 4.0 Cookbook, Packt Publishing*
- *Oracle APEX Best Practices, Packt Publishing*
- *Oracle Database 11g Performance Tuning Recipes: A Problem-Solution Approach, APress*

Surachart blogs at http://surachartopun.com and http://oraclethai.blogspot.com. You can reach him via Twitter (@surachart) or via LinkedIn at http://th.linkedin.com/in/surachartopun.

**Ronald Rood** is an innovating Oracle DBA with over 20 years of IT experience. He has built and managed cluster databases on about each and every platform that Oracle ever supported, from the famous OPS databases in Version 7 until the latest RAC releases, currently being 11g. Ronald is constantly looking for ways to get the most value out of the database to make the investment for his customers even more valuable. He knows how to the handle the power of the rich Unix environment very well, and this is what makes him a first class troubleshooter and solution architect. Apart from the spoken languages such as Dutch, English, German, and French, he also writes fluently in many scripting languages.

Currently Ronald is a principal consultant and Oracle ACE working for Ciber in the Netherlands where he cooperates in many complex projects for large companies where downtime is not an option. Ciber (CBR) is a global IT services company with a client-focused approach.

Ronald often likes getting involved in Oracle forums, writes his own blog (`http://ronr. blogspot.com`) called *From errors we learn...*, writes for various Oracle-related magazines and also has written a book, *Mastering Oracle Scheduler in Oracle 11g Databases*, *Packt Publishing*, where he fills the gap between the Oracle Documentation and the customers questions.

Ronald has lots of certifications, some of them are as follows:

- ▶ Oracle Certified Master
- ▶ Oracle Certified Professional
- ▶ Oracle Database 11g Tuning Specialist
- ▶ Oracle Database 11g Data Warehouse Certified Implementation Specialist

Ronald fills his time with Oracle, his family, sky-diving, radio-controlled model airplane flying, running a scouting group, and having a lot of fun.

*"A problem is merely a challenge that might take a little time to solve"*

**-Ronald Rood**

**Iloon Ellen-Wolff** started working with Oracle products 22 years ago, employed by several software houses in the Netherlands.

His experience goes back to Oracle Forms Version 2 and Report Writer. Almost 15 years ago, he started working for Oracle Support Services for the Developer competency (Oracle Forms, Oracle Reports and Application Express, APEX Listener, SQL*Plus, SQL Developer, and Oracle Database Service Cloud) assisting customers with solving their software problems.

During those years, he applied his gained knowledge in other ways such as in coaching new engineers, team leading, and teaching Application Express courses for Oracle University.

From the last two years, he is involved in the Oracle Cloud project. He is a member of the Platform as a Service readiness team and is involved in testing Application Express in the cloud and being a trainer in this area (Foundation Trainer).

One of his responsibilities in Oracle Support is Global Technical Lead Application Express. He works closely with Sustaining Engineering, Product Development, and Product Management from the Application Express team.

He is a frequent speaker for different Oracle User Groups (UKOUG, Dutch User Group, Norway User Group, Bulgaria User Group, and OBUG), and talks about Application Express and SQL Developer. He is also an Oak Table member since September, 2013 (http://www.oaktable.net/).

He is a specialist in the following areas:

- Database Service Cloud (PaaS)
- Application Express
- Apex Listener
- Oracle Forms
- SQL Developer
- Fusion Middleware Release 11/12

He has also co-authored the book *Oracle APEX Best Practices, Packt Publishing* (more information can be found at http://www.amazon.com/Oracle-APEX-Best-Practices-Nuijten/product-reviews/1849684006/ref=dp_top_cm_cr_acr_txt?showViewpoints=1).

He also blogs at http://iloonellen.blogspot.com.

# www.PacktPub.com

## Support files, eBooks, discount offers and more

You might want to visit www.PacktPub.com for support files and downloads related to your book.

Did you know that Packt offers eBook versions of every book published, with PDF and ePub files available? You can upgrade to the eBook version at www.PacktPub.com and as a print book customer, you are entitled to a discount on the eBook copy. Get in touch with us at service@packtpub.com for more details.

At www.PacktPub.com, you can also read a collection of free technical articles, sign up for a range of free newsletters and receive exclusive discounts and offers on Packt books and eBooks.

http://PacktLib.PacktPub.com

Do you need instant solutions to your IT questions? PacktLib is Packt's online digital book library. Here, you can access, read and search across Packt's entire library of books.

## Why Subscribe?

- ▸ Fully searchable across every book published by Packt
- ▸ Copy and paste, print and bookmark content
- ▸ On demand and accessible via web browser

## Free Access for Packt account holders

If you have an account with Packt at www.PacktPub.com, you can use this to access PacktLib today and view nine entirely free books. Simply use your login credentials for immediate access.

## Instant Updates on New Packt Books

Get notified! Find out when new books are published by following @PacktEnterprise on Twitter, or the *Packt Enterprise* Facebook page.

# Table of Contents

# Preface

Oracle Application Express is a rapid web application development tool that works with the Oracle database. Using features such as plug-ins and dynamic actions, APEX helps you build applications with the latest techniques in AJAX and JavaScript.

*Oracle APEX Cookbook, Second Edition*, shows you how to to develop and deploy reliable, modern, responsive web applications using only a web browser and limited programming experience.

With recipes covering many different topics, it will show you how to use the many features of APEX.

You will learn how to create simple web pages with forms and reports, and how to enhance the look of your applications by using style sheets. You will see how you can integrate things such as Tag Clouds, Google Maps, web services, and much more in your applications. Using plug-ins, dynamic actions, BI Publisher, Translations, and websheets, you will be able to enhance your applications to a new level in APEX.

You will learn how to enhance some of the visual aspects of your applications and use modern web browser techniques by implementing HTML5 and CSS3. The book explains how to build applications for mobile devices such as smartphones and tablets in APEX by using built-in techniques and enhancing them with features from the jQuery Mobile framework.

This book will show you how to be agile in the development of your web applications by using team development, debugging, and third-party tools.

After reading this book, you will be able to create feature-rich web and mobile applications in Application Express with ease and confidence.

# What this book covers

*Chapter 1, Creating a Basic APEX Application*, describes the basic steps to create an APEX application. We will learn to make an intranet application where employees can get information.

*Chapter 2, Themes and Templates*, presents some recipes which will make your application look better using themes and templates by creating your own theme, including images in it and so on.

*Chapter 3, Extending APEX*, shows us how to extend our applications with some nice features such as visual effects, a tag cloud, a Google map, and a data upload page.

*Chapter 4, Creating Websheet Applications*, teaches us how to create a websheet application, create a page in the application, add a navigation page to the websheet, and allow multiple users to access the websheet.

*Chapter 5, APEX Plug-ins*, describes five types of plug-ins: Item type, Region type, Dynamic Action type, Process type, and Authorization type.

*Chapter 6,* Creating *Multilingual APEX Applications*, shows us how we can fully translate an application using built-in functionalities to translate applications, without having to rebuild the application completely and adding something of our own to easily switch between languages.

*Chapter 7, APEX APIs*, shows us how to use APIs as they offer a lot of flexibility and speed in developing web applications.

*Chapter 8, Using Web Services*, teaches us how to use web services in APEX and how to publish a REST web service.

*Chapter 9, Publishing from APEX*, shows us how to export reports, get the output in some kind of digital format, and how to interact with BI Publisher.

*Chapter 10, APEX Environment*, contains recipes that will show how to set up and use a development environment, how to use version control, and how to deploy Application Express on a web container with the APEX Listener. Furthermore, it explains how to use error handling and how to use packaged applications.

*Chapter 11, APEX Administration*, shows you how to create a workspace, how to create users on the workspace, how to manage the workspaces, and a recipe to create table APIs.

*Chapter 12, Team Development*, explains how we can take advantage of the features in team development in our project. Each recipe will show how a part of team development can be put to use in a specific part of the project cycle.

*Chapter 13, HTML5 and CSS3*, contains recipes that show how to use modern web browser techniques by implementing HTML5 and CSS3.

*Chapter 14, APEX Mobile*, shows recipes to create a web application for mobile devices by using the jQuery Mobile templates. Features such as auto-detecting a mobile device, swiping, list view reports, and items such as a slider will all be discussed in this chapter.

# What you need for this book

APEX 4.0 or higher, and for some recipes, APEX 4.2 is required.

Oracle RDBMS database 10.2.0.3 or higher is also required.

Any one of the following Internet browsers:

- Microsoft Internet Explorer 7 or later
- Mozilla Firefox 3.5 or later
- Google Chrome 4.0 or later
- Apple Safari 4.0 or later

# Who this book is for

This book is aimed both at developers new to the APEX environment and at intermediate developers. More advanced developers will also benefit from the information at hand.

If you are new to APEX, you will find recipes to start development. If you are an experienced user, you will find ways to work smarter and more easily with APEX and enhance your applications.

A little knowledge of PL/SQL, HTML, and JavaScript is assumed.

# Conventions

In this book, you will find a number of styles of text that distinguish between different kinds of information. Here are some examples of these styles, and an explanation of their meaning.

Code words in text, database table names, folder names, filenames, file extensions, pathnames, dummy URLs, user input, and Twitter handles are shown as follows: "Again, we create a select list like before and name it P15_EMPLOYEES."

A block of code is set as follows:

```
begin
  dbms_network_acl_admin.create_acl (acl          => 'acl_user.xml'
  ,description => 'Description'
  ,principal   => 'APEX_040000'
  ,is_grant    => true
  ,privilege   => 'connect'
  ,start_date  => null
```

```
   ,end_date     => null);
   --
   DBMS_NETWORK_ACL_ADMIN.ADD_PRIVILEGE(acl           =>
     'acl_user.xml'
   ,principal => 'APEX_040000'
   ,is_grant  => true
   ,privilege => 'resolve');
   --
   DBMS_NETWORK_ACL_ADMIN.ASSIGN_ACL(acl   => 'acl_user.xml'
   ,host => 'name of website or host, i.e. soap.amazon.com');
   --
   commit;
end;
```

**New terms** and **important words** are shown in bold. Words that you see on the screen, in menus or dialog boxes for example, appear in the text like this: "At the **Create Application** radio group, leave this option to **From Scratch**."

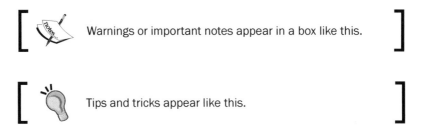

Warnings or important notes appear in a box like this.

Tips and tricks appear like this.

# Reader feedback

Feedback from our readers is always welcome. Let us know what you think about this book—what you liked or may have disliked. Reader feedback is important for us to develop titles that you really get the most out of.

To send us general feedback, simply send an e-mail to feedback@packtpub.com, and mention the book title via the subject of your message.

If there is a topic that you have expertise in and you are interested in either writing or contributing to a book, see our author guide on www.packtpub.com/authors.

# Customer support

Now that you are the proud owner of a Packt book, we have a number of things to help you to get the most from your purchase.

# Downloading the example code

You can download the example code files for all Packt books you have purchased from your account at `http://www.packtpub.com`. If you purchased this book elsewhere, you can visit `http://www.packtpub.com/support` and register to have the files e-mailed directly to you.

# Errata

Although we have taken every care to ensure the accuracy of our content, mistakes do happen. If you find a mistake in one of our books—maybe a mistake in the text or the code—we would be grateful if you would report this to us. By doing so, you can save other readers from frustration and help us improve subsequent versions of this book. If you find any errata, please report them by visiting `http://www.packtpub.com/submit-errata`, selecting your book, clicking on the **errata submission form** link, and entering the details of your errata. Once your errata are verified, your submission will be accepted and the errata will be uploaded on our website, or added to any list of existing errata, under the Errata section of that title. Any existing errata can be viewed by selecting your title from `http://www.packtpub.com/support`.

# Piracy

Piracy of copyright material on the Internet is an ongoing problem across all media. At Packt, we take the protection of our copyright and licenses very seriously. If you come across any illegal copies of our works, in any form, on the Internet, please provide us with the location address or website name immediately so that we can pursue a remedy.

Please contact us at `copyright@packtpub.com` with a link to the suspected pirated material.

We appreciate your help in protecting our authors, and our ability to bring you valuable content.

# Questions

You can contact us at `questions@packtpub.com` if you are having a problem with any aspect of the book, and we will do our best to address it.

# 1
# Creating a Basic APEX Application

In this chapter we will cover the following topics:

- ► Creating an APEX 4.0 application
- ► Creating a simple form page
- ► Creating a simple report page
- ► Implementing an interactive report
- ► Creating a chart
- ► Creating a map chart
- ► Creating a navigation bar
- ► Creating a list of values
- ► Including different item types
- ► Protecting a page using an authorization scheme
- ► Securing an application with Authentication
- ► Controlling the display of regions and items with Dynamic Actions
- ► Creating a computation
- ► Creating an automated row fetch with a page process
- ► Putting some validation in a form
- ► Creating a report with PL/SQL Dynamic Content

# Introduction

This chapter describes the basic steps to create an APEX application. Using APEX, it is really simple to create a basic application. The user interface is web-based and very intuitive. A lot of objects can be created using wizards which will guide you through the creation process.

Our aim is to make an intranet application where employees can get information. When starting the application, it shows a homepage with information such as weather, traffic company information, latest news, blogs, and so on. Employees can see their colleagues' profiles, just like in Facebook. Employees also have access to documents such as timesheets and project plans.

# Creating an APEX 4.0 application

This recipe describes the tasks needed to create an APEX 4.0 application. You should have APEX 4.0 installed or have an account on Oracle's online APEX environment at `http://apex.oracle.com` and your web browser should be a modern browser like Microsoft Internet Explorer 7 or higher or Mozilla Firefox 1.0 or later. The starting point is the **Oracle Application Express** home page:

## How to do it...

1. Click on the Application Builder icon on the left-hand side of the screen.

   You will see a page where you can choose between database applications or websheet applications. Furthermore, you see already created applications.

2. Click on the **Create** button on the right-hand side of the screen. Two options are shown. You can now choose between a database application and a websheet application. We select the database application.

   In APEX you have two ways of selecting and proceeding to the next step most of the time. Usually, there is an icon accompanied by a radio button. When you check the radio button, you must then click on the **Next** button to proceed. When you click on the icon, you automatically go to the next step. In this book, when there is the situation that you have to select one of the shown options, we will only tell which one of the options you should select. You can decide for yourself which way to select and proceed:

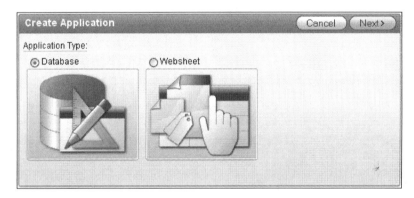

3. Select **Database**.

4. In the next step we can now choose between **From Scratch**, **From Spreadsheet**, and **Demonstration Application**. When you choose **Demonstration Application**, Oracle APEX creates an application which shows the possibilities of APEX. However, we want to create an application by ourselves, and we can install this demonstration application at a later time. For now, we select **"From Scratch"**.

5. Enter a name and an application ID . Preferably choose a name which covers the goal of the application. In our case, we call the application `Intranet`.

6. Application ID is a generated and unique identification number, but you can also use some other number for your convenience.

7. At the **Create Application** radio group, leave this option to **From Scratch**.

8. Finally, select the schema where the tables that you want to use for your application will reside and click on **Next**.

   The next step in the wizard is selecting pages. You can start with a blank page and, from that starting point, extend your APEX application. You can also choose to add reports and forms beforehand. At this point you don't actually define the content of the pages, you just create the "skeleton" of them.

9. We choose to add one blank page and proceed to the next step.

10. Now you can choose to include tabs in your application. Tabs are components that help you navigate through the application. For now, we are not going to use tabs, so select **No Tabs**.

The next step is the option to copy shared components from another application. **Shared components** are objects that can be used throughout the application, for example, a list of values or images. Because we create a simple application from scratch, we don't want to copy shared components from another application. Select **No**.

An **authentication scheme** is a means of allowing users access to our application. APEX offers different methods for this. More will be explained in another recipe. The scheme for this application will be selected in the next step.

1. Select the standard Application Express authentication scheme.

2. You can select the language used in your application, as well as where the user language should be derived from.

3. The last option in this step is the date format mask. Click on the **LOV** button next to the text item to get a list with possible date format masks and select one.

4. The last step in the wizard is the theme. Theme 1 and Theme 2 are basic themes. If you don't like all those colors, just select something like Theme 18. That is quite a simple theme.

5. We select **Theme 1** and that completes the **Create Page** wizard.

Now that we have completed the wizard, we can click on the **Create** button to confirm. The application will be created and we will see a number of pages, depending on how many pages we already created in step 6.

**Downloading the example code**

You can download the example code files for all Packt books you have purchased from your account at http://www.packtpub.com. If you purchased this book elsewhere, you can visit http://www.packtpub.com/support and register to have the files e-mailed directly to you

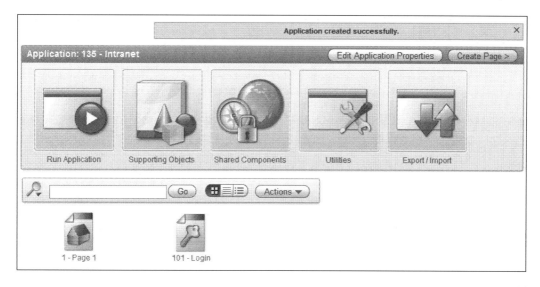

Depending on the type of authentication, we will also see page **101—Login**. This is the default page APEX navigates to when you run an application using authentication. It is generated automatically with all functionalities to allow users to log in to our application.

Click on the large **Run Application** button to go to the login page.

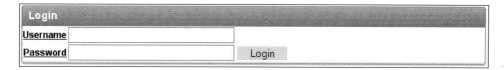

We can log in on this page with the same credentials we use to gain access to the APEX development environment. So enter this username and password and click on the **Login** button.

Well, that's it! We've created and run our first Oracle APEX 4.0 application. We can now click on the pages to define them, or we can add new pages to extend our application. We can also click on the Run Application icon to see what has actually been created. Since we only included an empty page, we will see something like this—an empty application except for a single, also empty page:

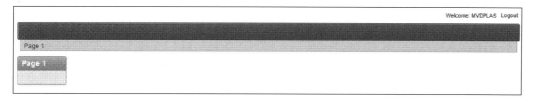

## How it works...

We have just created our first application. Even though it's just an empty shell, this is the starting point for all APEX applications. Creating content for our application is a whole different story and will be explained in the following recipes.

# Creating a simple form page

After you have created the application, it is time to create one or more forms and reports. First let's get started with a simple form. We will build a tabular form with insert, update, and delete possibilities.

## Getting ready

Make sure that the table our form is based on contains a Primary Key and a sequence to update the Primary Key. In this case, we will be using the EMP table, so we have to make sure it is available in our database schema.

Also, we have to make sure the application that we created in the previous recipe is available.

## How to do it...

The starting point for this recipe is the overview of the intranet application we created in the previous recipe.

1. Click on the **Create Page** button.

2. You will get an overview of page types. Select **Form**.

3. Now you get an overview of types of forms, such as forms based on a procedure, forms based on a table or view, or forms based on a query. Select **Tabular** form.

4. The next step is to choose the table owner and the allowed operations. Here you can decide what your form should do: update only, update and insert, update and delete, or all operations (update, insert, and delete). Select all operations.

5. Select the table or view your form should be based on. If you know the table name, you can type it in the text field. Otherwise, click on the button next to the field and select a table from the pop-up list. We choose the employees table, EMP.

6. Now you can select the columns, which should be visible in the form. You can select columns by clicking on the column while holding the *Ctrl* key. To select all columns, you can click on the first column and drag your mouse to the last column.

7. If a Primary Key constraint is defined on the table we use, then it will automatically be selected. Otherwise, select the primary key by hand. APEX needs to know this to be able to update the changed rows.

8. Next, you can choose which way the Primary Key is automatically filled. Maybe you created a trigger which updates the Primary Key in case it is empty. However, we choose to update the Primary Key via an existing sequence. Select this option, and in the following listbox, select the appropriate sequence and proceed to the next step.

9. Next, you can select which columns in the form should be updatable. Select the desired columns and click on **Next**.

10. In this step, you can give the page a name and a page ID. Furthermore, you can specify a region title, a region template, a report template and decide if your forms page should contain breadcrumbs. A **breadcrumb** is a navigation component that shows the path to the current page. Leave the options as they are and click on **Next**.

11. We are not going to use tabs, so leave this option on its default selection and click on **Next**.

12. Next, fill in the names that should appear on the buttons in the form and click next.

13. In this step, you must define the branches. **Branches** are links to other pages. It is important to know which ID a page had in order to fill in the branches at this point. Usually, the **Cancel** button branches to the main page of the application. But it's also possible to find the page to branch to by using the **LOV** button. For the **Page Submit** branch, select the page ID assigned to the page we want to branch to. Click on **Next**.

14. The last step in the wizard is the confirmation page. Check the data. If something is wrong, you can go back using the **Previous** button. Otherwise, click on the **Finish** button.

The form will be created and here you can choose to run the form to see how it looks or you can edit the form to define things. When running the form, it should look like the following:

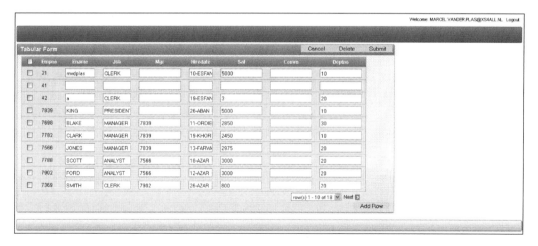

## How it works...

A tabular form is actually an updateable report. In the **Region** section, you can find the query that populates the data to show on the screen. By default, every row of the table is shown. We can restrict the result set by adding a `where` clause to this query.

When we edit the page, m we can see that the wizard created the four buttons and the processes for the data manipulation language (DML). The tree view shows an overview of the components the page is built up of. On the left-hand side we can see the components used for the rendering of the page (**Regions**, **Items**, and so on). It is built up in such a way that we can see the order of the components that are rendered when the page is loaded.

The middle section shows the components used for the processes on the page; in this case, these are validations, data manipulation, and branching. The right-hand side section shows an overview of all shared components used on this page, if any are available.

We can right-click on any component in the tree view to see the possible actions for that component:

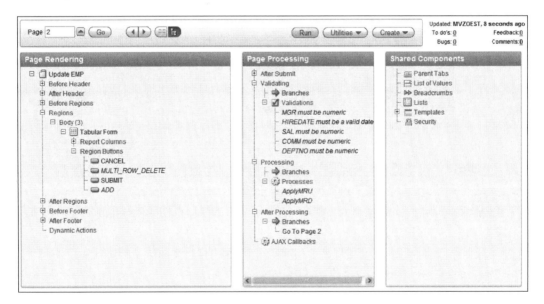

You can see that there are two multirow update processes. The first one is triggered by the Submit button and updates the changed rows. The **Add Rows** button initiates two processes: the second multirow update process and the add rows process. So, actually the **Add Rows** button submits the changes the user made so far and after that it creates an empty row.

The delete button initiates a JavaScript process that asks the user for confirmation. And this confirmation starts the delete process. This JavaScript function can be found in the **HTML header** section of the page properties.

## There's more...

You can also make a simple single record form. Here's how to do it.

In the **Application Builder**, click on the created application.

1. Click on **Create page**.
2. Click on the form icon.
3. Click on the form in the table or view.
4. Select the schema where the employees table resides and click on **Next**.
5. Enter the table name (in this case, it is EMP) and click on **Next**.
6. In the page number and page name dialogs, just leave the settings as they are and click on **Next**.
7. Select **Do not use tabs** and click on **Next**.
8. Select the Primary Key and click on **Next**.
9. Select **Existing** and select the desired sequence name in the listbox. Click on **Next**.
10. Select all of the columns and click on **Next**.
11. Change the button labels or leave them as they are and click on **Next**.
12. Enter the page numbers APEX should call when submitting or cancelling and click on **Next**.
13. In the confirmation dialog, click on **Finish**.
14. In the success message dialog, click on **Edit**.

# Creating a simple report

In our application we would also like to have an overview of all employees in the company. We can get this overview by creating a report. There are several types of reports and we just start with a simple report based on a query.

## Getting ready

The starting point is our created application. You need an existing table, like EMP.

## How to do it...

1.  In the **Application Builder**, go to the application we just created and click on the **Create Page** button.

2.  In the **Page Type** dialog, select **Report**.

3.  A page is shown where we can choose between the different types of reports. Options are: interactive reports, classic reports, reports based on a web service result, and wizard reports. We will choose classic reports.

    Some of the other types of reports will be covered in other recipes in this book. The next recipe is on interactive reports. In *Chapter 8, Using Web Services*, some examples of building reports on web services are explained. The **Wizard Report** option is not explained separately, because it just offers an easier, step-by-step way of building a report.

4.  In the next step you can assign a page number and a page name to the report. Furthermore, you can indicate whether you would like to have breadcrumbs on your report page. Leave the **Breadcrumb** option to **Do not use breadcrumbs on page** and click on **Next**.

5.  In this step you can choose to include tabs in your report page. We leave it to **Do not use tabs**. Click on **Next**.

6.  In this step you must enter a query in the textarea. You can use the Query Builder to help you build your query or you can also enter it manually. We use the following query:

    ```
    select *
      from emp
    ```

7.  After you have entered the query, click on **Next**.

8.  In the next step, you can define a report template, the region name, a number of rows displayed per page, and whether the user should be able to print the report on paper or spool it to a comma-separated file. Leave the options as they are and click on **Next**.

9.  In the last step, you see the confirmation page. If the choices made are not satisfactory, click on the **Previous** button to go back and modify the options. Otherwise, click on the **Finish** button.

The report is ready now. You can edit the report to define the settings or you can run the report to see how it looks. The result should be something like the following:

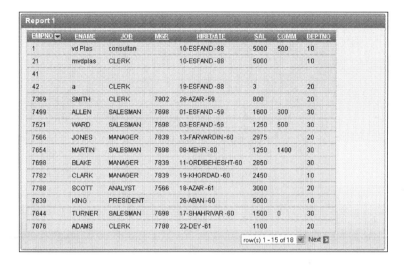

## How it works...

When you look at the page in the **Application Builder**, you will see that APEX created a **Reports** region.

1.  Right-click on the region name of the report and click on **Edit** to see the details of the report.
2.  In the **Region** source you can see the query you just entered. If you want to see the column details, click on the **Report Attributes** tab:

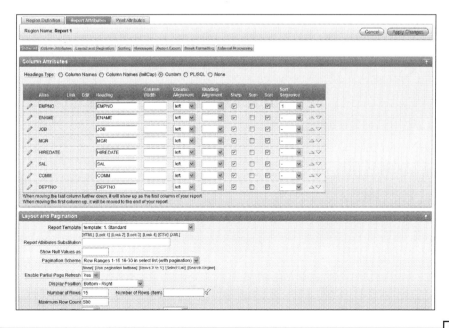

3. Here you can modify the column heading, the heading alignment, or the names of the columns. To get more into details about a column you can click on the pencil icon next to the column name.

   Sometimes in a project, the business case for a report changes. Instead of a classic report, the customer would like an interactive report. In case there are two options, remove the **Current Report** region and create a new one based on an interactive report or just migrate the current report using built-in functionalities.

   When we are looking at the **Region Definition** tab of the **Edit Region** page, we can see a **Tasks** list on the right-hand side of the screen. One of the options is **Migrate to Interactive Report**. This migration is not a Holy Grail, but can save a lot of time in the migration process.

4. Click on the **Migrate to Interactive Report** link.

5. In the following page, enter EMPNO in the **Unique Column** field and click on the **Migrate** button to see what happens.

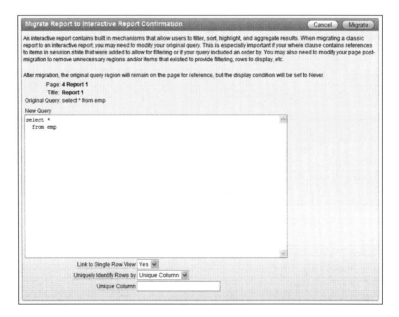

In the tree view of the page, we can see that the old **Report** region still exists but it's labeled **Disabled**. The new interactive report is added as we can see it in the following screenshot:

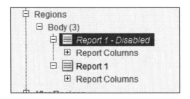

More on interactive reports is explained in the following recipe.

## See also

▶ *Chapter 8, Using Web Services* explains (among many other things) how to create a report on web service references.

# Implementing an interactive report

In this recipe, we are going to create an interactive report and show you how to use it. An interactive report is a special kind of report, which offers a lot of options to the user for filtering, sorting, publishing, and much more.

## Getting ready

It's always a good idea to start by creating a view that already selects all columns you want to show in your report. This simplifies the query required for your report region and separates the logic from presentation in your application architecture.

In this recipe, we are going to base the interactive report on the APP_VW_CONTACTS view that joins the tables for contacts, addresses, and communications. The query for this view is as follows:

```
select ctt.firstname
     , ctt.lastname
     , ctt.contact_type
     , ads.address_type
     , ads.address_line1
     , ads.address_line2
     , ads.postcode
     , ads.city
     , ads.state
     , ads.country
     , aac.default_yn
     , cct.id contact_id
     , ads.id address_id
  from app_contacts ctt
     , app_addresses ads
     , app_ads_ctt aac
 where aac.ctt_id = ctt.id
   and aac.ads_id = ads.id
[9672_01_01.txt]
```

We will also need a named LOV later on in the recipe. To create it, follow the next steps:

1. Go to **Shared Components** and then to **Lists of Values**.

2. Click on **Create** to make a new LOV.

3. Create it from scratch and call it ADDRESS_TYPE; it should be a dynamic LOV.

4. The query that it's based on is as follows:

```
select rv_meaning display_value
     , rv_low_value return_value
  from app_ref_codes
 where rv_domain = 'ADDRESSES'
[9672_01_02.txt]
```

## How to do it...

The starting point for this recipe is an empty page, so the first thing that we're going to do is create a new region to contain the interactive report.

1. Create a new region by right-clicking on the **Regions** label and selecting **Create**:

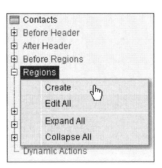

2. Select **Report** as the type of region.

3. Then select **Interactive Report** as the report implementation.

4. Give the region a title **Contacts**.

5. Select the value for **Region Template APEX 4.0 – Reports Region**. Keep the default values in the other fields.

6. As the source for the region, enter the SQL Query:

```
SELECT *
  FROM app_vw_contacts
[9672_01_03.txt]
```

7. Leave the other options with the default values.

8. Click on **Create Region** to finish this part of the recipe.

As you can see in the tree view, we now have a new region with all columns from the view:

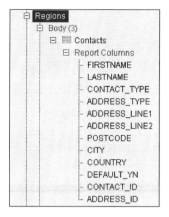

When we run the page now, we can already see some data. APEX also generated a toolbar above the report that we can use to filter data or change the way it is presented:

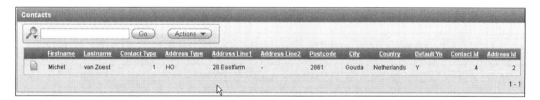

The next step is to alter the report, so we can customize the column labels and change the way some of the data is presented.

9.  In the tree view of **Page Definition**, right-click on the **Contacts** region and select **Report Attributes** from the pull-down menu.

10. Change the heading for the columns:

    ❏ **Firstname** as `First Name`

    ❏ **Lastname** as `Last Name`

    ❏ **Default Yn** as `Default Address?`

11. Click on **Apply Changes** to confirm the following changes.

    This changes the labels for some of the columns in the report. Next, we will change the presentation of the data inside one of the columns.

12. Expand the tree view to show the content of **Report Columns** of the **Contacts** region.

13. Right-click on `ADDRESS_TYPE` and click on **Edit**.

14. Change the item **Display Text As** to `Display as Text` (based on LOV and escape special characters).

15. Under **List of Values**, select **Use Named List of Values to Filter Exact Match** from the pull-down **Column Filter List of Values**.

16. Select **ADDRESS_TYPE** as the value of **Named List of Values**.

17. Click **Apply Changes**.

When we take a look at the page by clicking on we can see the changes to the column names and the **Address Type** no longer shows the abbreviation, but the full text:

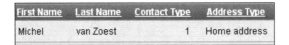

| First Name | Last Name | Contact Type | Address Type |
|---|---|---|---|
| Michel | van Zoest | 1 | Home address |

## There's more...

After the developer is done with creating an interactive report, the user will have a host of possibilities in the action menu to change the way the information is presented and filtered. These possibilities can be granted or revoked by the developer to an extent.

To see these options, right-click on the region and click on the option named **Edit region attributes**. When scrolling down this screen, you can see there are two sections: **Search Bar** and **Download**:

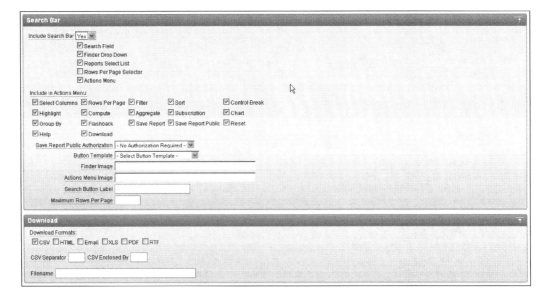

The first section holds the options that can be used in the **Search Bar**. When a user clicks on the **Action** button in the **Search Bar**, a menu will unfold revealing all the possible options. Data can be filtered, sorted, highlighted, and aggregated for instance. It's also possible for the user to generate a chart.

They can even save the changes made to the report for personal or public use, so other users can benefit as well:

The second section holds the file types that can be used to download the information in the interactive report. These include well-known formats such as CSV, PDF, and XLS:

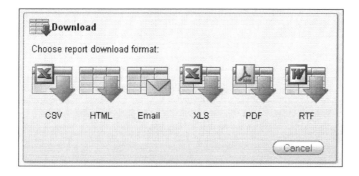

# Creating a chart

In many reports it's required to show some (or all) of the figures in charts. This will give users the opportunity to quickly see the data and possibly take actions accordingly.

This recipe will show how to create a chart and some possibilities to configure them.

## Getting ready

In the earlier recipes, we created the regions while building a new page. Of course, it's also possible to add regions on existing pages. To do so in this example, first prepare an empty page which will hold the region with the chart.

## How to do it...

1. Create a new region by right-clicking on the **Regions** label and choose **Create**.
2. Select **Chart** and click on **Next**.
3. Choose **Flash chart** and click on **Next**.
4. Select **Pie & Doughnut** and click on **Next**.
5. Select **3D Pie** and click on **Next**.
6. Enter **Employees in a department** in the title, leave the other fields with the default values and click on **Next**.
7. Enter **Employees in a department** in the **Chart** title, leave the other fields the default values and click on **Next**.

   We are going to select all employees per department, so we will enter a query that will get us that data into the chart.

8. Enter the following query into the SQL Query field:

```
select null link
     , dept.name label
     , COUNT(emp.ID) value1
  from APP_EMPLOYEES emp
     , APP_DEPARTMENTS dept
 where emp.dept_id = dept.id
 group by dept.name
[9672_01_04.txt]
```

9. Click on **Create Region**.
10. Run the page.

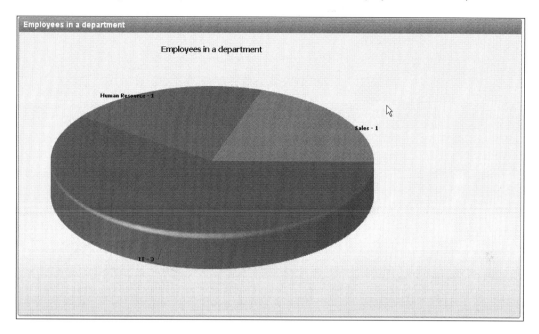

## There's more...

There are a number of possibilities to change and enhance this chart. Besides the 3D pie we have created here, there are dozens of other chart types. But there is a catch. Once a chart is created, the number of types it can be changed to is limited. When we would like to use a completely different chart type, the chart region has to be re-created.

This recipe can be easily expanded with a link to another page which can be clicked inside the chart.

To do this, first navigate to the **Chart Series** by expanding the tree view under the **Chart** region or by clicking on the edit link in the chart properties page. Edit the query on which the chart is based and change the first column. If we, for example, would have a page with ID 888, a query with a link to that page would look like the following:

```
select 'f?p=&APP_ID.:888:&APP_SESSION.:::NO::P888_DEPT_ID:'||dept.id
link
     , dept.name label
     , COUNT(emp.ID) value1
  from APP_EMPLOYEES emp
     , APP_DEPARTMENTS dept
 where emp.dept_id = dept.id
 group by dept.name, dept.id
[9672_01_05.txt]
```

We have chosen to show a dynamically generated link here. A few of the parameters need an explanation:

- ▸ `APP_ID` is the ID for this application.
- ▸ `APP_SESSION` is the ID for the current session.
- ▸ `P888_DEPT_ID` is the fictitious item on page 888 that holds the `dept_id`.

It is also possible to create a link by altering the **Action Link** region on the **Chart Series** page. The same items will be filled by this process, but it is easier to use when it is a relatively simple application:

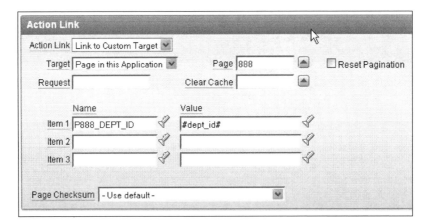

# Creating a map chart

A new type of chart available in Application Express 4.0 is the map chart. This allows users to present data on a geographical map. APEX 4.0 offers many maps from a world overview to maps of single countries.

Map charts allow applications a new way to visualize location-related data without much programming.

In this recipe, we will show you how to create a map that lists all contacts in the United States by state.

## Getting ready

First we need to have a structure ready in our database tables that holds at least one geography-related column (for example, country, state, or province names). This will be the pointer for our chart to which it can relate its map.

For this recipe, we will reuse the `APP_VW_CONTACTS` view. This view holds a column called `STATE` that we can use in our chart.

## How to do it...

Our starting point is again an empty page. The first thing to do is to add a new region.

1.  Right-click on **Regions** and select **Create**.

2.  Select **Map** as the **Region Type**.

    This will bring up a window with a couple of main categories of maps. Selecting one of these categories will bring up a list of sub categories that can be drilled down even further.

3.  Select **United States of America** and click on **Next**:

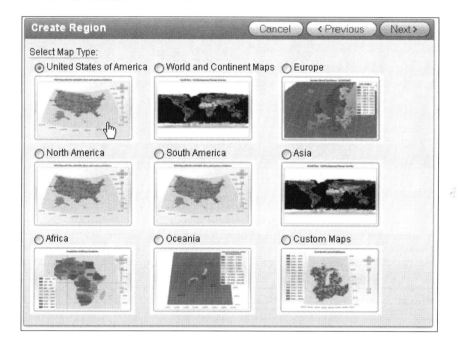

4.  In the following list select click on the **+** sign to open **Country Maps** and click on **States**:

5.  Enter **Contacts by State** for the title and leave the rest with their default values and click on **Next**.

6.  Enter the same text as the **Map Title**.

7.  Enter the following query in the appropriate SQL Query area:

```
select null link
     , STATE label
     , COUNT(CONTACT_ID) value
  from  APP_VW_CONTACTS
 group by STATE
[9672_01_06.txt]
```

8.  Click on **Create Region**.

9.  Run the page to see the result:

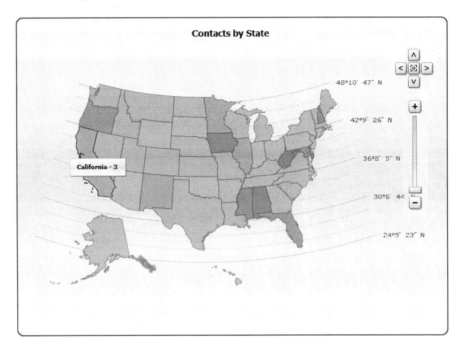

As we can see, each state that contains one or more contacts is highlighted. APEX also generates labels containing the state name and number of contacts if there is room for it. The other labels can be viewed by hovering over the state with the mouse pointer.

## How it works...

Application Express uses AnyChart 5 for displaying its charts. This is different from earlier versions of APEX, so migrating applications that make use of charts from Version 3.x to 4.0 is a little more complicated than migrating other functionalities.

When using a Map chart it is important that a column for the label is used that contains the name of the geographical region that you want highlighted on the map. For the standard maps provided by APEX, it's not allowed to use abbreviations, but it has to be the full name (for example, New York instead of NY and Virginia instead of VA).

## There's more...

Just like any other chart type, it is possible to create links to other pages. This can be used to create, for instance, a drill-down type of structure. We could create a series of pages from a world map, to a continent map, to a country map, and so forth.

How such a link can be created is explained in the chart recipe before this one.

# Creating a navigation bar

The navigation bar is the area of an APEX application that is normally placed into the header of each page (unless the template is changed of course). As a standard, the Logout link is provided here, so users can quickly log out of the application from any page.

This recipe will show how a navigation bar can be customized. This will allow users to quickly reach certain pages in the application.

## Getting ready

In this recipe we are going to see how you can create a quick link to a contact page. Before we can do that, we first need to have this page ready.

1. Create a new blank page. Name it `Contact` and assign page ID `999` to it.
2. Create a new HTML region on this page and enter the following text into it:

   ```
   For more information send an e-mail to info@packtpublishing.com
   ```

   For the second part of the recipe, we need an icon available. This can be any available icon as long as it measures 32 x 32 pixels. The `Images` directory of APEX offers some examples such as `fndtip11.gif`.

3. Go to **Shared Components**.
4. Click on **Images**.
5. Click on **Create**.
6. Select your application.
7. Select the image `fndtip11.gif` on your filesystem by using the **Browse** button.

8. Click on **Upload**.

   Furthermore, check your page template. In the **Navigation Bar Entry** section you should see at least the tags for image, alt, width, and height. For example:

   ```
   <a href="#LINK#"><img src="#IMAGE#" alt="#ALT#" height="#HEIGHT#"
   width="#WIDTH#" />#TEXT#</a>
   [9672_01_06A.txt]
   ```

9. To check the page template, go to a page and click on the **Page Template** link on the right-hand side of the page (in the **Templates** section). Scroll down to the **Subtemplate** section and check the **Navigation Bar Entry** textarea.

## How to do it...

The navigation bar can be found in **Shared Components**. To reach it, navigate to **Shared Components | Navigation Bar Entries**.

As a default, there is already a logout entry available. Our new entry will be added here:

1. Click on the button **Create**.
2. Select **From Scratch** and click on **Next**.
3. Select **Navigation to URL** and click on **Next**.
4. In the **Entry Label**, enter Contact and leave the rest on default. Click on **Next**.
5. Enter 999 into **Page** and default the other fields. Click on **Next**.
6. Click on **Create**.

   As you can see, a new entry is created next to the **Logout** entry. This means we are done and can now test it by running the application:

Instead of a link text it is also possible to use images. This can be helpful when developing, for example, a multi language application with a short list of languages. Instead of writing the full language name, we can use small icons depicting the available language.

In this example, we will only show you how to create a navigation bar icon and reuse our **Contact** page for this. Later on in the book, we will show you the details of how to create a language switch.

7. Go to **Shared Components | Navigation Bar Entries** and click on the button **Create**.

8. Select **From Scratch** and click on **Next**.

9. Select **Navigation to URL** and click on **Next**.

   This time we need to enter some more information on this screen.

10. Alter the **Sequence** to **15**.

11. In the **Entry Label** enter nothing.

12. In **Icon Image Name**, click on the button to the right of the field and select the icon **fndtip11.gif**.

   ❑ Alternatively, you can enter #APP_IMAGES#fndtip11.gif into the field.

13. Enter Contact into **Image ALT**.

14. Enter 32 for both **Image Height** and **Width**:

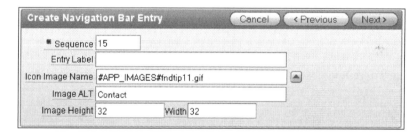

15. Click on **Next**.

16. Enter 999 into **Page** and default the other fields. Click on **Next**.

17. Click on **Create**.

You will notice a new entry in the list of the navigation bar. When running the application, this will be shown with the selected icon.

## There's more...

New in Application Express is the possibility to add a feedback link to the navigation bar. This will allow visitors of the application to quickly send feedback to the application developers or administrators.

1. Create a new navigation bar entry **From Scratch**.

2. Select **Feedback** and click on **Next**.

3. In the next screen, find the **Tasks** section to the far right and click on **Create Feedback Page**:

4. Set the page number to 102, leave everything else at default, and click on **Create**.

5. The focus will be returned to the navigation bar overview, so we have to repeat the first two steps.

6. Now select page 102 from the **Feedback Page** pull down list, enter 20 into the **Display Sequence**, and click on **Create**.

If you were to run the application now, no feedback link would be visible, because we have to allow the feedback option first.

So click on **Edit Application Properties** and find the option **Allow Feedback**. Set the pull down to **Yes** and click on **Apply Changes**. Now the application is ready to receive some feedback from its visitors:

## See also

- ▸ *Chapter 6, Creating Multilingual APEX Applications*, will cover translating your application and offering quick language switching to the visitors.
- ▸ *Chapter 12, Team Development*, will show how feedback can be used to the advantage of the development team.

# Creating a list of values

When you use forms with items that are Foreign Keys to other tables, it would be handy to derive the Primary Key from the lookup table instead of having to enter this ID manually in the text field. Or, when dealing with lots of similar, predefined data, you don't want to enter the same values over and over again. In those cases, you would want to use items such as listboxes, quick picks, or lists of values which display the data of the lookup items where the user can easily pick the right value.

In this recipe, we'll create a list of values. A list of values can not only be a list of predefined static values but it can also be a dynamic list with data retrieved from a table. We will create a static list of values. A list of values is a shared component so it can be used in more pages.

## Getting ready

The starting point is an existing application like the one we created. To define a list of values, you don't need to have a page. However, to make use of a list of values, you must define an item with a reference to the list of values. We will make a list of values on the JOB column.

## How to do it...

There are two ways to start the Create List of Values wizard. The first one is in the **Edit** page.

On the right-hand side of the screen, under **Shared Components**, click on the **Add** icon under **List Of Values**.

The second one is via **Shared Components**:

1. In the **Application Builder**, navigate to **Shared Components | List Of Values**. On the **List Of Values** page, click on the **Create** button.

2. You can create a list of values from scratch or you can copy an existing list of values and make some modifications to the newly created list of values. In our case, we will create a list of values from scratch. Click on **Next**.

3. Enter a name for the list of values, Jobs for example, and select **Dynamic** or **Static**. Choose **Static** and click on **Next**.

In the next step, you can enter the desired values. There are two types of values: the display value and the return value. The display value indicates how it is displayed and the return value is the value which will be returned into the text item the list of values is called from:

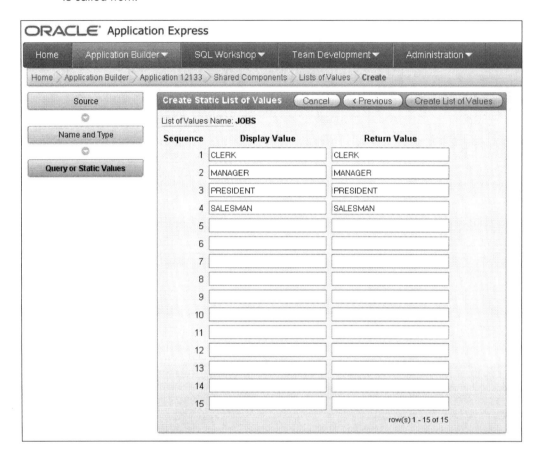

After you have entered the values, click on the **Create List of Values** button.

The list of values is created and can now be used by items. To assign an existing item to the list of values, go to the page where you want to include your list of values. In this case, we go to the tabular form based on the EMP table that we created in the *Creating a simple form page* recipe.

4.  Click on the **Regions** section on the **Report** link. Click on the pencil icon near the Job column.

5.  In the **Tabular Form Element** section, select **select list (named lov)** at the **Display As** field.

6. Next, in the **List Of Values** section, at the **Named Lov** field, select the list of values you just created.

7. Click on the **Apply Changes** button.

8. Run the form to see the result. It should look like the following:

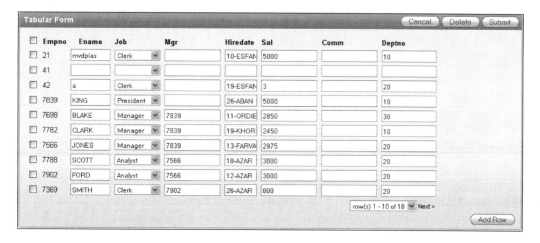

## How it works...

The list of values serves as a source for items types such as a list box or pop-up list of values. A list of values contains two columns: a display column and a column with the return value. This return value will be the actual data which will be stored in the item which is assigned to the list of values.

A list item can also be created directly upon a report column or item, but then is not reusable.

## There's more...

Another possibility is to use a previously defined list of values as a basis when creating a new item. This is useful in situations where you want to reuse a list of values on more than one occasion. A question that requires the answer Yes or No for example, can return on many pages in an application:

1. Go to the page where you want to have the item.

2. Right-click on the **Items** section of the region where the item should go and select **Create Page Item**.

3. In the **Select Item Type** dialog, click on the **Select List**.

4. In the next step, enter a name for the item. You may also enter a sequence number and the region where the item should appear. Click on **Next**.

5. In this step, provide some additional information such as the label, the height, and the alignment. Click on **Next**.

6. Next, define what APEX should do when you select some value from the list. You can redirect the user to another page or you can submit the page. Another option in this step is the indication whether APEX should allow multiselection. Leave this option to **No** and click on **Next**.

7. In the next step, enter the name of the existing list of values that you want to use in the **Named LOV** field. Leave the other options and click on **Next**.

8. In the last step, define the source of the item. Leave the options and click on the **Create Item** button.

# Including different item types

In APEX, it is possible to use many different item types. Some of these we've already seen in other recipes. In this recipe we're going to talk about some of the advanced item types such as shuttles and HTML editors and how to interact with them.

## Getting ready

To start with this recipe, create an empty page with ID 15 and put an HTML region with the name IT Employees on it.

## How to do it...

The first example of an advanced item type is the shuttle list. We will use this list to add employees to the IT department. The shuttle will show a list of available employees on the left-hand side and a list of employees already in the IT department on the right-hand side.

1. Create a new item on your page by right-clicking on the **IT Employees** region and selecting **Create Page Item**.

2. Select **Shuttle** and click on **Next**.

3. Name the item P15_IT_SHUTTLE and click on **Next** until you reach the **List of Values** page in the wizard.

4. Enter the following query to populate the left side of the shuttle:

```
select username display_value
     , id return_value
  from app_employees
 where dept_id <> 3
[9672_01_07.txt]
```

5.  After clicking on **Next**, you will be asked to enter a value for **Source Value**. This will populate the right-hand side of the shuttle. For this, we will use **PL/SQL Function Body** as the **Source Type** that will return a list of usernames delimited by colons:

```
declare
   v_list apex_application_global.vc_arr2;
begin

   select username return_value
     bulk collect
     into v_list
     from app_employees
   where dept_id = 3;

   return(apex_util.table_to_string(v_list));
end;
[9672_01_08.txt]
```

6.  Click on **Create Item** to finish the wizard.

Now the item will be populated with the employees:

The right-hand side of the shuttle item can also be populated by the default value that can be defined on the item's properties.

Another type of item we want to discuss here is the Cascading Select Item. Let's say we want to make a list of all employees. This is potentially a very long list, so before showing the employees, we first want to select the department we are working with.

First, we create the item that shows all departments for our company:

1.  Create a new page item.

2.  Use item type **Select List**.

3.  Name it P15_DEPARTMENTS.

4.  Give it a label and click on **Next** until you reach the LOV query, and enter the following SQL:

```
select name display_value
     , id return_value
  from app_departments
[9672_01_09.txt]
```

5.  Now create the item.

The next part is to create the select list for the employees in the department. Again, we create a select list like before and name it P15_EMPLOYEES.

Now when we reach the LOV wizard screen, we enter the following SQL:

```
select firstname||' '||lastname display_value
     , id return_value
  from app_employees
 where dept_id = :P15_DEPARTMENTS
[9672_01_10.txt]
```

Also on this screen, change the value of **Cascading LOV Parent Item(s)** to P15_DEPARTMENTS. Click on **Next** and then on **Create Item**.

When we now run the page and select a **Department**, we can see that the **Employees** list changes immediately.

 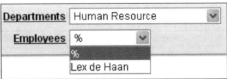

# Protecting a page using an authorization scheme

In some cases, you might want to restrict access to certain parts of your application to certain users. For example, not everyone should have access to the Form Page where you can alter the salaries. In such a case, you can protect your page using an authorization scheme.

## Getting ready

Before starting with the recipe you should have a table created in the database with usernames and roles. Let's say you have the following table APP_USERS:

```
ID         NUMBER(5)
USERNAME   VARCHAR2(50)
PASSWORD   VARCHAR2(50)
ROLE       VARCHAR2(10)
```

The table contains two rows. One is a user with admin privileges (role is ADMIN). The other one is a user with the no extra privileges (role is DEFAULT).

## How to do it...

1. Go to **Shared Components**.

2. Click on the **Authorization Schemes** link. You can find it in the **Security** section.

3. Next, you might see the authorization schemes that have already been created. If no authorization schemes have been created in the past, you see an empty page. Click on the **Create** button.

4. Next, select **From Scratch** and click on **Next**.

5. Next, enter a name for this authorization scheme and enter the conditions in the **Authorization Scheme** section.

    In our case, we name the scheme AUTH_ADMIN. The scheme type could be a PL/SQL function returning Boolean or an EXISTS SQL query. You have to create this function or query by yourself. The code could be included in the **Expression 1** textarea but you can also make a call to a function stored in the database. In our case, we put the code in here and we choose for the EXISTS SQL query. You see the query as follows:

```
select  1
from    app_users
where   username = :APP_USER
and     role = 'ADMIN'
[9672_01_11.txt]
```

    The query returns 1 if the username is the current user (:APP_USER) and the user has admin privileges.

6. Also, enter the error message APEX should display if the query returns no rows. Click on the **Create** button.

7. In the **Evaluation Point** section, select **Once per page view** to validate the authorization scheme. This will make APEX check the authorization for every call that is made to pages (or other components) using this scheme.

8. The other option is **Once per session**. This is much more efficient, because the check is only done once (at the start of the session). But when it's possible that the session state changes or there is anything else that is not consistent during the session, this option is not reliable.

9. The authorization scheme is now ready. Now, page access must be restricted by this authorization scheme.

10. Go to the page that requires authorization and click on the **Edit** icon (the pencil) in the **Page** section.

11. Go to the **Security** section and select the **Authorization Scheme** we just created (AUTH_ADMIN) in the **Authorization Scheme** list element.

That's it. The page now requires authorization to be accessed. Run the page to see how it works. Also see what happens if you do an update on the APP_USERS table:

```
update app_users
set    role     = 'DEFAULT'
where  username = ...;
```

Or

```
update app_users
set    role     = 'ADMIN'
where  username = ...;
[9672_01_12.txt]
```

Don't forget the commit.

## How it works...

Every time you navigate to this page, APEX executes the query in the **Authorization Scheme**. If the query returns one row, everything is fine and the user is authorized to view this page. If the query returns no rows, the user is not authorized to view the page and the error message is displayed.

## There's more...

You don't have to go to the **Shared Components** to create an Authorization Scheme. It can also be done when you are on a page. In the **Security** section on the right-hand side of the screen, click on the Add icon. The **Create Authorization Scheme** wizard will be started.

# Securing an application with Authentication

Application Express comes with three standard ways to authenticate users on applications. We can use the credentials of database users, we can use the credentials of users defined within APEX itself, or we can use the credentials defined in the Database Access Descriptor. In this recipe, we will show how to add our own Authentication Scheme to this list.

An Authentication Scheme controls access to an entire application as opposed to an Authorization Scheme that controls access to individual components inside the application.

Simply put, an Authentication Scheme is what is called when a user clicks on the **Login** button.

## Getting ready

First, we need a table to store the data for our users. In our application, this table will be APP_USERS. It contains columns for username and password, so we can create a very basic authentication scheme. Make sure this table is ready before continuing in this recipe.

Enter at least one row of data into the table that we can use to login at the end of the recipe.

Also we need two functions in place. APP_HASH is a function that will use a hashing algorithm and a salt to mask the real password. To make it more secure, the current date can be used in the algorithm, but this is enough for our example.

In a production environment, it is probably a good idea to wrap this code, because it can help intruders gain access to the application.

```
create or replace function app_hash (p_username in varchar2, p_
password in varchar2)
return varchar2
is
  l_password varchar2(4000);
  l_salt varchar2(4000) := 'DFS2J3DF4S5HG666IO7S8DJGSDF8JH';

begin

  l_password := utl_raw.cast_to_raw(dbms_obfuscation_toolkit.md5
  (input_string => p_password || substr(l_salt,10,13) || p_username ||
    substr(l_salt, 4,10)));
  return l_password;
end;
[9672_01_13.txt]
```

APP_AUTH is a function that will check if the user is valid and if the password is entered correctly:

```
create or replace function app_auth (p_username in VARCHAR2, p_
password in VARCHAR2)
return BOOLEAN
is
  l_password varchar2(4000);
  l_stored_password varchar2(4000);
  l_expires_on date;
  l_count number;
begin
  select count(*)
    into l_count
    from app_users
   where upper(username) = upper(p_username);

  if l_count > 0
  then
    select password
      into l_stored_password
      from app_users
      where upper(username) = upper(p_username);

    l_password := app_hash(p_username, p_password);

    if l_password = l_stored_password
    then
      return true;
    else
      return false;
    end if;
  else
    return false;
  end if;

end;
[9672_01_14.txt]
```

## How to do it...

The first thing we have to do is add the new authentication scheme to the list of existing schemes:

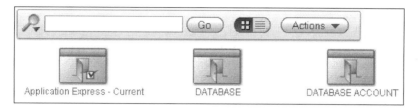

1. Click on the **Create** button.
2. Choose **From Scratch** and click on **Next**.
3. Name it **Application Authentication** and click on **Next.**
4. Click on **Next** on the following two screens as well.
5. Select **Page in This Application** and page 101 on the **Invalid Session Target** and click on **Next** until you reach **Credentials verification method**.
6. Select **Use my custom function to authenticate** and enter `return app_auth` in **Authentication Function**.
7. Click on **Next** until you reach **Logout URL**.
8. The **Logout URL** is `wwv_flow_custom_auth_std.logout?p_this_flow=&APP_ID.&amp;p_next_flow_page_sess=&APP_ID.:1`
9. Click on **Next** and then on **Create Scheme**.

The last step is to make the new Authentication Scheme the current for the application. To do this, navigate to the tab **Change Current** on the **Schemes Overview** screen. Select the new scheme from the list and click on the **Make Current** button.

You can now log in to the application using a username and password from the `APP_USERS` table.

# Controlling the display of regions and items with Dynamic Actions

Dynamic Actions are control items that dynamically can affect the display of regions or items on a page. There are several situations when you want to show or hide items. For example, a text item asking for a maiden name should only be displayed when the person is female and married. In other cases, it is irrelevant to ask for a maiden name (on the other hand, with homosexual marriages it's possible for a man to have a "maiden" name, and in some cases a man can adopt the family name of his wife, but let's not make this example more difficult than necessary).

The same applies to the **Commission** field in the employees table. This item should only be enterable when the employee's job is a salesman. Let's build the functionality for this last situation.

## Getting ready

You should already have an application and a simple single record form on the employees table.

## How to do it...

1. Right-click on the **Dynamic Actions** link in the leftmost section and click on **Create**.

2. Select **Standard** and proceed to the next step.

3. Enter a name for this dynamic action. For example, D_JOB_COMM_SHOW. Click on **Next**.

4. In the next screen, the **Selection Type** is **Item(s)** and in the **Item(s)** field, enter the name of the item holding Job. You can use the **List of Values** button to select the right Page Item.

5. In the **Condition list** box, select **equal to**.

6. In the **Value** textarea, enter **SALESMAN**. Click on **Next**.

7. Select **Show** as the **True Action** and go to the next step.

8. In the next screen select **Item(s)** in the **Selection Type**. In the shuttle item that now appears, move the name of the commission field to the right.

9. Click on the **Create** button.

You have now created a dynamic action which shows the **Commission** field when the job is **SALESMAN** and hides the **Commission** field when the job is not **SALESMAN**.

## How it works...

The **Dynamic Actions** are actually event handlers in HTML. There are several event handlers.

Because these events are HTML (or rather JavaScript) they are handled client side. This has the advantage that the page doesn't have to be reloaded completely when an action is triggered to show or hide items.

| Event | Meaning |
|---|---|
| After refresh | Item has been refreshed (that is, by page refresh) |
| Before refresh | Fires before item has been refreshed (that is, by page refresh) |
| Blur | User navigates to another item |
| Change | User navigates to another item and the value of the item has changed |

| Event | Meaning |
|---|---|
| Click | User clicks on the item with a pointing device (like a mouse) |
| Dblclick | User double-clicks on the item with a pointing device |
| Focus | User navigates to the item via the tab key or a pointing device |
| keydown | User clicks on a key on the keyboard |
| keypress | User clicks on a key on the keyboard (=onkeyDown followed by onkeyUp) |
| keyup | User releases the key after having pressed it |
| load | The browser loads all content |
| mousedown | User clicks on the mouse button when the mouse pointer is over the item |
| mouseenter | User clicks on the item with the pointing device |
| mouseleave | User moves away the mouse from the item |
| mousemove | User moves the mouse while the mouse pointer is over the item |
| mouseover | User moves the mouse pointer over the item |
| mouseout | User moves away the mouse pointer from the item |
| nmouseup | User releases the mouse button after having it pressed |
| submit | Form is submitted |
| Resize | Document view is resized |
| Scroll | Document view is scrolled |
| Select | User selects some text in a text field |
| Submit | Form is submitted |
| Unload | Page is unloaded |

In our example, we use the onchange event handler. So, when the user changes the value in JOB, the onchange is triggered and it calls the action to show or hide the **COMMISSION** field, depending on the value in JOB. If it is **SALESMAN** then show commission, else hide commission.

## There's more...

You can control the display of more than one item at a time. Simply separate the items by a comma in the items field.

You can also control the display of regions. So, you can show or hide a complete report. Instead of item, select region and the name of the region in the affected element section when defining an action.

# Creating a computation

Computations are events that will prepare items with data. As the name implies, computations can "compute" how data is to be shown on screen or how data is handled after submitting. Computations can be triggered during page rendering, but they can also be used in the **After Submit** process.

This example will show an implementation of a computation, but there are many more possible uses for computations.

## How to do it...

Start by creating a normal text item on the form that was created in the second recipe of the first chapter. This is a normal form based on the EMP table. Normally, a user would have to manually enter the commission. What we are going to do is to create a computation that will automatically enter an amount into this field, based on a percentage of the salary and a bonus for people that work in the Sales department.

First, identify the item that holds the commission column.

The next step is to find the moment when we want to execute the computation. In this case, before the page is submitted but after the **Save** button is pressed. So in this case we will create the computation **After Submit**.

1.  Right-click on the **Computations** under **After Submit** in the **Page Processing** component and click on **Create**:

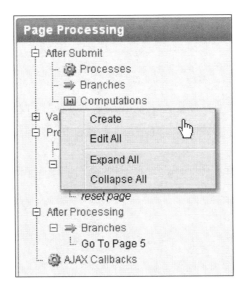

2. Choose **Item on this page** and press **Next**.

3. Select **P5_COMM** from the **Compute Item** select list, select **PL/SQL Function Body** from the **Computation Type** select list and click on **Next**.

4. The next step is to enter the **PL/SQL** code for this computation:

```
declare
   l_comm number;
begin
   if :P5_DEPTNO = 30
   then
      l_comm := :P5_SAL * 1.10;
   else
      l_comm := :P5_SAL * 1.05;
   end if;
   return l_comm;
end;
[9672_01_15.txt]
```

5. Click on **Create**.

The computation is now done. It can be tested by selecting an existing record from the list of employees and altering its salary and then saving the data. Another option is to create a completely new employee. You will see that an employee under the Sales department with dept no. 30 will receive a 10 percent commission whilst employees from all other departments will receive 5 percent.

## There's more...

Computations can be used for far more situations than preparing an item before saving it to the database.

An example of another implementation can be an item that will show the current date when the page loads, or an item that will show a total amount when certain other amount items are entered. Used with dynamic actions, computations can be very powerful.

# Creating an automated row fetch with a page process

When you create a Single Record form, you probably would like to see that the form automatically retrieves data on startup. You can do that with an automated row fetch. In this section, we will create a page process with an automated row fetch. We're going to make a form where users can update their data.

## Getting ready

We will use the EMP table so make sure it exists, together with the Primary Key. Create a simple form page:

1. In the **Application Builder**, click on the **Create Page** button.

2. Select the Blank page and click on **Next**.

3. Assign a number and enter a name in the **Page Alias** field. The page number is automatically filled by APEX.

4. In the next step, enter a name for this page and click on **Next**.

5. In the **Tabs** dialog, select **No** and click on **Next**.

6. In the **Page Confirmation** dialog, click on **Finish**.

The page is now ready and we can start creating a region with items.

1. Click on the icon of the new page.

2. Create a region by right-clicking on the **Regions** link and clicking on **Create**.

3. Select **HTML** and click on **Next**.

4. In the **Type Of HTML** dialog, select **HTML** and click on **Next**.

5. In the next step, enter a title for the region and click Next.

6. In the **HTML text region source** step, leave all options and click on **Create Region**.

   A region is created and now we will add some items to this region. We will start with the Primary Key of the table.

7. Right-click on the name of the region and select **Create Page Item**.

8. Select **Text Item** and click on **Next**.

9. In the next step, select **Text Field** and click on **Next**.

10. Next, enter a name for this item. Since this item will display the Primary Key we give it the same name as the Primary Key column, empno. So, the item will be named P11_EMPNO (11 is the page number, this can be different depending on your situation). Enter this name in the text field and click on **Next**.

11. In the next step, you can enter a label for this text item. Enter **empno** and click on **Next**.

12. In the **Source** dialog, in the **Source Type** listbox, select **Database Column** and enter EMPNO in the **Item Source Value** textarea. Mind the capitals, otherwise it will not work.

13. Click on the **Create Item** button.

The item has now been created.

Next, create another item. Let's say Ename.

1. Right-click on the name of the region and select **Create Page Item**.

2. Select **Text Item** and click on **Next.**

3. In the next step select **Text Field** and click on **Next**.

4. Next, enter a name for this item. Enter P11_ENAME (again, change 11 to the page number in your situation) in the text field and click on **Next**.

5. In the next step you can enter a label for this text item. Enter ename and click on **Next**.

6. In the **Source** dialog, in the **Source Type** listbox, select **Database Column** and enter ENAME in the item **Source Value** textarea. Mind the capitals, otherwise it will not work.

7. Click on the **Create Item** button.

The item has now been created.

## How to do it...

1. In the page you just created, expand the **After Header** section and right-click the **Processes** link. Now click on **Create**.

2. Select **Data Manipulation** and click on **Next**.

3. Select **Automated Row Fetch** and click on **Next**.

4. Enter a name for this process. In the **Point** listbox, select **On Load – After Header**. Click on **Next**.

5. In the next step, enter the table name, the item containing the Primary Key column value, and the Primary Key column. In our case, the table name is EMP and the item containing the Primary Key column value is **P11_EMPNO**. The Primary Key column is the column in the table that is part of the Primary Key. In our case it is EMPNO. Again, mind the capitals, otherwise it won't work.

6. Click on the **Create Process** button. The automated row fetch has been created and you can run the page to see what happens.

## How it works...

The automated row fetch is executed when the page is run but after the page header section has been generated by APEX. A row is fetched by using the Primary Key value stored in the page item P11_EMPNO. If this item is empty in the session state, no row will be fetched at all.

When a row is fetched, the column values are put in internal arrays (memory cache), but will not be committed into session state itself. The session state is only populated when the page is submitted (using the values stored in the page items). This has to do with performance (insert/delete session state) for example, clicking a "cancel" link.

In this case, running the page without `P11_EMPNO` having a value will produce a page with empty items.

# Putting some validation in a form

When you fill in a form, the entered data must be validated, just to make sure that it is correct. Date fields, number fields where the number should not exceed some defined limit, items with a certain format like a telephone number or an e-mail address, all this data has to be validated. In APEX you can use validations to check the user input.

## Getting ready

For this recipe we will use a user profiles form where the user can enter some personal information. Make sure you have access to the `app_user_profiles` table and the `app_ups_seq` sequence. You can create a user profiles form using these steps:

1. Go to your application.
2. Click on **Create page**.
3. Select **Form**.
4. Select **Form on a table or view**.
5. Select the table/view owner and click on **Next**.
6. In the **table/view name** field, enter `app_user_profiles`. Click on **Next**.
7. Click again on **Next**.
8. Select **do not use tabs** and click on **Next**.
9. In the Primary Key column 1, select **ID**. Click on **Next**.
10. Select **Existing sequence**. In the **Sequence** list box, select **app_ups_seq**. Click on **Next**.
11. Select **all columns** and click on **Next**.
12. Click on **Next**.
13. Enter the page numbers APEX should navigate to if the form is submitted or cancelled. You can use the page number of the home page, mostly 1, for both. But you can also use the same page number as this page. Click on **Next**.
14. Click on **Finish**.

Let's put some validation on the items. We are going to put validation on birthday, e-mail, and a Twitter account. For the check of the Twitter account you must first create the following procedure:

```
create or replace procedure app_search_user (p_search   in  varchar2
                                            ,p_result   out varchar2)
is
  l_request      utl_http.req;
  l_response     utl_http.resp;
  l_tweet_url    varchar2(255) := 'http://api.twitter.com/1/users/
lookup.xml';
  l_content      varchar2(255) := 'screen_name='||p_search;
  l_line         varchar2(1024);
  l_result       varchar2(100) := 'no user';
  l_user         varchar2(100) := 'your user name';
  l_password     varchar2(100) := 'your password';
begin
  -- build the request statement
  l_request    := utl_http.begin_request(url    => l_tweet_url
                                         ,method => 'POST');
  -- set header
  utl_http.set_header(r     => l_request
                     ,name  => 'Content-Length'
                     ,value => length(l_content));
  -- authenticate the user
  utl_http.set_authentication(r        => l_request
                             ,username => l_user
                             ,password => l_password);
  -- write the content
  utl_http.write_text(r    => l_request
                     ,data => l_content);
  -- get the response
  l_response := utl_http.get_response(r => l_request);
  begin
    loop
      utl_http.read_line(r           => l_response
                        ,data        => l_line
                        ,remove_crlf => true);
      if instr(l_line,'<screen_name>') > 0
      then
        l_result := 'user found';
      end if;
    end loop;
  exception
    when utl_http.end_of_body
```

```
      then
         null;
    end;
    utl_http.end_response(r => l_response);
    p_result := l_result;
  exception
    when others then
      utl_http.end_response(r => l_response);
      p_result := 'request failed';
      raise;
end app_search_user;
/
[9672_01_16.txt]
```

This procedure makes a call to the Twitter API and searches for the Twitter username which was passed through. The request sent looks like the following URL:

```
http://api.twitter.com/1/users/lookup.xml?screen_name=<twittername>
```

Here, `<twittername>` is the Twitter username you are checking. The result is an XML or JSONresponse. In this case, if the Twitter username exists, the procedure gets an XML response with a tag `<screen_name>`, which holds the username. If the Twitter username does not exist, the procedure gets an XML response with an error tag. The procedure makes use of the `utl_http` package so the database user must be granted execute rights to this package. Also, it is important to define the **Access Control List** (**ACL**) if your database version is 11g. To grant access, log in as SYS user and execute the following procedure:

```
begin
  dbms_network_acl_admin.create_acl (
    acl           => 'utl_http.xml',
    description => 'HTTP Access',
    principal     => '<oracle username>',
    is_grant      => TRUE,
    privilege     => 'connect',
    start_date    => null,
    end_date      => null
  );

  dbms_network_acl_admin.add_privilege (
    acl           => 'utl_http.xml',
    principal     => '<oracle username>',
    is_grant      => TRUE,
    privilege     => 'resolve',
    start_date  => null,
    end_date      => null
```

```
   );

  dbms_network_acl_admin.assign_acl (
     acl         => 'utl_http.xml'
     host        => 'api.twitter.com'
     lower_port => 80
     upper_port => 80   );
   commit;
end;
/
[9672_01_17.txt]
```

## How to do it...

1.  In the **Page** view, go to the **Page Processing** section and right-click on **Validating**. Select **Create Validation**.

2.  Select the **Validation Level**. In our case, we choose **Item Level**.

3.  Select the **Birthday** item.

4.  In the **Select a validation method** dialog, select the PL/SQL validation method.

5.  In the type of **PL/SQL** validation dialog, select **PL/SQL** error.

6.  The sequence number has already been issued but you can change it to your own comfort. You can also enter a name for the validation. These two fields are mandatory. In the third field, the display location, you can select where the error message should appear. Click on **Next**.

7.  In the **Validation Text** area, enter the following code:

    ```
    if :Pxx_BIRTHDAY > (sysdate - numtoyminterval(13,'YEAR'))
    then
        raise_application_error (-20001,'You must be at least 13 years
    old to register.');
    end if;
    [9672_01_18.txt]
    ```

xx is the page number. This code checks if the entered date is greater than the current system date minus 13 years. If so, the person is younger than 13 years and is not allowed to register. In that case an error message should be issued. You can enter the error message in the **Error Message** textarea. In the next step, optionally you can specify the conditions when the validation should take place.

The first validation is ready now. The next validation is the e-mail.

1.  Right-click on **Validating**. Select **Create Validation**.

2.  Select item level validation and click on **Next**.

3.  Select the e-mail item.

4.  In the next step, select a regular expression.

5.  Check the sequence number and the name of the validation. Click on **Next**.

6.  In the **Regular Expression** field, enter the following:

```
([[:alnum:]]+\.?){2}@([[:alnum:]]+\.?){3,4}/?
```

With regular expressions you can force a user to conform to a certain format when entering data. You can, for example, check on the format of telephone numbers, URLs, dates and, in this case, correct e-mail addresses. E-mail addresses should at least have the at sign (@) and a dot (.), such as abcd@abcd.com. But an e-mail address can have more dots, and numbers are also allowed. [[:alnum:]] indicates that characters and numbers are accepted. The + sign means that it can match 1 or more times. The dot followed by the question mark indicates that a dot can match 0 or more times. The {2} indicates that it must match at least two times. Behind the at sign again, numbers, characters, and dots are allowed.

1.  In the **Error Message** textarea, enter the error message: The email address is not valid.

2.  Skip the condition and click on the **Create** button.

The second validation has now been created. Now let's go to the validation of the Twitter account.

1.  Right-click on **Validating**. Select **Create Validation**.

2.  Select the item level validation.

3.  Select the Twitter item.

4.  Select the **PL/SQL** validation method.

5.  Select function returning error text.

6.  Enter the sequence number and a name for the validation and select where the error message should appear. Make sure that the sequence number is higher than the sequence from the previous validations. Validations are processed in the order of these sequence numbers; lowest sequence numbers are processed first.

7.  In the next step, in the validation text area, enter the following code:

```
declare
  l_result varchar2(100);
begin
  app_search_user(:P15_TWITTER,l_result);
  if l_result = 'user found'
```

```
    then
       return null;
    else
       return 'no valid user';
    end if;
  end;
  [9672_01_19.txt]
```

This PL/SQL code calls the stored procedure with the Twitter username as a parameter and gets a result back. If the Twitter username exists, "user found" is returned, otherwise "no valid user" is returned. In the latter case, an error message should be issued. You can enter the error message in the **Error Message** textarea.

In the **Conditions** dialog, leave the options as they are and click on the **Create** button.

## How it works...

On submitting the form, APEX validates the items. In the case of the birthday, it executes the PL/SQL code where the entered birthday is checked. In the case of the e-mail address, the item containing the e-mail address is checked against the regular expression.

## There's more...

You can also validate multiple rows of an item in a tabular form. If one or more rows fail validation, APEX indicates this by showing the concerned items in red with an error message in the **Notification** area. Also, you can validate at page level.

There are different validation methods. See the following table:

| Validation method | Meaning |
| --- | --- |
| SQL | Enter a `where exists` SQL query, a `not exists` SQL query or a SQL expression SQL query |
| PL/SQL | Enter a PL/SQL expression, PL/SQL error (`raise application_error`) a function returning Boolean or a function returning error text |
| Item not null | Item should not be empty |
| Item string comparison | Compare the value of the item with a predefined string |
| Regular expression | Item value should meet a certain format, like a date format (`dd/mm/yyyy`) or an IP address (`xxx.xxx.xxx.xxx`) |

## See also

  ▶   For more information on regular expressions, go to `http://psoug.org/reference/regexp.html`

# Creating a report with PL/SQL Dynamic Content

APEX offers many item types and templates to use when designing an application. Sometimes this isn't enough, for example, when you have an existing web application built with mod PL/SQL that you want to reuse.

It's possible by using built-in packages such as HTP or HTF, or by using some native APEX code to create these types of pages directly in PL/SQL.

## How to do it...

In this example, we are going to build a report without using any items, but only PL/SQL code.

On an empty page, create a new region:

1. Choose a **PL/SQL Dynamic Content** region type.
2. Name it Employees.

The PL/SQL Source is the most important part of this region. With this, we will be building up the report. To show how this works, we will first create the region without any layout.

Enter the following as the PL/SQL and click on **Next**, and then on **Create Region**:

```
declare
  cursor c_emp
      is
          select apex_item.hidden(1,emp.id) id
               , apex_item.display_and_save(2,emp.firstname) firstname
               , apex_item.display_and_save(2,emp.lastname) lastname
               , apex_item.display_and_save(2,emp.username) username
               , apex_item.display_and_save(2,dept.name) department
               , apex_item.display_and_save(2,job.abbreviation) job
               , apex_item.display_and_save(2,job.description) job_desc
            from app_employees emp
               , app_departments dept
               , app_jobs job
           where emp.dept_id = dept.id
             and emp.job_id  = job.id;
begin
  for r_emp in c_emp
  loop
    htp.p(r_emp.id);
    htp.p(r_emp.firstname);
```

```
        htp.p(r_emp.lastname);
        htp.p(r_emp.username);
        htp.p(r_emp.department);
        htp.p(r_emp.job);
        htp.p(r_emp.job_desc);
     end loop;
end;
[9672_01_20.txt]
```

When the page is run, all data from each employee is placed on one continuous line. To change this and make it look more like a report, we will add some HTML encoding, using the `htp` package.

Change the code inside the begin-end to the following:

```
htp.tableopen;

for r_emp in c_emp
loop
    htp.tablerowopen;
      htp.tabledata(r_emp.id);
      htp.tabledata(r_emp.firstname);
      htp.tabledata(r_emp.lastname);
      htp.tabledata(r_emp.username);
      htp.tabledata(r_emp.department);
      htp.tabledata(r_emp.job);
      htp.tabledata(r_emp.job_desc);
    htp.tablerowclose;
  end loop;

  htp.tableclose;
[9672_01_21.txt]
```

This looks a lot better and gives us a starting point to apply a better layout:

**Dynamic content**

| | | | | | |
|---|---|---|---|---|---|
| Steven | King | sking | Sales | CEO | Chief Executive Officer |
| Neena | Kochhar | nkochhar | IT | MGR | Manager |
| Lex | de Haan | ldehaan | Human Resource | CLERK | Clerk |
| Marcel van der Plas | mvdplas | IT | | CONS | Consultant |
| Michel van Zoest | mvzoest | IT | | CONS | Consultant |

Applying layout can now be done on multiple levels. For starters, the APEX_ITEM package can be used to select different item types in the cursor query. We have now used APEX_ITEM. DISPLAY_AND_SAVE to show the data as text only, but we could also use item type TEXT to make it a text field.

On a second level, we can start using classes from the CSS that is used by the application. These can be applied to the items, tables, tablerows, and so forth. How this can be done as explained in *Chapter 2, Themes and Templates*.

# 2
# Themes and Templates

In this chapter we will cover the following topics:

- ▸ Creating your own theme
- ▸ Importing a theme
- ▸ Creating a custom template
- ▸ Including images in your application
- ▸ Referencing CSS classes in your application
- ▸ Controlling the layout

## Introduction

Now that we have an application we would like to give it more looks. Maybe the application has to adhere to certain corporate layout standards. Or maybe you just want to add some more colors. Using themes and templates it is possible to give your application some cosmetic changes. A theme is a collection of templates and a template is a collection of components ranging from pages and reports to controls like calendars. A template consists of a header template, a body template, and a footer template. A template also contains some subtemplates, for example, for the success message.

In this chapter, we will present some recipes which will make your application look better.

# Creating your own theme

When working with themes, there are some important things to know. First of all, there is the theme export SQL file in which all templates of the theme are included. Secondly, there are the images that belong to your theme. And thirdly, there are the .css files. CSS is an abbreviation of Cascading Style Sheet and describes the style of the elements in a web page. For example, the font of the text or the color of the background. In the stylesheet there are also references to images. It is important that the references in these files are correct, otherwise you will see no style at all, just plain text.

When you want to create your own theme you can do two things: start from scratch or copy an existing theme and adapt it. Starting from scratch is more work as you have to create all the templates as well. Copying and modifying an existing theme costs less time but if you have to change a lot in order to get the desired layout, you might as well start from scratch.

## Getting ready

If you use the embedded PL/SQL gateway to run APEX, you must have FTP access to the host where APEX resides. You can enable FTP by specifying the FTP port. Log in to SQL*Plus as sys or system and execute the following query:

```
Select dbms_xdb.getftpport() from dual;
[getftpport.sql]
```

The result should be a number, like 2100. In that case, that is the port to which you can connect with your FTP client. You need the database system account with the system password to connect to FTP. If the result is 0, there is no port open and you have to set the port number. You can do that with the following command:

```
Exec Dbms_xdb.setftpport(2100);
[setftpport.sql]
```

In this example, you set the FTP port number to 2100. You can choose the port number by yourself but be aware that if you choose the standard port 21, you might encounter problems if another FTP service is running on the host.

By the way, you can also get and set the HTTP port number. The HTTP port number is used to access APEX. Instead of getftpport() and setftpport(), you use gethttpport() and sethttpport().

To access the FTP, use an FTP client like FileZilla. Use the following parameters:

| Parameter | Value |
| --- | --- |
| Host | Name of the database host |
| Port | 2100 |
| Server type | FTP |
| Login type | Normal |
| User | System |
| Password | <your system password> |

When you log in to the FTP, go to the `images` directory. It is possible that you see other directories starting with images and a number which obviously looks like a date and a sequence number. Those are the image directories from previous releases from APEX and it means that your current APEX version has been upgraded.

In the images directory, you can see the themes directories. There you can make your own new theme by adding a directory in which you can upload your images and `.css` stylesheets.

In this recipe, we will use an existing theme and adapt it to our own standards. For this recipe make sure theme 18 is installed. theme 18 is a simple theme which you can find in the repository. If you haven't installed it, do it now:

1. In Application Builder, go to the application you are working on. In the application go to the **Shared Components**.

2. In Shared Components, go to the **Themes**. You can find the themes in the user interface section.

3. In the themes page, click on the **Create** button.

4. Select **From the repository** and click on **Next**.

5. Select **theme 18** and proceed to the next step.

6. In the last step, confirm by clicking on the **Create** button.

## How to do it...

1. First we have to make an export of the theme you want to copy. So go to **Application | Shared Components | Themes** and click on **Export Theme**. You can find export theme on the right side of the screen, under tasks.

2. In the next step, in the **Export Theme** list box, select **theme 18**. In the file format list box, you can enter UNIX or DOS. If you are using Microsoft Windows as your computer's operating system, select DOS and click on the export theme button. If you use Linux or UNIX as your operating system, select **UNIX**. Click on the **Export Theme** button.

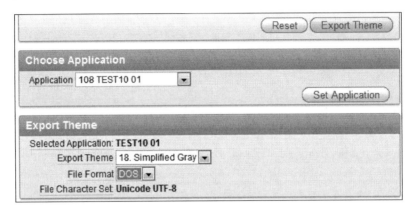

The theme will now be downloaded as an SQL file and you will be asked to enter a directory where the file will be stored.

3. Next, create a directory on your local filesystem. We will call the new theme `theme_115`, so create a directory with that name.

4. Open your FTP client and log on to the `localhost`.

5. Go to the `directory /images/themes/theme_18` and transfer (download) the contents to your local directory called **theme_115**.

6. In the CSS files, replace all occurrences of **t18** with **t115** and save the files. Don't forget to check if the references in the stylesheets are pointing to the newly created theme directory.

7. Locate the exported theme (it is an SQL file) and open it. Replace `theme_18` with `theme_115`, replace `t18` with `t115` and save the file under the name `theme_115.sql`.

8. Transfer (upload) the entire directory `theme_115` to the FTP server under the directory `/images/themes`. So after the upload you should see a directory `theme_115` on the host, like in the following screenshot:

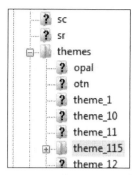

9. In the application builder, go to your application and click on **Export/Import**.

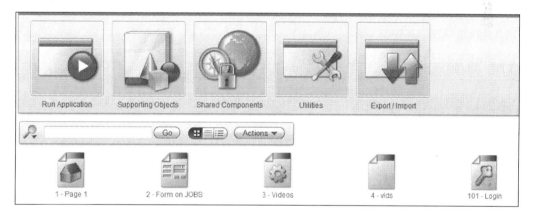

10. Select **Import** and proceed to the next step.

11. In the import file item, enter the filename of the theme (SQL file) you just modified. In our case it is `theme_115.sql`. You can also use the search button to locate and select the file.

12. At the file type listbox, select **Theme Export**. Click on **Next**. The theme will be imported.

13. After the import has been successful, the new theme has to be installed to use it. So, click on **Next**.

14. In the last step, you will be asked to enter the application where the new theme has to be installed. Furthermore, you can opt between **Replace existing theme** and **Create new theme**. Select **Create new theme** and click the **Install Theme** button.

15. Now, the new theme has been created but it probably does not have the ID 115. In that case you can modify the theme ID. In the theme page, click **Change Identification Number** on the right side of the screen, under **Tasks**. You can then select the theme and the new ID you would like to assign. In this case, that would be 115. Click **Next**.

16. To confirm, click the **Change theme ID** button in the last step.

Your theme is now ready to use and as a last step, you must switch to the new theme:

1. Go to the **Themes** page.

2. Click the **Switch Theme** button.

3. In the **Switch to theme** listbox, select the new theme and click **Next**.

4. If everything is OK (the status column shows **OK** checks) you can click **Next** and switch theme to confirm. If there is something wrong, for example, missing templates (this can happen if an existing application has a reference to a template class which doesn't exist in the newly applied theme), the status will show error for the type of template which is missing. In that case, check if everything is complete or select another theme.

Your newly created theme is now active. Run the application to see what it looks like. Actually, you should see no change compared to the theme 18, as you just made a copy of Theme 18.

## How it works...

We made an export of a theme and imported it under another name into APEX. We also created a new directory with the images and the CSS files in it. So far nothing special, it is actually a copy of the other theme. But now we can adapt this new theme and add our own style to it, leaving the original theme intact.

# Importing a theme

The themes that come with APEX offer enough different styles and layouts to give your application a unique and satisfying look. However, if your application must conform to a specific corporate layout or your application must look the same as another APEX application, you can import a theme. APEX offers an easy way to import and use a theme. You can find several themes (free or commercial) on the Internet.

## Getting ready

Make sure you have already downloaded the theme and put it on your filesystem.

## How to do it...

1. In the application builder, go to the application you are working on.

2. Click on the **Export/Import** button.

   Select **Import**. In the next step, enter the name and path of the theme. You can also use the Find button to locate the file. An APEX import or export theme file is just a `.sql` file. You can even view the contents of the file. It should begin with something like this:

```
set define off
set verify off
set serveroutput on size 1000000
set feedback off
WHENEVER SQLERROR EXIT SQL.SQLCODE ROLLBACK
begin wwv_flow.g_import_in_progress := true; end;
/

--      AAAA        PPPPP   EEEEEE  XX      XX
--     AA  AA      PP  PP   EE        XX  XX
--    AA    AA     PP  PP   EE         XX XX
--   AAAAAAAAAA    PPPPP    EEEE        XXXX
--   AA      AA    PP       EE         XX XX
--   AA      AA    PP       EE        XX    XX
--   AA      AA    PP       EEEEEE   XX      XX
prompt   Set Credentials...

begin

   -- Assumes you are running the script connected to SQL*Plus as the Oracle use
   wwv_flow_api.set_security_group_id(p_security_group_id=>990412166842593);

end;
/

begin wwv_flow.g_import_in_progress := true; end;
/
begin

select value into wwv_flow_api.g_nls_numeric_chars from nls_session_parameters

end;

/
begin execute immediate 'alter session set nls_numeric_characters=''.,''';

end;
```

3. In the file type radio group, select **Theme Export**. Optionally, you can select the file character set but most of the time Unicode UTF-8 is sufficient. Click on **Next**. The file will be imported.

4. If the file has been successfully imported, you get a successful message. This does not mean that you can use it already. The theme has to be installed first. Click on **Next** to install now.

5. In the next step, you can click on the **Install into application** listbox to select the application where it has to be installed. Click on the **Install theme** button.

6. After successfully installing the theme, you will see the other installed themes. The active theme is marked with an asterisk (*). If you want to make the newly installed theme the current one, click on the **Switch theme** button in the upper-right corner.

7. In the switch to theme listbox, select the desired theme. Click on **Next**.

8. In the next step you get an overview of the templates and the status of the templates. If there is any problem check the templates and the classes. If everything is ok, click on the **Next** button.

9. In the last step, click on **Switch theme** to confirm. You can now run your application to see what it looks like.

## How it works...

A theme consists of templates. There are nine different types of templates:

1. Breadcrumb
2. Button
3. Calendar
4. Label
5. List
6. Page
7. Popup lov
8. Region
9. Report

In the template you can edit the contents. You can make more templates of a certain type. For example, you can make two templates of type label. However, only one can be set as default for use in an application. Up till APEX 3.2, APEX makes use of an HTML table with the `<td>`, `</td>`, `<tr>` and the `</tr>` tags. As from version 4.0, APEX also uses div-based templates. It will load pages faster with better accessibility.

In a template you see substitution strings, keywords between pound signs (#), which Oracle replaces on rendering. Examples of substitution strings are title, user, and error message. The substitution strings appear in the form of:

`#SUBSTITUTION STRING#`

So with the pound signs at the beginning and the end of the string and in uppercase. For example the substitution string `#TITLE#` will be replaced with the title of the page, and `#REGION_POSITION_02#` will be replaced by the contents of the region where the display point (you can find it under the user interface section on the region definition) is set to region position 2.

# Creating a custom template

When you create a theme from scratch, you also have to link the templates to the theme. You can copy templates from another theme to your newly created theme. But you can also create new templates from scratch. We will create a new template in this recipe.

## Getting ready

We can go on with theme 115 that we made in the first recipe, so make sure you already created this theme.

## How to do it...

1. In **Application Builder**, go to the application you are working on. After that, go to the **Shared components**.
2. In the shared components page, click on **Templates**.
3. Click on the **Create** button to start the wizard.
4. In the next step you see nine types of templates. Select the **Region template**.
5. Click on **From scratch** and click on the **Next** button.

6. Enter a name for this new template, that is, `cust_rep_reg`. You can also select the theme this new template should be part of. And finally, select the template class. In our case, we select the **Reports** region. Click the **Create** button to finish the wizard.

| Region | | | | |
|---|---|---|---|---|
| Region | Borderless Region | 0 | - | - |
| | Borderless Region | 0 | 35 hours ago | admin |
| | Bracketed Region | 0 | - | - |
| | Bracketed Region | 0 | 35 hours ago | admin |
| | Breadcrumb Region | 1 | - | - |
| | Breadcrumb Region | 0 | 35 hours ago | admin |
| | Button Region with Title | 0 | - | - |
| | Button Region with Title | 0 | 35 hours ago | admin |
| | Button Region without Title | 0 | - | - |
| | Button Region without Title | 0 | 35 hours ago | admin |
| | Chart List | 0 | - | - |
| | Chart Region | 0 | - | - |
| | Chart Region | 0 | 35 hours ago | admin |
| | cust_rep_reg | 0 | 2 minutes ago | admin |
| | Form Region | 2 | - | - |

7. The new template has now been created and you can see it in the list. Edit the new template by clicking on the template name (**cust_rep_reg**).

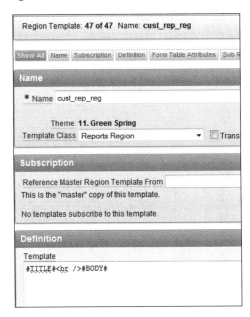

8. You can use HTML in combination with the substitution strings to create a layout. Oracle replaces the substitution strings with the component values. You can find the substitution string at the bottom of the page:

## Substitution Strings

Substitution strings are used within templates to reference component values. This report de

| Substitution | Referenced | From | Description |
|---|---|---|---|
| #TITLE# | Yes | Template | Region Title |
| #EDIT# | No | | Edit Button |
| #EXPAND# | No | | Expand Button |
| #CREATE# | No | | Create Button |
| #CREATE2# | No | | Create2 Button |
| #CLOSE# | No | | Close Button |
| #BODY# | Yes | Template | Region Body |
| #SUB_REGION_HEADERS# | No | | Sub Region Headers |
| #SUB_REGIONS# | No | | Sub Regions |
| #FORM_OPEN# | No | | HTML Form Open |
| #FORM_CLOSE# | No | | HTML Form Close |
| #HELP# | No | | Help Button |
| #DELETE# | No | | Delete Button |
| #COPY# | No | | Copy Button |
| #NEXT# | No | | Next Button |
| #PREVIOUS# | No | | Previous Button |
| #CHANGE# | No | | Change Button |
| #REGION_ID# | No | | Unique Region Id |
| #REGION_STATIC_ID# | No | | Region Static Id |
| #REGION_ATTRIBUTES# | No | | Region Attributes |
| #SUB_REGION_ID# | No | | Static Id of Sub Region |
| #SUB_REGION_TITLE# | No | | Title of Sub Region |
| #ENTRIES# | No | | Sub Region Header Entries |
| #SUB_REGION# | No | | Sub Region |

9. You can use the following example to enter in the definition section:

```
<table class="t115Region" id="#REGION_STATIC_ID#" #REGION_
ATTRIBUTES# border="0" cellpadding="0" cellspacing="0" summary=""
width="97%" style="border:none;">
<tbody class="ReportsRegion">
<tr>
<th class="t115RegionHeader">#TITLE#</th>
```

```
<th class="t115ButtonHolderHeader" width="100%">#CLOSE# 
 #PREVIOUS##NEXT# #DELETE##EDIT##CHANGE##CREATE##
CREATE2##EXPAND##COPY##HELP#</th>
</tr>
<tr>
<td class="t115RegionBody" colspan="2"
bgcolor="lightgrey">#BODY#</td>
</tr>
</tbody>
</table>
[T115region.txt]
```

This template code is a copy of the original code from theme 18, but with the background color set to light grey.

Substitution strings should be written in uppercase and should begin and end with a #-sign. As from APEX 4.0, new templates use the `<div>` tag. The older templates from APEX 3.2 and before used the`<table>` - `<tr>` - `<td>` tags.

10. Click on the **Apply changes** button.

11. If you want to use the new template, you have to change the pages/regions which will use this new template. Suppose you have a page with a tabular form. Click on the page you want to edit.

12. Click on the region you want to edit.

13. In the template listbox, select the new template, **cust_rep_reg**. You can find the template listbox in the user interface section.

14. Click on the **Apply changes** button. The region will now use this new template.

## There's more...

You can make your newly created template the default template for that specific component type. Just go to the **Shared components** page, go to the themes, and select the theme you want to edit. On the right side of the screen, under **Tasks**, click on **Edit theme**. You will see the component defaults. In the region listbox, select the new template. Click on the **Apply changes** button. The new template is now the default for the region component type.

# Including images in your application

A web application will look better when you use images. Of course, APEX 4.0 supports the use of images in web pages. You can easily upload images to the APEX host with your FTP client. To connect to the APEX host, see the description at the beginning of this chapter. You should copy your images to the images directory. APEX uses a shortcut or prefix for this path. Mostly it is /i/ but you can change that. Go to shared components and click on the edit definition link on the right side of the screen, under **Application**. In the name section you can find this image prefix text item where you can modify the prefix. It is advised to always use the substitution string #IMAGE_PREFIX# instead of /i/ when referring to images in templates or button images to safeguard the URI to the images when modifying the virtual directory on the HTTP server (EPG or Apache).

There is another way to upload images to the APEX environment. In the application builder, go to the application you are working on. Click on the **Shared components** icon. In the **Files** section, click on the **Images** link. You have workspace and application images.

## Getting ready

1. First you have to import the images into the APEX environment.

2. There are two ways to import images. We will discuss the images upload via APEX.

3. Go to the application builder and select an application.

4. Click on the **Shared components** icon.

5. Click on the **Images** link in the files section at the bottom of the screen.

6. Click on the **Create** button.

7. In the next step, you can choose whether the image should be available just for one application or for the entire workspace. If you want your image to be available throughout the entire workspace, leave the application listbox to no application associated. Otherwise, select an application. We want the image to be available to the entire workspace, so select **No application associated** in the **Application** listbox. Click on the **File** button to locate and select the image to be uploaded from your file system.

8. Click on the **Upload** button to upload the image. The image will be uploaded and after that you see the icon of the image to indicate that the image file has been successfully uploaded.

9. If you want more images to be uploaded, repeat these steps.

## How to do it...

First, let's include an image of the company's logo. To include a logo in the top-left corner, follow these steps:

1. In the application builder, go to the shared components by clicking on the **Shared components** icon.

2. Click on the **Edit definition** link on the right side of the screen, under **Application**.

3. Go to the **Logo** section and select **Image** as the **Logo Type**.

4. In the **Logo:** text field, enter the name of the image. It can be any image file type like a Bitmap (.bmp), a JPEG (.jpg), a PNG (.png), or a GIF (.gif) file. The image filename should be prefixed #IMAGE_PREFIX# when the image resides as an external resource, #APP_IMAGES# when uploaded as application image and #WORKSPACE_IMAGES# when uploaded as workspace image. We uploaded a workspace image so prefix the image filename with #WORKSPACE_IMAGES#.

5. In the **Logo Attributes** text field, you can define the width and height of the image. The logo area in the top-left corner is a fixed height area so if your image is too large, you might set the width and height. In this case, we set it to the following:

```
Width="200" height="30"
[Img_size.txt]
```

6. Run the page. You should see a logo, something like this:

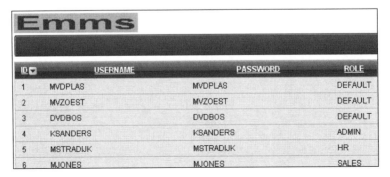

Now we will include an image in a region, just for the illustration.

Suppose you have an HTML region, you can use the following to show an image:

```
<img src="#WORKSPACE_IMAGES#emms.GIF">
[Img_wsi_emms.txt]
```

## How it works...

If you uploaded the image with an application specified, you can use #APP_IMAGES# as well:

```
<img src="#APP_IMAGES#emms.GIF">
[Img_ai_emms.txt]
```

However, if you uploaded the image for the workspace, so with no application specified, you can only use #WORKSPACE_IMAGES#.

If you uploaded the images to the images directory using FTP, you can use #IMAGE_PREFIX#. This is a substitution string for the images directory or /i/ if you specified the image prefix.

## There's more...

You can also include images by specifying the complete URL from another website. Create a HTML region and include the following in the region source:

```
<img src="http://www.example.com/frontpageimage.jpg">
[Img_ex.txt]
```

Where http://www.example.com/frontpageimage.jpg is the reference to an image on a host. Be careful though, as some website owners don't like it when images on their web pages are used on another web page. Loading images can be very bandwidth consuming, which in the end can lead to extra costs for the website owners.

When you upload images to APEX, the images are stored in the database. When you use images copied via FTP or copied to the web server, the files are actually physically there. However, the images that are stored on the web server load faster and can be cached by the browser.

# Referencing CSS classes in your application

Cascading Stylesheets offer an easy way to quickly change the look and feel of a web application. They hold information about colors, sizes, borders, and fonts. Working with stylesheets is a good way to separate the style and the actual content of a webpage. The HTML document should only contain text and HTML tags.

In this recipe, we will make a simple stylesheet, upload it to the APEX environment, and use it in our application. We will change the buttons and the background of the region. All this is done by referencing classes in the stylesheet.

## Getting ready

We will use the user profiles page we made in *Chapter 1, Creating a Basic APEX Application* so make sure this page is ready. For the buttons we will use other background images. You can make them yourself or you can copy some from the Internet (mind the copyrights). You can find them anywhere. Make sure these buttons have the same size as the original buttons. Once you have made the images you have to upload them using the FTP client. Copy the images to the /images/ directory.

For this example, we will use theme 1. If you haven't installed theme 1 yet, follow these steps:

1. Go to the **Shared Components**.

2. In the user **Interface** section, click on the **Themes** link.

3. Click on the **Create** button.

4. Select **From the repository** and click on **Next**.

5. Select **theme 1**.

6. Click on the **Create** button. The theme will now be created but it still isn't the active theme, so click on the **Switch theme** button.

7. In the **Switch to theme** listbox, select **theme 1** and click on **Next**.

8. In the next dialog you see the templates and the status. If the status is OK for all templates, click on **Next**.

9. In the last step, click on the **Switch theme** button. Theme 1 is now the active theme and this is indicated by an asterisk (*) near the theme.

## How to do it...

1. Create a new text file and put the following in it:

```
.bgregion {
border: 1px solid;
background-color:lightblue;
}

button {
border: 0;
cursor: pointer;
font-weight: normal;
padding: 0 10px 0 0;
text-align: center;
```

```
}

button span {
position: relative;
display: block;
white-space: nowrap;
font-size: 13px;
padding: 0 4px 0 15px;
}

button.button_custom {
background: transparent url('../images/rb_a.GIF') no-repeat scroll
top right;
color: black;
display: block;
float: left;
font: normal 12px arial, sans-serif;
font-face:bold;
height: 24px;
margin-right: 6px;
padding-right: 18px; /* sliding doors padding */
text-decoration: none;
}

button.button_custom span {
background: transparent url('../images/rb_span.GIF') no-repeat;
display: block;
line-height: 14px;
padding: 5px 0 5px 18px;
}
[buttons.css]
```

2.  Save the file and give it a name, that is, `custom_theme.css`.

3.  In the application builder, go to the application you are working on.

4.  Click on the **Shared components** icon.

5.  In the **Files** section, click on the **Cascading style sheets** link.

6.  Click on the **Create** button.

7.  In the next step, click on the **File** button.

8.  A file dialog appears. Locate your created custom theme stylesheet and select this file.

9.  You can also enter some comments in the notes text area. After that, click on the **Upload** button.

10. The stylesheet will be uploaded and if you have succeeded, you will see an icon with the name **custom_theme.css**.

11. Go to the application and click on the **Userprofiles** page.

12. In the page section, click on the Edit icon (the pencil on the upper right corner).

13. Click on **Show all**.

14. In the HTML header and body attribute section, enter the following in the HTML header text area:

```
<link href="#WORKSPACE_IMAGES#custom_theme.css" rel="stylesheet"
type="text/css">
[Link_css.txt]
```

15. This tag will be included in the webpage so that we can reference the styles from the stylesheet. Click on the **Apply changes** button.

16. In the **Templates** section, click on the region template.

17. Replace **rc-content-main** with **bgregion**. You can find **rc-content-main** in the div just before the #BODY# substitution string.

18. Click on the **Apply changes** button.

19. Click on the button template.

20. In the **Definition** section, replace **button-gray** with **button_custom** in the template text area.

21. Click on the **Apply changes** button.

22. Run the page. You should see other buttons and a light blue background.

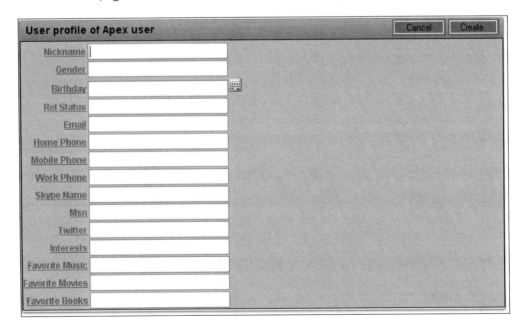

## How it works...

In the HTML tags, you can reference to the stylesheet. This can be done in three ways:

1. Declare tags in the stylesheet, such as :

   ```
   H1{font-family: verdana, arial; font-size: 200%; color: darkblue}
   [Font_verdana.css]
   ```

2. This causes every <H1> tag in the HTML document to be formatted with an Arial-like font, a font-size of 200%, and in the color dark blue.

3. Name the objects in the HTML document and give it the same name as declared in the stylesheet:

   ```
   #reportarea {background-color:lightyellow}
   [Bg_ly.css]
   ```

4. Include a `div` in your HTML document and name it `reportarea`:

   ```
   <div id="reportarea">some text</div>
   [Div_reportarea.txt]
   ```

5. This causes to display a `div` with a light yellow background.

6. Reference by using classes.

7. Declare a class in the stylesheet:

   ```
   .divbackground{border: 1px solid;
   background-image:url(background.gif);
   background-position:left top;}
   [div_bkg.css]
   ```

8. Include a `div` in your HTML document and use the class attribute to reference to `divbackground`:

   ```
   <div class="divbackground">some text</div>
   [Div_class_bkg.txt]
   ```

This displays a div with a solid line and a background image with the name `background.gif`. The image starts at the upper-left corner of the div.

In our webpage, we referenced using classes in the stylesheet. First, we referenced to the `bgregion` class and for the buttons we referenced the `button_custom` class.

There are two images used for the buttons. The first image, `bg_span.gif` is the actual background with the button label. The second image, `bg_a.gif` will be put on the right side of the first image. In this way, you will see two images that together look like one button. In this way, the button width is variable and dependent on the length of the label.

Be careful when you switch to another theme. You will possibly lose your template settings. You can avoid this by exporting the theme.

# Controlling the layout

One of the most difficult tasks of web programing is the control of the layout. In previous versions of APEX, tables were used to place the items on the desired positions. You can use an HTML editor to see a preview of the layout. As from APEX 4.0, new themes are introduced that use divs to position the different components. Divs are almost necessary to be able to use dynamic actions layout. The biggest advantage from div-based layout over table-based layout is that you can precisely position components of the web page.

In this recipe, we will create a page with a report region showing the application users and a chart region with the number of roles used. The two regions will be displayed next to each other.

## Getting ready

Just make sure that theme 1 is the active theme.

## How to do it...

1. In the application builder, go to your application.
2. Click on the **Create page** button.
3. Select **Report** and in the next step, select **Classic report**.
4. Leave the page number or assign a number yourself and enter a name for the page. Click on **Next**.
5. Select **Do not use tabs** and click on **Next**.
6. In the text area, enter the following query:

```
select  id
    ,       username
    ,       password
    ,       role
from    app_users;
[select_app_users.sql]
```

7. Click on **Next**.
8. Enter a name for the region (that is, **Users**) and click on **Next**.
9. In the last step, click on the **Finish** button.

10. Your page has now successfully been created and you see a success message.

11. Click on the **Edit page** icon.

12. In the regions section, click on the **Add** icon in the upper right corner of the section.

13. Select **Chart**.

14. In the next step, select **HTML chart**.

15. In the title text item, enter User roles. Click on **Next**.

16. In the query text area, enter the following query:

```
select null link
     ,    role label
     ,    count(id) value
from    app_users
group by role
[select_aur_role.sql]
```

You can also use the query builder. Click on the build query button to start a wizard which helps you to create your query.

17. Click on the **Create region** button.

18. The region will be created and you now have two regions. When you run the page, you will see that the chart region is positioned below the **Users** region. Maybe you want to place the region next to the **Users** region. That can be done in several ways.

19. Click on the **Edit page** button at the bottom of the page.

20. In the **Regions** section, click on the **User roles** link to edit the region.

21. In the **User Interface** section, select **2** in the **Column list** box.

22. Click on the **Apply changes** button and run the page to see how it looks.

23. You can see that the regions are displayed next to one another. There is also another way to control the position of the regions.

24. Click on the **Edit page** button at the bottom of the page.

25. In the templates section, click on the **Page template** link.

26. In the definition section you see HTML code for the header, the body, and the footer of the page. To see how this actually looks you could use an HTML editor and copy-paste the code in the editor. However, you can also get a preview of the template. Click on the **Preview template** link in the tasks section on the right side. You can see a preview that is a little bit more clear when you go to the page, click on the **User** roles link in the regions section, and click on the flashlight that is located after the **Display** point listbox in the **User Interface** section.

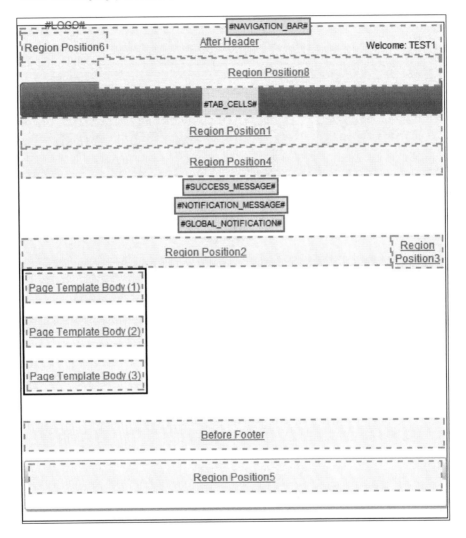

In this preview for theme 1, you can see the region position 2 and region position 3 are positioned next to each other but that region position 3 is smaller. Let's see how this looks when we position the chart region on region position 3:

1. Close the preview pop-up window and go back to your page.

2. In the **Regions** section, click on the **Users region** to edit the region.

3. In the **User Interface** section, select **Page template region position 2** in the **Display Point** listbox.

4. Click on the **Apply changes** button.

5. In the **Regions** section, click on the **User roles** link to edit the region.

6. In the user interface section, select **Page template region position 3** in the **Display Point** listbox. Select **1** in the **Column** listbox (we changed this to 2 in the beginning of this recipe). Click on the **Apply changes** button.

7. Run the page and see what the page looks like.

## How it works...

The screenshot shown in the previous paragraph shows the various positions in the region. You can also see these positions in the display point listbox in the **User Interface** section when you click on a region in the application builder.

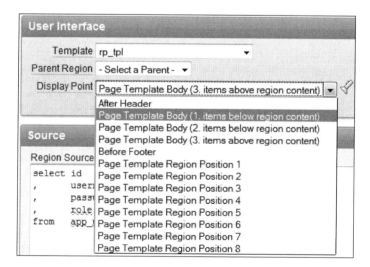

In this way you can control where the content of a region is displayed. If you position two regions at the same position, like we first did in this recipe, the last region will be displayed below the first region. You can put them next to each other by using the column listbox, which you can find behind the display point listbox in the user interface section. The first region will be positioned in column 1 and the second region will be positioned in column 2.

## There's more...

Alternatively, you can change the entire layout, just by changing the HTML code in the template. So, if you would like to display the success message at the bottom of the page, go to the definition section of the template and enter the substitution string #SUCCESS_ MESSAGE# in the footer text area.

By the way, did you notice that in theme 1, region position 5 by default is displayed twice, one time in the body and the second time in the footer? This means that if you set a region's display point to region position 5, you will see this region twice!

# 3
# Extending APEX

In this chapter, we will cover:

- ▸ Adding JavaScript code to your application
- ▸ Creating a tag cloud with AJAX
- ▸ Creating visual effects with JavaScript libraries
- ▸ Enhancing your application with the Google API
- ▸ Including Google Maps
- ▸ Embedding multimedia objects in your application
- ▸ Creating a region selector
- ▸ Sending mail via APEX
- ▸ Uploading and downloading files
- ▸ Calling APEX from an Oracle Form
- ▸ Creating a data upload page
- ▸ Using shipped files

## Introduction

In the first two chapters we described the tasks to create a basic APEX web application. In this chapter we will extend our application with some nice features such as visual effects, a tag cloud, and a Google map.

Many of these features are made possible with the use of JavaScript. JavaScript enables dynamic features such as dynamic list of values, drag-and-drop functionality, and different effects on popping-up and disappearing of items.

Since APEX 4.0, many of these JavaScript features can be built using plug-ins. However, for some features, you still need to use JavaScript. By the way, you also need to have good knowledge of JavaScript if you want to make use of the extensive possibilities of Google Maps.

# Adding JavaScript code to your application

JavaScript can also be used for client validation. We will build a validation on the `salary` field. When the user raises the salary by more than 10 percent, an alert box will appear where the user can confirm the salary.

## Getting ready

Make sure you have a tabular form based on the EMP table. At least the `salary` column should be present in the form.

## How to do it...

1.  In the **Application Builder**, go to the page based on the EMP table.

2.  In the **Regions** section, click on the **Report** link:

3.  Click on the Edit icon (the pencil) near the **SALARY** column:

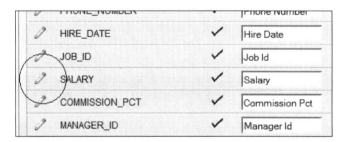

4.  In the **Column Attributes** section, enter the following in the **Element Attributes** text field:

    ```
    onfocus=remember_oldsal(this.value); onchange=validate_sal(this.
    id,this.value);
    [9672_03_01.txt]
    ```

5. Click on the **Apply Changes** button, and after that click again on it.

6. In the **Page** section, click on the Edit icon.

7. In the **HTML Header** and **HTML Body Attribute** section, enter the following in the **HTML Header** textarea:

```
<script type="text/javascript">
  var oldsal = 0;
  function remember_oldsal(salary)
  {
    oldsal = salary;
  }

  function validate_sal(sal_id, salary)
  {
    if (salary > (oldsal * 1.10))
    {
      var r = confirm("Are you sure you want to change this salary
to " + salary);
      if (r == false)
      {
        $("#"+sal_id).val(oldsal);
      }
    }
  }
</script>
[9672_03_02.txt]
```

The header now contains two JavaScript scripts and a variable declaration. This variable declaration is necessary because if the variable had been declared in a function, it wouldn't have been accessible. The function REMEMBER_OLDSAL copies the salary when the user navigates to the salary field. The function VALIDATE_SAL calculates the old salary raised by 10 percent, and if the new salary is greater than the old salary plus 10 percent, a popup alert is displayed. If the Cancel button is clicked (r == false), the value of the variable oldsal is copied to the salary column. Otherwise, newly entered salary is kept as is.

8. Click on the **Apply Changes** button.

9. Run the form and see what happens if you change a salary by more than 10 percent.

## How it works...

Everything you put in the **HTML Header** section will be presented in the HTML header of the page. You can see this by right-clicking on the page and selecting **View Source**. You will then see the HTML code which is used to present the page. On the top of the code, you can see your JavaScript code.

The JavaScript functions can be called from objects in the web page. For example, you can call a JavaScript function when the user navigates to a text item or when the body of a web page is loaded.

Items can be identified by an ID or a name, and you can get or set the value of items with the jQuery function `$("#ITEM").val()`, in the following manner:

```
Variable = $("#P18_ID").val();
```

To do the same prior to APEX 4, you had to use the following:

```
Variable = document.getElementById(id).value;
```

You can also put values into the items with the following function:

```
$("#P18_ID").val(5000);
```

Or, use the following prior to APEX 4:

```
document.getElementById(id).value = 5000;
```

And you can also use the following jQuery syntax to copy values between items:

```
$("#P18_NAME").val($("#P18_TEXT").val());
```

In APEX, you can add a call to a JavaScript function in the **Element Attributes** section of the item.

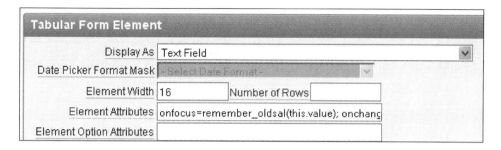

## There's more...

There are various ways to include JavaScript code in the page. You can not only put JavaScript code in the HTML header of the page or the region source, but you can also put some JavaScript code in the item. Go to the item and type your code in the **HTML** section.

Since APEX 4, working with JavaScript has been made easy with the use of dynamic actions, region display selectors, and plug-ins. This recipe is included only to show how JavaScript works in APEX, but if you can, use the new features. They will save you a lot of work.

# Creating a tag cloud with AJAX

**Asynchronous JavaScript and XML (AJAX)** is a method of communication between a client and the server where the website resides. AJAX makes it possible to dynamically respond to actions on the client side. For example, it is possible to directly check an e-mail address while you are typing! Or set a color of an object when clicking on another object. Ajax is most used to dynamically fetch data from the server to use it on the web page.

Until APEX 4.0, using Ajax in your web page required advanced programming with JavaScript. But since APEX 4.0, it is a lot easier to use AJAX with the help of dynamic actions. We will make a page with a tag cloud and a region where you can see the news articles. When you click on a tag in the tag cloud, APEX will show the articles that are related to the selected tag. This information is an AJAX call and is implemented using a dynamic action.

## Getting ready

We will create a new page. Make sure you have created, and have access to the tables APP_NEWS, APP_TAGS, and APP_TGS_NWS.

## How to do it...

1. Go to your application and click on the **Create Page** button.

2. Select **Blank page**.

3. Enter a page alias, for example `tagnews`, and click on **Next**.

4. Enter a name for the page, for example, `News articles by tags`, and click on **Next**.

5. Select **No** and click on **Next**.

6. Click on **Finish**.

7. Click on the Edit icon.

8. In the **Regions** section, click on the Add icon.

9. Select **PL/SQL dynamic content**.

10. Enter a title for the region, in this case `Tag cloud`. Click on **Next**.

11. In the **PL/SQL Source** textarea, enter the following code:

```
declare
  --
  cursor c_tags is
    select tns.tgs_id
    ,      tgs.tag
    ,      count(tns.tgs_id) num_of_times
    from   app_tgs_nws tns
    ,      app_tags     tgs
    where  tgs.id = tns.tgs_id
    group by tns.tgs_id, tgs.tag
    order by 1;
  --
  l_min_num number(3);
  l_max_num number(3);
  l_size    number(2);
  l_multiplx number(2);
begin
  select min(num_of_times) min_num
  ,      max(num_of_times) max_num
  into   l_min_num, l_max_num
  from   (select tns.tgs_id
          ,      tgs.tag
          ,      count(tns.tgs_id) num_of_times
          from   app_tgs_nws tns
          ,      app_tags     tgs
          where  tgs.id = tns.tgs_id
```

```
             group by tns.tgs_id, tgs.tag);
    --
    l_multiplx := round(72/l_max_num);
    --
    for r_tags in c_tags
    loop
       l_size := round(l_multiplx * r_tags.num_of_times);
       sys.htp.print (q'!<a onmouseover="this.style.
cursor='pointer';" onclick=document.getElementById("PXX_TAG").
value="!'||r_tags.tag||'";
style="font-size:'||to_char(l_size)||'px; text-
decoration:none;">'||r_tags.tag||'</a>');
       sys.htp.print ('   ');
    end loop;
end;
[9672_03_05.txt]
```

Replace XX in PXX_TAG by the page number. The onmouseover event is necessary to change the cursor as if it were pointing to a link. The onclick event copies the value of the tag that is clicked on to the hidden item PXX_TAG. This is needed to build the query. The item will be referenced in the dynamic action. But first we need to create the item through the following steps:

1. Click on the **Create Region** button. The tag cloud region is now ready. Now we will create the hidden item.

2. In the **Items** section, click on the Add icon.

3. Select **Hidden** and click on **next**.

4. In the **Item Name** text item, enter the name PXX_TAG where XX is the page number you are creating. You can see the page number on the first line of the **Create Item** section.

5. In the **Region** listbox, select the tag cloud region you just selected. Click on **Next** two times.

6. Click on the **Create Item** button. The hidden item is ready. Now we will create the region for the news articles.

7. In the **Regions** section, click the Add icon.

8. Select **HTML**.

9. Again, select **HTML** and click on **Next**.

10. Enter a title for the region, for example Related articles, and click on **Next**.

11. Leave the **Region Source** empty and click on the **Create Region** button.

The last step is the creation of the dynamic action.

1. In the **Dynamic Actions** sections, click on the Add icon.
2. Select **Advanced**.
3. Enter a name for this action, for example `show_articles`, and click on **Next**.
4. In the **Event** listbox, select **Click**.
5. In the **Selection Type** listbox, select **Region**.
6. In the **Region** listbox, select the tag cloud region and click on **Next**.
7. In the **Action** listbox, select **Set Value**. A **Settings** section appears.
8. In the **Set Type** listbox, select **PL/SQL function body**.
9. In the **PL/SQL function body** textarea, enter the following code:

```
declare
cursor c_nws is
   select title
   ,       text
   from    app_news
   where   upper(text) like '%'||upper(:PXX_TAG)||'%';
--
l_text varchar2(32000) := '';
begin
for r_nws in c_nws
loop
   l_text := l_text || '<h1>' || r_nws.title || '</h1>';
   l_text := l_text || '<br>';
   l_text := l_text ||    replace(r_nws.text,:PXX_TAG,'<b>'||:PXX_
TAG||'</b>');
   l_text := l_text || '<br>';
   l_text := l_text || '<br>';
end loop;
return l_text;
end;
[9672_03_06.txt]
```

Replace XX in PXX_TAG by the page number. This script loops through the records of a query. The query selects the records where the text contains the tag where the user clicked on. The results of the query are displayed using the htp.p function.

1. In the **Page Items to Submit** text field, enter PXX_TAG where XX is the page number.
2. In the **Escape Special Characters** listbox, select **No** and click on **Next**.

In the next step we must set the affected objects:

1.  In the **Selection Type** listbox, select **Region**. In the **Region** listbox, select **HTML region (related articles)**. Click on the **Create** button.

2.  In the **Processes** section, click the Add icon.

3.  Select **PL/SQL** and click on **Next**.

4.  Enter a name for the PL/SQL process, for example `populate_tags`.

5.  In the **Point** listbox, select **On Load – Before Header** and click on **Next**.

6.  In the **PL/SQL** textarea, enter the following code:

```
declare
  cursor c_app_tags
  is
    select id
    ,      tag
    from   app_tags
    order by id;
  --
  cursor c_instr(b_tag in varchar2)
  is
    select id
    ,      instr(upper(text),upper(b_tag)) tag_found
    from   app_news;
begin
  delete from app_tgs_nws;
  --
  for r_app_tags in c_app_tags
  loop
    for r_instr in c_instr(r_app_tags.tag)
    loop
      if r_instr.tag_found > 0
      then
        insert into app_tgs_nws
        values (r_app_tags.id,r_instr.id);
      end if;
    end loop;
  end loop;
  --
  commit;
end;
[9672_03_25.txt]
```

The preceding piece of code populates the intersection table between APP_NWS and APP_TAGS. First, the table is truncated, and then, the code loops through the text of the APP_NWS table to search for the tags from the APP_TAGS table. If it finds a match, a row is inserted into the APP_TGS_NWS table. This process is started each time the user enters this page. In this way, changes in the APP_NWS table are immediately visible. So, when a row is inserted into the APP_NWS table with a text that contains something like APEX, the tag cloud will show the APEX tag bigger.

7. Click on the **Create Process** button.

The page is now ready. Run the page and see how the articles change when you click on a tag.

## How it works...

We use the `<a>` tag where we put some extra JavaScript code. First, there is the `onmouseover` event which changes the cursor style to a pointer (the "hand"). Second, there is the `onclick` event which copies the tag to the hidden item.

In the dynamic action, a PL/SQL function is executed which loops through a cursor of a query that selects all records with articles related to the tag (the `like` operator is used). In the dynamic action, the `set_value` function is used to replace the content of the affected region by the content of the variable `l_text`.

Actually the affected region (`Related articles`) is a div, and the dynamic action is an AJAX process that retrieves the data from the server (the query) and puts them in the div. In JavaScript, you would use the following line of code for divs:

```
$('divid').html("some text or HTML code");
```

The following JavaScript code would be used for items:

```
$('#P_ITEM').val('some text');
```

The last case is similar to a dynamic action where the affected object is an item.

You can test all this yourself:

1. Go to the page and click on the Edit icon in the **Page** section.

2. In the **HTML Header** and **Body Attribute** section, enter the following in the HTML header textarea to create a JavaScript function:

```
<script type="text/javascript">
function set_div(){
document.getElementById("dynamicdiv").innerHTML = "This is some
text in a div";
}
</script>
[9672_03_07.txt]
```

3. Click on the **Apply Changes** button.

4. To assign an ID for the `Related articles` div (region), click on the **Related articles** region. In the **Attributes** section, enter `dynamicdiv` in the **Static ID** text field and click on the **Apply Changes** button.

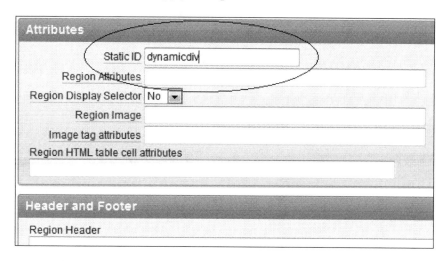

5. To create a text item, in the **Items** section, click on the Add icon.

6. Select **Text field** and click on **Next**. In the **Item Name** text field, enter a name and in the **Region** listbox, select the **tag cloud** region. Click three times on **Next**. Then click on the **Create Item** button.

7. Click on the newly created item. In the **Element** section, enter the following in the HTML form element attributes:

```
onblur=set_div();
[9672_03_08.txt]
```

The `onblur` event fires when the user navigates out of the item by using the *Tab* key, the *Enter* key, or by clicking the mouse pointer somewhere else.

8. Click on the **Apply Changes** button.

Run the page. Click on the item you just created and navigate out of the item using the *Tab* or *Enter* key. The div should show the text `This is some text in a div`. This is just an example to show you what a dynamic action actually does. Don't mind the strange `onblur` event on the item used to trigger an event. An `onclick` event was not possible as the entire tag cloud had an `onclick` event triggering the dynamic action to set the `Related articles` region.

The static ID for the div is necessary, otherwise APEX generates its own ID which looks something like `R431819100396833156` and then you have to find the div ID using the page source of the web page.

# Creating visual effects with JavaScript libraries

JavaScript libraries can be used to make your web page catchy. You can use JavaScript libraries to pop up or disappear items. But JavaScript libraries can also be used when you want to implement the drag-and-drop functionality.

There are several JavaScript libraries. The most well-known JavaScript library is jQuery. In Apex 4.0, jQuery is built-in and can be directly accessed, so you don't have to download and install it. However, when you want to use a JavaScript library such as **scriptaculous**, you have to download and install it.

Since jQuery is built-in, we will use it to demonstrate the making of an accordion. We will create an accordion where we put in some information, and by clicking on it, you can see the different sections.

## Getting ready

We will use the APP_EVENTS table, so make sure this table is accessible.

## How to do it...

First we create a region template:

1. Navigate to **Shared Components | Templates**.
2. Click on the **Create** button.
3. Select **Region** and click on **Next**.
4. Select **From Scratch** and click on **Next**.
5. Enter a name for the region, for example accordion.
6. In the **Template Class** listbox, select **Custom 1**.
7. Click on the **Create** button.

8. In the list of templates, click the **accordion** template.

| Region | accordion | 2 | 3 hours ago | admin | - | - | 4 | | |
|---|---|---|---|---|---|---|---|---|---|
| | Borderless Region | 0 | 7 weeks ago | test1 | - | - | 20 | | |
| | Borderless Region | 0 | - | - | - | - | 11 | | |
| | Borderless Region | 0 | 7 weeks ago | admin | - | - | 18 | | |
| | Borderless Region | 0 | 24 hours ago | admin | - | - | 4 | | |
| | Bracketed Region | 0 | 7 weeks ago | admin | - | - | 18 | | |
| | Bracketed Region | 0 | 7 weeks ago | test1 | - | - | 20 | | |

9. In the **Definition** section, enter the following in the **Template** text field:

```
<div id="#REGION_STATIC_ID#" #REGION_ATTRIBUTES#>
#BODY##SUB_REGION_HEADERS##SUB_REGIONS#
</div>
<link rel="stylesheet" href="#IMAGE_PREFIX#libraries/jquery-
ui/1.8/themes/base/jquery.ui.accordion.css" type="text/css" />

<script src="#IMAGE_PREFIX#libraries/jquery-ui/1.8/ui/minified/
jquery.ui.accordion.min.js" type="text/javascript"></script>

<script type="text/javascript">
apex.jQuery(function() {
apex.jQuery("##REGION_STATIC_ID#").accordion();
});
</script>
[9672_03_26.txt]
```

10. In the **Sub Regions** section, enter the following code in the **Template** text field:

```
<h3><a href="#">#SUB_REGION_TITLE#</a></h3>
<div>#SUB_REGION#</div>
[9672_03_27.txt]
```

11. Click on the **Apply Changes** button.

The template is ready now. The next step is to create a region and a sub-region:

1. Go to the page where you want the accordion to appear.
2. In the **Regions** section, click on the Add icon.
3. Select **HTML** and click on **Next**.
4. Again select **HTML** and click on **Next**.
5. Enter a title for the region, for example `accordion`.
6. From the **Region template** listbox, select **accordion** (the template we just created).
7. Click on **Next**.
8. Click on the **Create Region** button.

That was the region. Now we will create the sub-region:

1. In the **Regions** section, click on the Add icon.
2. Select **HTML** and click on **Next**.
3. Again select **HTML** and click on **Next**.
4. Enter a title for the sub-region, for example `Welcome`.
5. From the **Region Template** listbox, select **No Template**.
6. From the **Parent Region** listbox, select the parent region we just created, that is, **accordion**.
7. Click on **Next**.
8. In the **HTML Region Source**, enter some text.
9. Click on the **Create Region** button.

That was the first slice. Now we will create a second slice:

1. In the **Regions** section, click on the Add icon.
2. Select **Report** and click on **Next**.
3. Select **SQL Report** and click on **Next**.
4. In the **Title** text field, enter **Events**.
5. In the **Region Template** listbox, select **No Template**.
6. In the **Parent Region** listbox, select the parent region we created, that is **accordion**.
7. Click on **Next**.
8. In the **Query** textarea, enter the following query:

```
select  event
,       location
from    app_events;
[9672_03_28.txt]
```

9. Click on the **Create Region** button.

10. The accordion is ready now. Run the page and see how it looks. Mine looks something as shown in the following screenshot:

## How it works...

This recipe consists of two parts: creating a template of type region and creating regions and sub-regions. The region is the placeholder for the accordion and the sub-regions are the slices. In the template we put some HTML and JavaScript code that is needed to reference the jQuery containing the code for the accordion, and to call the `accordion` function.

In the template, the div gets the ID from the #REGION_STATIC_ID# substitution variable. The `accordion` function uses that ID to render the accordion on the proper region. The jQuery call to the accordion includes the div ID, prefixed by the hash sign (#). That is why you see two hash signs in the call to the accordion:

```
apex.jQuery("##REGION_STATIC_ID#").accordion();
```

The first is the hash prefix and the second is the enclosing hash sign of the substitution variable.

The displayed data has to conform to the following layout:

```
<div id="accordion">
    <h3><a href="#">seminar</a></h3>
    <div>30-MAR-2010: Apex day, Zeist, Netherlands</div>
    <h3><a href="#">workshop</a></h3>
    <div>07-JUN-2010: APEX 4.0 workshop</div>
</div>
```

The first and the last line are part of the parent region. Everything in between is part of the sub-region (the slices). In the preceding example, you see two slices. Since the `<h3>`, `<a>`, and the `<div>` tags are in the template, you only have to put the text into the sub-region to display as desired.

## There's more...

You can make the accordion dynamic by using a PL/SQL dynamic content region where you use `sys.htp.p` to display the data including the `<h3>`, `<a>`, and `<div>` tags:

1. In the **Regions** section, click the Add icon.

2. Select **PL/SQL dynamic content**.

3. Enter a title for the region, for example `Events`.

4. In the **Region Template** listbox, select the **accordion** template.

5. Click on **Next**.

6. In the **PL/SQL Source** textarea, enter the following code:

```
declare
  cursor c_aet is
    select rownum line
    ,       event_type
    ,       event_date
    ,       event
    ,       location
      from    (select decode(row_number() over (partition by event_
type order by event_type),1,event_type,null) event_type
              ,       event_date
              ,       event
              ,       location
             from app_events);
begin
  for r_aet in c_aet
  loop
    if r_aet.event_type is not null
    then
      if r_aet.line != 1
      then
        sys.htp.p('</div>');
      end if;
      sys.htp.p('<h3><a href="#">'||r_aet.event_type||'</a></
h3>');
      sys.htp.p('<div>');
    end if;
```

```
      sys.htp.p('<b>'||to_char(r_aet.event_date,'DD-MM-YYYY')||'</
  b>'||': '||r_aet.event||', '||r_aet.location);
      sys.htp.p('<br>');
    end loop;
  end;
  [9672_03_29.txt]
```

This code selects from the APP_EVENTS table and displays the date and the event. Therefore it uses sys.htp.p to display the data, including the necessary tags. By using the accordion template, everything will be displayed in an accordion.

You can select the slices by clicking on them. However, you can change the call to the accordion so that you only have to hover over the slices instead of clicking on them. In the accordion template, change the following line of code:

```
apex.jQuery("##REGION_STATIC_ID#").accordion();
```

Into:

```
apex.jQuery("##REGION_STATIC_ID#").accordion({event:"mouseover"});
```

Besides the accordion, jQuery offers other cool "widgets", such as a slider or a progressbar. For more information, take a look at http://www.jquery.com.

# Enhancing your application with the Google API

In the previous recipe you could see how a JavaScript library such as jQuery can be used within APEX. Other JavaScript libraries can also be used, but they need first to be downloaded and installed. To make life easier for people who intend to use the various JavaScript libraries, Google introduced the **Google API**. Google puts the most well known JavaScript libraries online so you can reference them now without installing them into your own APEX environment! By the way, you can also use the JavaScript libraries in other languages such as PHP or just plain HTML with JavaScript.

To demonstrate this, we will make use of the `scriptaculous` library. Suppose you have the following intranet home page:

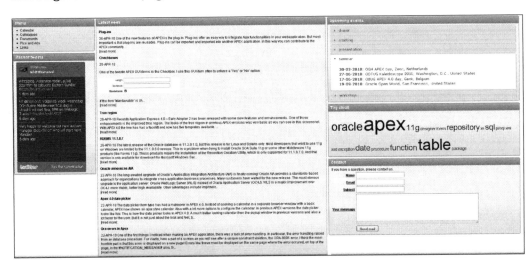

We will let the **Latest news** section pulsate on loading the homepage.

## How to do it...

1. In the **Application Builder**, edit page **1**.

2. In the **Page** section, click on the Edit icon.

3. In the **HTML Header** section, enter the following code in the **HTML Header** textarea:

```
<script src="http://www.google.com/jsapi" type="text/
javascript"></script>
<script type="text/javascript">
google.load("prototype", "1");
google.load("scriptaculous", "1");
function pulsate_news() {
    Effect.Pulsate('news', {'pulses' : 15, 'duration' : 3.0});
    }
google.setOnLoadCallback(pulsate_news);
</script>
[9672_03_11.txt]
```

First, you need to load the libraries. This can be done with the `google.load()` function. The first argument is the library and the second argument is the version. In this case, we will use Version 1 of the `scriptaculous` JavaScript library. By the way, `scriptaculous` makes use of the `Prototype` library, so this library has to be loaded first. The function `pulsate_news()` calls the `pulsate` effect, and the function `pulsate_news` is called by the `google.setOnLoadCallback()` function. The first argument of the `pulsate_news()` function is the ID of the affected div. The second argument is a list of options you can set. In this case, the news region pulsates 15 times in 3 seconds.

4. Click on the **Apply Changes** button.

Now we must set the ID of the affected div to `news`.

1. Click on the edit region link of the latest news region.
2. In the **Attributes** section, enter `news` in the **Static ID** text field.
3. Click on the **Apply Changes** button.
4. Run the page and see the **Latest news** region pulsate.

## How it works...

Load the necessary libraries with the `google.load` function. After that, create a function that calls the effect. To start the effect, use `google.setOnLoadCallBack`. The last step is to give the affected object (a div or an item or other DOM object) an ID that will be used in the call to the JavaScript effect.

## There's more...

For APEX 4.2, replace the code in step 3 by the following:

```
<script src="//ajax.googleapis.com/ajax/libs/prototype/1.7.1.0/
prototype.js"></script>
<script src="//ajax.googleapis.com/ajax/libs/scriptaculous/1.9.0/
scriptaculous.js"></script>
```

Add the following to the **Execute when Page Loads** textarea in the JavaScript section:

```
Effect.Pulsate('news', {'pulses' : 15, 'duration' : 3.0});
```

## See also

▸ For more information on the Google API or `scriptaculous`, take a look at http://code.google.com/intl/nl/apis/ajaxlibs/documentation/index.html, http://code.google.com/apis/ajax/playground/?exp=libraries, or http://script.aculo.us.

# Including Google Maps

In your APEX application it is possible to include a Google map. A Google map can be very useful, for example, for contact details or directions. It is not only simple to include a map, but you can also extend the map with several functions. In former releases of APEX, you needed to create a PL/SQL dynamic region with JavaScript embedded in the PL/SQL code. Since APEX 4.0, you can use plug-ins. We will show you how to include the Google map with plug-ins. In this recipe we will create a Google map with markers representing the locations from the APP_CUSTOMERS table.

## Getting ready

Make sure you have access to the APP_CUSTOMERS table. Also, make sure you have an API key to get the Google map working. If you haven't got any, request one at https://developers.google.com/maps/documentation/javascript/tutorial?hl=nl#api_key.

## How to do it...

First of all, you have to define a plug-in.

1.  In the **Application Builder**, go to your application and click on the Shared Components icon.

2.  In the **User Interface** section, click on the **Plug-ins** link.

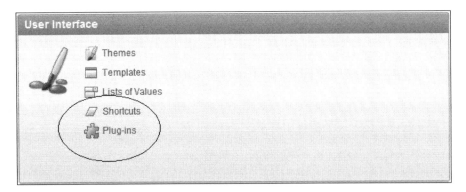

3.  Click on the **Create** button.

4.  In the **Name** section, enter a name in the **Name** text field, for example Google map.

5.  In the **Internal Name** text field, enter a unique name. If you want to make your plug-in publicly available, this name must be unique worldwide. In that case, it is advisable to use your company's fully qualified domain name reversed. For example `com.packtpub.apex.google_map`.

6.  In the **Type** listbox, select **Region**.

7.  Click on the **Create** button. The plug-in has now been created and now we must define the attributes.

8.  In the **Custom Attributes** section, click on the **Add Attribute** button.

9.  In the **Name** section, enter `Width` in the **Label** text field.

10. In the **Settings** section, select **Integer** in the **Type** listbox.

11. Select **Yes** in the **Required** listbox.

12. In the **Display Width** text field, enter `4`, and in the **Maximum Width** text field, enter `4`.

13. In the **Default Value** textarea, enter `600`.

14. Click on **Create And Create Another**.

15. In the **Name** section, enter `2` in the **Attributes** text field.

16. Enter `Height` in the **Label** text field.

17. In the **Settings** section, select **Integer** in the **Type** listbox.

18. Select **Yes** in the **Required** listbox.

19. In the **Display Width** text field, enter `4` and in the **Maximum Width** text field, enter `4`.

20. In the **Default Value** textarea, enter `400`.

21. Click on **Create**.

The attributes have now been defined. Now we will enter the code which is needed to display the Google map.

1.  In the **Source** section, enter the following code in the **PL/SQL Code** textarea:

```
function render_google_map (
    p_region               in apex_plugin.t_region,
    p_plugin               in apex_plugin.t_plugin,
    p_is_printer_friendly in boolean )
return apex_plugin.t_region_render_result
is
cursor c_cmr is
    select cust_street_address1||', '||cust_city geoloc
    from    app_customers
    where   cust_street_address1 is not null
    order by customer_id;
    --
```

```
    l_width       apex_application_page_regions.attribute_01%type :=
p_region.attribute_01;
    l_height      apex_application_page_regions.attribute_02%type :=
p_region.attribute_02;
    l_code        varchar2(32000);
    i             number(3) := 0;
begin
apex_javascript.add_library (
    p_name           => 'maps?file=api& v=3&key=YOURKEY',
    p_directory      => 'http://maps.google.com/',
    p_version        => null,
    p_skip_extension => true );
--
sys.htp.p('<div id="'||p_region.static_id||'_map"
style="width:'||l_width||'px; height:'||l_height||'px"></div>');
--
l_code := 'var map = null;
    var geocoder = null;
    if (GBrowserIsCompatible()) {
    map = new GMap2($x("'||p_region.static_id||'_map"));
    map.setCenter(new GLatLng(36.902466,-84.202881), 5);
    map.addControl(new GLargeMapControl());
    map.addControl(new GMapTypeControl());
    geocoder = new GClientGeocoder();';
--
for r_cmr in c_cmr
loop
    l_code := l_code || 'geocoder.getLatLng(' ||''''||
        r_cmr.geoloc ||''''||','||
        'function(point) {
            var baseIcon = new GIcon(G_DEFAULT_ICON);
            baseIcon.shadow =
            "http://www.google.com/mapfiles/shadow50.png";
            baseIcon.iconSize = new GSize(20, 34);
            baseIcon.shadowSize = new GSize(37, 34);
            baseIcon.iconAnchor = new GPoint(9, 34);
            baseIcon.infoWindowAnchor = new GPoint(9, 2);
            var letteredIcon = new GIcon(baseIcon);
            letteredIcon.image = "http://www.google.com
            /mapfiles/marker'||chr(65+i)||'.png";
            markerOptions = { icon:letteredIcon };
            var marker = new GMarker(point,markerOptions);
            map.addOverlay(marker);
            });';
```

```
    i := i + 1;
  end loop;
  --
  l_code := l_code || '}';
  --
  apex_javascript.add_onload_code (p_code => l_code);
  --
  return null;
  end render_google_map;
  [9672_03_12.txt]
```

Replace YOURKEY by your own Google API key. This code will be explained in the next paragraph.

2. In the **Callbacks** section, enter `render_google_map` in the **Render Function Name** text field.

3. Click on the **Apply Changes** button. The plug-in has been created and can now be used within our web page.

4. In the **Application Builder**, go to your application.

5. Click on the **Create Page** button.

6. Select **Blank Page**.

7. In the **Page Alias** text field, enter a name, for example, `Google map`, and click on **Next**.

8. Enter a name for the page and click on **Next**.

9. Select **No Tabs** and click on **Next**.

10. Click on the **Finish** button to confirm.

The page has now been created. Now you can create a region with the Google map:

1. Click on **Edit Page**.

2. In the **Regions** section, click on the Add icon to create a new region.

3. Select **Plug-ins**.

4. Select the plug-in you just created and click on **Next**.

5. Enter a title for the region and click on **Next**.

6. In the next step, enter the width and the height of the map. The default values are shown but you can enter other dimensions. Click on **Next**.

7. Click on the **Create Region** button.

Now the region with a Google map has been created. To show the actual addresses of the markers, we will now create a Reports region.

In the **Regions** section, click on the Add icon.

1. Select **Report** and click on **Next**.

2. In the **Report Implementation** dialog, select **Classic report**.

3. Enter a title for this region, for example `Locations`. Alternatively, you can select 2 in the **Column** listbox if you want to display the report next to the map. Click on **Next**.

4. In the **Query** textarea, enter the following query:

```
select chr(64+rownum) label
,      cust_first_name
,      cust_last_name
,      cust_street_address1
,      cust_city
,      cust_state
,      cust_postal_code
from app_customers
order by customer_id
[9672_03_13.txt]
```

5. Click on the **Create Region** button.

6. The page is now ready. Run the page to see the result as shown in the following screenshot:

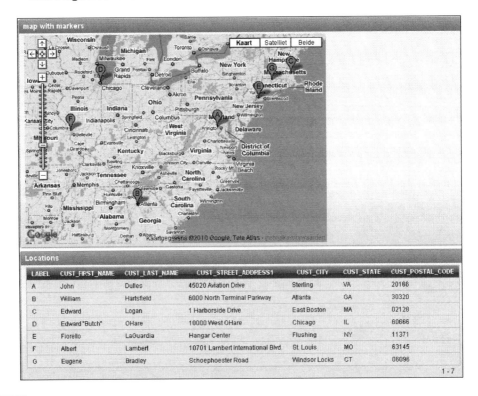

## How it works...

For this recipe we make use of a region type plug-in. The plug-in contains the code to put a map in the region. This is a PL/SQL code with JavaScript embedded. The JavaScript code is the actual code to put the map on the screen.

The function `render_google_map` starts with a cursor with the query on table `app_customers`. The street address and the city are concatenated so that this can be used in the JavaScript code. In the **Declare** section you also see the attributes which were created with the plug-in: `width` and `height`. They are referenced using the `apex_plugin` types.

The code starts with a call to `apex_javascript.add_library`. In this call, the URL for the Google map is built. The next step is the creation of a div. This div is given an ID and this ID will be remembered so that the Google Maps API can put the map in this div. In the div, the `width` and the `height` attributes are used to define the size of the map.

In the JavaScript code, a new map is created with the generated ID. This map is centered using the `map.setCenter` command where the coordinates and the zoomlevel are set. The `map.addControl` command sets the navigational buttons and the zoombuttons on the upper-left corner of the map. The geocoder is used to search the location which is fetched from the query. This is done with the `geocoder.getLatLng` function. The `baseicon` functions define the markers on the map. For every character there is an image available on `www.google.com`. For example, if you want to put a marker with the letter A on the screen, use `http://www.google.com/mapfiles/markerA.png`.

The `map.addOverlay` function sets the marker on the map.

This JavaScript code is put in a variable and will be used in the call to `apex_javascript.add_onload_code`.

## There's more...

The Google Maps API offers a lot of possibilities. You can make markers clickable so that a balloon with the location details will be shown. You can also use overlay functions such as a path which graphically connects locations with a colored line. For more information take a look at the Google Maps API website.

## See also

- For more information on plug-ins refer to *Chapter 5, APEX Plug-ins*.
- If you want to learn more from the Google Maps API, take a look at `http://maps.google.com` and `https://developers.google.com/maps/?hl=us`.

# Embedding multimedia objects in your application

Flash or Shockwave plug-ins or YouTube videos can add that sparkling touch to web pages. It is nice to know that it is possible to include these multimedia objects into APEX web pages. Actually, it is quite simple to implement. To demonstrate this, we will create a web page where a user can select a movie from a listbox and see the requested video.

## Getting ready

Make sure you have access to the APP_VIDEO table and that the table contains some records to test.

## How to do it...

1. In the **Application Builder**, click on the **Create Page** button.
2. Select **Blank Page**.
3. Enter a page alias, for example, Videos and click on **Next**.
4. Enter a name for the page, for example, Videos. In the **Optional HTML Regions** section, enter a name in the first text field, for example select video. Click on **Next**.
5. Select **No Tabs** and click on **Next**.
6. Click on **Finish** to confirm the settings.

The page has now been created together with an HTML region. Now we will create a listbox and a PL/SQL dynamic region:

1. Click on the Edit icon.
2. In the **Items** section, click on the Add icon.
3. Select **Select List**.
4. Enter a name for the select list, for example, PXX_VIDEO (XX is the page ID). Click on **Next**.
5. Click again on **Next** (leave the options as they are).
6. In the **Page Action when Value Changed** listbox, select **Submit Page**. Click on **Next**.

7. Click on the **Create dynamic list of values** link. A pop-up window appears.

8. Select the table/view owner and click on **Next**.

9. In the **Table** or **View** text field, select **APP_VIDEO**. You can use the button next to the field to select a table or view. Click on **Next**.

10. In the **Display Column** listbox, select **Name**. In the **Return Value** listbox, select **url**. Click on **Next**.

11. Click on the **Finish** button.

12. Click on **Next**.

13. As a last step, click on the **Create Item** button.

Now we will create the PL/SQL dynamic region:

1. In the **Regions** section, click on the Add icon.

2. Select **PL/SQL dynamic action**.

3. Enter a title for the region, for example, showvid.

4. In the **Region Template** listbox, select **No template**.

5. In the Parent Region listbox, select **showvid** (that is the region you just created). Click on **Next**.

6. In the **PL/SQL Source** textarea, enter the following code:

```
Sys.htp.p('<object width="640" height="385">');
Sys.htp.p('<param name="movie" value="'||:PXX_VIDEO||'&hl=nl_
NL&autoplay=1&fs=1&">');
Sys.htp.p('</param>');
Sys.htp.p('<param name="allowFullScreen" value="true">');
Sys.htp.p('</param>');
Sys.htp.p('<param name="allowscriptaccess" value="always">');
Sys.htp.p('</param><embed src="'||:PXX_VIDEO||'&hl=nl_
NL&autoplay=1&fs=1&" type="application/x-shockwave-flash"
allowscriptaccess="always" allowfullscreen="true" width="640"
height="385">');
Sys.htp.p('</embed>');
Sys.htp.p('</object>');
[9672_03_14.txt]
```

The PL/SQL code makes use of the `htp.p` function to output HTML and JavaScript to the screen. The result is the same code you should get when you want to embed a YouTube video:

And the code looks like the following:

```
<object width="640" height="385">
<param name="movie" value="http://www.youtube.com/v/
vwx814B9ed8&hl=nl_NL&fs=1&">
</param>
<param name="allowFullScreen" value="true">
</param>
<param name="allowscriptaccess" value="always">
</param>
<embed src="http://www.youtube.com/v/vwx814B9ed8&hl=nl_NL&fs=1&"
type="application/x-shockwave-flash" allowscriptaccess="always"
allowfullscreen="true" width="640" height="385">
</embed>
</object>
[9672_03_15.txt]
```

First, the `object` tag tells APEX that a multimedia object such as an image or a movie will be included in the web page. The size of the object can be set with the `width` and `height` parameters. The next step in the code is the declaration of parameters. The `allowscriptaccess` parameter is necessary to enable the playing of a video on a different website than `youtube.com`. The `embed` tag is the actual inclusion of the multimedia object and `src` is the source of the object. In this case, the source is a URL to a movie at `youtube.com`. All this code will be showed as HTML using the `htp.p` function. To be able to use this code to show more videos, the listbox will be concatenated to the code.

7. Well, the code has been entered, so click on the **Create Region** button.

The page is now ready. Run the page and see the result:

## How it works...

This web page makes use of the embedded code which you can get from the YouTube website. We could have put this code into an HTML region; that works too. But in that case the URL of the YouTube video is hardcoded and cannot be changed by the user. With the use of the `htp.p` function you can make the code dynamic by concatenating the URL.

In the recipe, you could also see that the PL/SQL dynamic region has a parent HTML region. This is done to make it look as if all the objects are put together into one region, which looks better.

You can pass some more parameters to the player such as autoplay, genie menu (showing related videos after playing the video), enabling the fullscreen mode, or starting in High Definition (HD) whenever available.

## There's more...

In this recipe we showed you how to embed a YouTube movie in your web page. It is also possible to embed other plug-ins such as a Flash plug-in, a Twitter widget, or a Weather widget. Websites like Twitter offer you the HTML code which you have to include in your web page, and similar to this recipe, you can use the `htp.p` function to send this HTML code to the screen.

You can also make a Region plug-in and give it some attributes such as movie, object width, and object height.

## See also

► For more information on the YouTube API, take a look at `http://code.google.com/apis/youtube/player_parameters.html`.

# Creating a region selector

Sometimes, a web page can be very chaotic, especially when there are many items on the screen. In that case, it may be a good idea to group items into logical sections. The sections can be displayed separately to save room for the rest of the items. We will make a web page where the user can edit the user profile. This user profile will be divided into three categories: person, communication, and favorites. The user will be able to click on a button to see only the category the user is interested in.

## Getting ready

We will use the table `APP_USER_PROFILES`, so make sure this table exists and is accessible.

## How to do it...

First, make a form based on a table:

1. Click on the **Create Page** button.
2. Select **Form**.
3. Then select **Form on a table or view**.

4.  Select the table/view owner and click on **Next**.

5.  Enter the name of the table. You can use the button next to the field to select the table. Click on **Next**.

6.  Enter a page name, for example, `User profile`.

7.  Enter a region title, for example, `user`.

8.  In the **Region Template** listbox, select **APEX 4.0 – Reports region**. Click on **Next**.

9.  Select **Do not use tabs** and click on **Next**.

10. Select the Primary Key column of the table. In this case, it is named `ID`. Click on **Next**.

11. Select **Existing Trigger** and click on **Next**.

12. Select **All Columns** and click on **Next**.

13. In the next step, you can enter different names for the button labels. Click on **Next**.

14. Enter the page numbers APEX should navigate to after the user has clicked the **Cancel** or **Create** buttons. For example, you can enter page 1 for the **Cancel** button, which means that APEX returns to page 1 if the user clicks on the **Cancel** button. Click on **Next** to continue.

15. Click on **Finish** to confirm.

The page is now ready, but we will now split the various items into three categories:

1.  Click on the Edit icon.

2.  Create a new region (click the Add icon in the **Region** section).

3.  Select **HTML**.

4.  Select **HTML** as the type of region.

5.  Enter a title for the region. We will call this region `Person`.

6.  In the **Region Template** listbox, select **APEX 4.0 – Region without title**. Click on the **Create** button.

7.  Repeat the steps two more times: one for **Communication** and one for the **Favourites**. In the end you should have four regions: **User, Person, Communication**, and **Favourites**.

8.  Make sure you switch to **Tree View**.

9.  Drag the items **ID, gender, birthday**, and **rel_status** to the **Person** region.

10. Drag the items **email, home_phone, mobile_phone, work_phone, Skype_name, msn, twitter**, and **nickname** to the **Communications** region.

11. Drag the items **Interests, favourite_music, favourite_movies**, and **favourite_books** to the **Favourites** region.

Now we have three regions with items from the APP_USER_PROFILES table. It will look like the following:

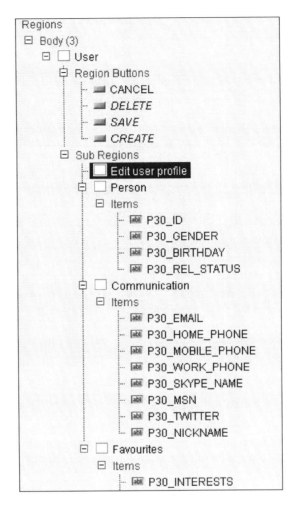

In order to create a region selector we will have to indicate that the regions can be selected by the region selector:

1. In the **Regions** section, click on the **Edit Region** link for the **Person** region.

2. In the **Attributes** section, select **Yes** in **Region Display Selector**.

3. Click on the **Apply Changes** button.

4. Apply the same to the **Communication** and the **Favourites** regions.

The last step is to create a region selector:

1. In the **Regions** section, click on the Add icon to create a new region.
2. Select **Region Display Selector**.
3. Enter a name for the region title, for example, `Edit user profile`.
4. Click on the **Create** button.

**Region Display Selector** is now ready but we will include the region into the **User** region so that it looks like this all is part of one region:

1. Click on the **Region Display Selector** region in the **Regions** section.
2. In the **User Interface** section, select the **User** region in the **Parent Region** listbox.
3. Click on the **Apply Changes** button.

Now we will do the same for the other three regions:

1. Click on the **Person** region in the **Regions** section.
2. In the **User Interface** section, select the user region in the **Parent Region** listbox.
3. In the **Template** listbox, select **APEX 4.0 – Region without title**.
4. Click on the **Apply Changes** button.
5. Repeat this step for the other regions: **Communication** and **Favourites**.
6. The page is ready now. Run the page and try it out:

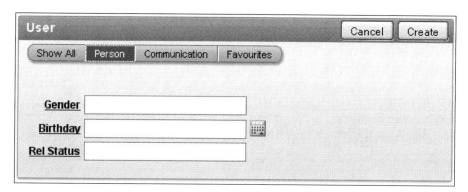

## How it works...

**Region Display Selector** is actually an unnumbered list. This list contains list items and each list item has a reference to a region. In HTML, this looks like the following:

```
<ul id="96054411561206575_RDS" class="apex-rds">
<li class="apex-rds-first apex-rds-selected"><a href="#SHOW_
ALL"><span>Show All</span></a></li>
```

```
<li><a href="#R96048122465171863"><span>Person</span></a></li>
<li><a href="#R96048531469174507"><span>Communication</span></a></li>
<li class="apex-rds-last"><a href="#R96050120519180839"><span>Favour
ites</span></a></li>
</ul>
```

The `<a>` tag has a reference to a region. The regions are actually divs with an ID. You can find the ID's in the code behind the hash (#) sign. You can assign your own ID by entering your own ID in the **Static ID** text field in the **Attributes** section of the region. In that case, you would have seen something like the following:

```
<li><a href="#person"><span>Person</span></a></li>
```

You can also see the `<span>` tag. The `div` and `span` tags are almost identical, with the difference that a `div` tag applies to a section of a document of the page and a `span` tag applies to the inline text but it keeps the formatting of the outside text. That is a default behavior but this can be changed by the use of cascading style sheets.

Furthermore, you saw that the three regions with items have the region without title template. This is done because otherwise you would have seen the entire region including the title, which is too much information in this little space.

The three regions with items and the **Region Display Selector** all have the same parent: the **User** region. This is not necessary. You can also display them as separate regions.

# Sending mail via APEX

Sending mails is an important feature in a web application. You can use it when you want to confirm something, you want to send information to the user, or the user wants to send your company an e-mail with an inquiry. In this recipe we will make a section on the home page where users can request information via e-mail.

## Getting ready

Your database should be able to send outbound e-mails. Therefore, check that your database is configured for sending e-mails.

## How to do it...

1. In the **Application Builder**, go to page **1** of your application.

2. In the **Regions** section, click on the Add icon to create a new region.

3. Select **HTML**.

4. Select **HTML** again. This time it's for the type of HTML region.

5. Enter a title for this region. For example, Contact and click on **Next**.

6. In the textarea, enter the following text: If you have any questions, please mail us.

7. Click on the **Create Region** button.

8. In the **Items** section, click the Add icon to create a new item.

9. Select **Text Field** and click on **Next**.

10. Enter a name for this item. In our case this would be P1_NAME.

11. In the **Region** listbox, select the region you just created and click on **Next**.

12. Enter a name for the label. Click two times on **Next**.

13. Click on the **Create Item** button.

14. The first item is now ready. You should also create the following items using the previous steps:

    ❑   P1_EMAIL

    ❑   P1_SUBJECT

    ❑   P1_TEXT

    But for this last item, select **Text Area** instead of **Text Field** as the item type.

15. Next create a button. In the **Buttons** section, click on the Add icon.

16. Select the region for this button. In our case, we select the region we just created. Click on **Next**.

17. Select **Displayed among this region's items** as the position.

18. Enter a name for this button, for example P1_SENDMAIL.

19. Check the **Beginning on new line** checkbox.

20. In the **Label** field, enter Send mail.

21. In the **Button Style** listbox, select **HTML button**.

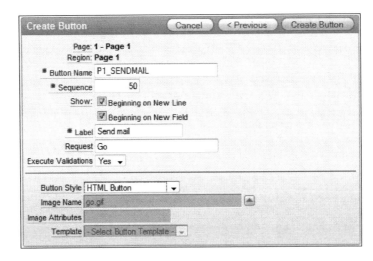

22. Click on the **Create** button.

We now have a region with the necessary text items and a button to send the mail. Now we must create the process:

1. In the **Processes** section in the middle of the screen, click on the Add icon.

2. Select **Send E-mail** and click on **Next**.

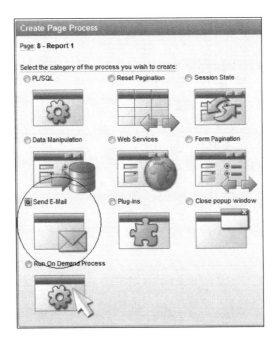

3. Enter a name for this process and click on **Next**.

4. In the **From** field, enter &P1_EMAIL. (with the dot at the end).

5. In the **To** field, enter your company's e-mail address.

6. In the **Subject** field, enter &P1_SUBJECT. (with the dot at the end).

7. In the **Body Plain Text** field, enter &P1_TEXT. (with the dot at the end).

8. Further, you can choose to have APEX send the mails immediately by selecting **Yes** in the **Send Immediately** listbox at the bottom.

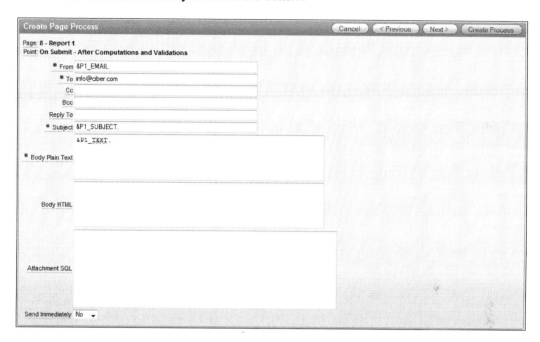

9. Click on **Next**.

10. Enter a success and a failure message and click on **Next**.

11. In the **When Button Pressed** listbox, select the button you just created.

12. Click on the **Create Process** button.

The **Contact** region with items and a send button is now ready. Run the form and try to send an e-mail:

## How it works...

The actual work is done by the `apex_mail.send` function and this function is called in the `page` process. This `page` process is of type `Email` and all you have to do is to enter all details in the text fields. However, you can make it dynamic by using substitution variables like `&P1_NAME.` (don't forget the dot at the end).

# Uploading and downloading files

Sometimes it is very handy to be able to upload and download files in a web application. For example, an intranet site where users can upload their own images, or a product catalog with images of the products. We will create a web page where users can upload and download important documents such as templates of letters, fax sheets, telephone directories, and so on.

## Getting ready

Make sure you have access to the `APP_DOCUMENTS` table. Also make sure the directory parameter in the call to `bfilename` points to an existing directory and that at least read access is granted. To create a directory with read access, execute the following commands (under the sys or system user) in sqlplus:

```
Create directory <<directory>> as 'c:\documents';

Grant read on directory <<directory>> to <<user>>;
[9672_03_17.txt]
```

Where <<directory>> is the name of the directory you want to create in the database. This is a virtual directory and you can give any name. <<user>> is the name of the Oracle user the read rights should be granted to. You can also use public if you want all users to be able to read from that directory.

## How to do it...

1. In the **Application Builder**, go to your application and click on the **Create Page** button.

2. Select **Report** and then select **Classic Report**.

3. Enter a page name for the report, for example Documents.

4. Select **Do not use tabs** and click on **Next**.

5. In the **PL/SQL** textarea, enter the following query:

```
select id
    ,      description
    ,      filename
    ,      dbms_lob.getlength("DOC_CONTENT") doc_content
from   app_documents
[9672_03_18.txt]
```

6. Click on **Next**. In the next step, click on **Next**.

7. Click on **Finish** to confirm the creation of the report.

The report is ready but you have to do one more thing:

1. Click on the Edit icon.

2. In the **Regions** section, click on the **Edit Report Columns** link.

3. In the **Column Attributes** section, click on the Edit icon right before the column named doc_content.

4. In the **Column Formatting** section, enter the following in the **Number/Date Format** text field:

```
DOWNLOAD:APP_DOCUMENTS:DOC_CONTENT:ID:
[9672_03_19.txt]
```

5. The format mask must be filled with parameters in the following order and separated by colons:

```
DOWNLOAD:<TABLE_NAME>:<BLOB COLUMN NAME>:<PRIMARY KEY COLUMN
NAME>:
[9672_03_20.txt]
```

6. Alternatively, you can use the **Blob download format mask** link below the **Number/Date Format** text field.

7. Click on the **Apply Changes** button. The page is ready now. Run the page to test the download:

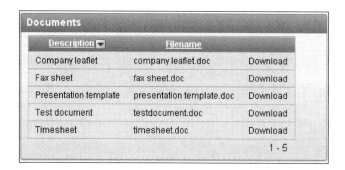

So far we have created the download page. To create an upload page, perform the following steps:

1. In the **Application Builder**, go to your application and click on the **Create Page** button.

2. Select **Form**.

3. Then select **Form on a table or view**.

4. Click on **Next**.

5. In the **Table/View Name** text field, enter the name of the table. In our case enter `APP_DOCUMENTS`.

6. In the next step, enter a page name and a region name and click on **Next**.

7. Select **Do not use tabs** and click on **Next**.

8. Select the Primary Key column `ID` of `APP_DOCUMENTS`, and click on **Next**.

9. Select **Existing Sequence** and in the **Sequence** listbox select the sequence **DCM_SEQ**.

10. Click on **Next**.

11. In the **Select column(s)** listbox, select **DESCRIPTIONS**, **DOC_CONTENT**, and **FILENAME** and click on **Next**.

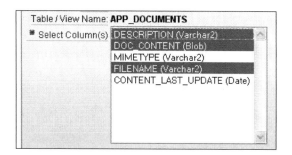

12. In the next step, leave the options as they are and click on **Next**.

13. Enter the ID's of the pages APEX should navigate to when submitting or cancelling and click on **Next**.

14. Click on **Finish** to confirm. The page is almost ready now. Click on the Edit icon.

15. In the **Items** section, click on the **doc_content** item.

16. In the **Source** section, enter the following in the **Source Value** textarea:

    ```
    DOC_CONTENT:MIMETYPE:FILENAME:CONTENT_LAST_UPDATED::
    [9672_03_21.txt]
    ```

    The parameters represent the blob column, the column containing the mimetype (indicates what type of file has been uploaded, for example image or WordPad), the column containing the filename, and the column containing the date last updated.

    By the way, you can also use the **Blob download format mask** link below the textarea to enter the source value.

17. Click on the **Apply Changes** button. The page is ready now. Run the page to see the result:

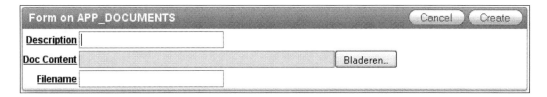

## How it works...

You just created an upload page and a page where you can download files. As you can see in the upload page, the blob column is represented by an item of type file browse. At runtime, this field gets a button which shows a file dialog on clicking. If the record already contains an uploaded file, you will also see a download link which makes it possible to download the file.

In the report page, along with the download link there are two things important. First, the column in the query. For the blob column, the function `dbms_lob.getlength()` is used. Second, the column formatting needs a special type of formatting. These two things make APEX put a download link on the screen.

## There's more...

We discussed the uploading and downloading of files that are stored in a blob in a table. You can also download files from the filesystem on the server.

Create a page with a HTML region with nothing in it. In that page, create an on load-before header page process of type PL/SQL and include the following code:

```
declare
  l_name     varchar2(100) := 'testdocument.doc';
  l_filename bfile;
  v_length   number(8);
begin
  l_filename := bfilename('DIR',l_name);
  v_length   := dbms_lob.getlength(l_filename);
  --
  begin
    owa_util.mime_header('application/octet',false);
    sys.htp.p ('Content-length: ' || v_length );
    sys.htp.p('Content-Disposition: attachment; filename="'||l_
name||'"');
    owa_util.http_header_close;
    wpg_docload.download_file(l_filename);
  exception
    when others then
      raise;
  end;
end;
[9672_03_22.txt]
```

The preceding script uses the function `bfilename` to locate the file. The `owa_util.mime_header` function indicates the mimetype of the file to be downloaded. This mimetype tells APEX what type of file is to be downloaded. The `htp.p` function is used to pass the length of the file and the filename. The actual download starts with the call to the function `wpg_docload.download_file()`.

Since the page process is an on load-before header process, the download of the file will start as soon as you run this page. You don't want that, so you have to make another page or take an existing page and create a link to the download page.

# Calling APEX from an Oracle Form

Sometimes you may want to call an APEX web page from within an Oracle Form. For example, when you want to redirect the user to another system which is built in APEX. Or the user wants to show a report which was already created in APEX—no need to create it twice and by the way, calling an Oracle Report basically goes the same as calling an APEX web page. With the Form's built-in `web.show_document` it is possible to call a web page from within a Form. We will make use of this function to demonstrate how to call an APEX report (overview of customers with a Google map) from an Oracle Form.

## Getting ready

Make sure you have a running Forms environment. Open an existing Form from where you want to call an APEX web page.

Have a look at your APEX URL. You can find it in the upper region of your browser and it looks like the following:

The URL starts with the hostname followed by the port number. The host and the port number are separated by a colon. After `apex/` you can see `f?`. APEX always starts with this and after the question mark you see `p=4550`. P is a parameter and stands for the application ID. In this case you see application `4550`. That is actually the APEX builder (yes, the APEX builder is also an application). After that, you see several more numbers, all separated by a colon. The number directly after the application ID is the page ID. After the page ID comes the session ID. You don't need to remember this number as APEX generates this ID every time you call this page. After the session ID, you can pass more parameters, even your own page items with their values.

Now that you know this, you can easily build your URL when you want a certain page in your APEX application to be called by an Oracle Form. Suppose your application ID is `12133` and the page ID you want to call is `10`. And let's say your APEX host is `apexhost` on port `8000`, then your URL must be `http://apexhost:8000/apex/f?p=12133:8`.

Remember this URL as you need it later in the recipe.

## How to do it...

1. In your Form, create a button.

2. Under this button, create a **WHEN-BUTTON-PRESSED** trigger.

3. In the trigger, enter the following code:

```
web.show_document('http://apexhost:8000/apex/f?p=12133:10','_
blank');
[9672_03_23.txt]
```

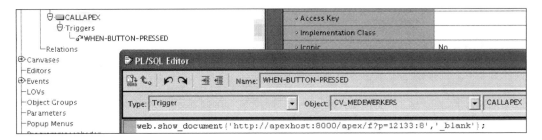

As you can see, the first parameter in the `web.show_document` function is the URL we just built.

Basically, that's all. Compile the trigger and the form and run it.

## How it works...

With the Form's built-in `web.show_document` you can call a web page from within Oracle Forms. `web.show_document` has two parameters. The first parameter is the URL of the called website. The second parameter sets the location of the called web page:

| Parameter | Meaning |
| --- | --- |
| `_blank` | Web page will be shown in a separate browser window |
| `_self` | Web page will replace the Forms application in the browser |
| `<framename>` | Web page will be shown in a frame named `<framename>` in a HTML page |

## There's more...

The called web page in APEX can contain items. These items can be filled with values you pass from the Oracle Form. Suppose you have a web page with an overview of the customers and you only want to see the customers from the United States. You could do the following, provided that in the APEX page an item exists called `P8_COUNTRY` and that this item is used in the `where` clause of the query (that is, `where country = :p8_country`):

Replace the code in the **WHEN-BUTTON-PRESSED** trigger with the following code:

```
declare
  l_country varchar2(100) := 'United States';
  l_url     varchar2(255) := 'http://apexhost:8000/apex/
f?p=12133:8:::NO::P8_COUNTRY:';
begin
  l_url := l_url || l_country;
  web.show_document(l_url,'_blank');
end;
[9672_03_24.txt]
```

The seventh parameter is the name of the item which can be given a value when calling the page. After the item name and the colon comes the value of the item, in this case `United States`.

You can also make a web page where Forms and APEX are integrated together. And it is possible to pass parameters in both directions. You can find a lot of blogs on the Internet regarding this subject.

# Creating a data upload page

Since Version 4.0, APEX offers the possibility to create a Data Upload wizard. This wizard is actually a visual representation of SQL Loader. But now you can import data from spreadsheets in a user-friendly way. In this recipe we will show you how easy and powerful this Data Upload wizard can be. We will create a page where a user can upload dealer address data.

## Getting ready

Make sure you have access to the `app_dealers` table and that you have an `.csv` file and an `.xls` file with the following layout:

```
DLR_NAME
DLR_ADDRESS
DLR_CITY
DLR_STATE
DLR_COUNTRY_CD
```

We enclosed two sample files along with this book.

## How to do it...

1. In the **Application Builder**, click on **Create Page**.

2. In the **User Interface** radio group, select **Desktop**.

3. Click on the Data Loading icon.

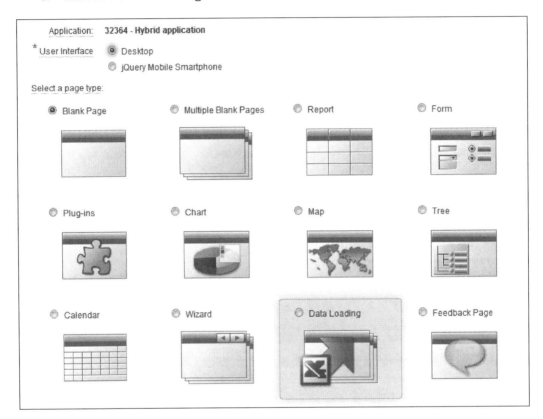

4. In the **Data Load Definition Name** text field, enter a name for the definition, for example, `load_dealers`.

5. In the **Table Name** listbox, select **APP_DEALERS**.

6. In the **Unique Column 1** listbox, select **DLR_ID** and click on **Next**.

7. In the next step you can add a transformation rule. Suppose you want to store the city name in capitals, you can select **To Upper Case** in the **Type** listbox and move the **city** column to the right-hand side panel in the **Select columns** shuttle. Click on **Next**.

8. In the next step you can add a lookup. A **lookup** can be useful if you don't want to store the value from the file but from a lookup table. For example, when the country code is stored in the file, you could use a country table to lookup the country code in that table and return the country name. Click on **Next**.

9.  In this step you can change the name of the pages or regions that have been created for this Upload wizard. Change it or leave the default and click on **Next**.

10. Select whether you want to use an existing tab and tabset, or create a new tab within an existing tabset, or use no tabset at all and then click on **Next**.

11. Enter to which pages APEX should navigate to when clicking on the **Cancel** or **Finish** buttons. You can also change the names of the buttons in this step then click on **Next**.

12. Click on **Create**.

The Upload wizard is ready. Run it and test it. You can upload a `.csv` file or you can copy and paste from your Excel sheet.

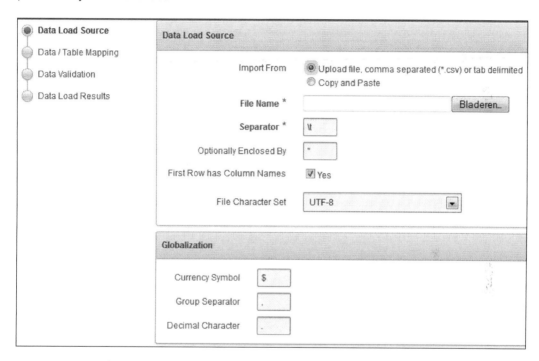

# Using shipped files

When you just create an application, you might find it a little bit "normal". Maybe you want to improve the look and feel. By default, you can benefit from the built-in jQuery, but there's more.

APEX 4.2 comes shipped with a number of CSS and JavaScript files. These files help the user to make applications look better and even offer support for the most popular browsers. Note that Microsoft Internet Explorer does not seem to work on all new features.

Another thing is that APEX ships with only one mobile template, the blue one. Although you could use the jQuery Themeroller, APEX already has a variation on the existing jQuery mobile templates.

When you have access to the APEX installation, take a look at the `libraries` folder which can be found in the `images` folder. Amongst the folders, you can also find a folder named `ios-inspired-theme`. It contains a CSS file that can be used in the existing jQuery Mobile template. In this recipe we will show you how to use this CSS file to get a different mobile theme.

## Getting ready

You have a working mobile application with a list view report as described in *Chapter 14, Mobile*.

## How to do it...

1. Go to **Shared Components**.
2. In the **User Interface** section, click on **Templates**.
3. In the **Page Template** row, click on the Copy icon.

4. Enter a name for the new template, for example `ios_style_page`.
5. Click on the **Copy** button.
6. The template is copied now. Find the template and click on the link:

7. Add the following line to the code, between the `#HEAD#` substitution string and the closing `head` tag:

```
<link rel="stylesheet" href="/i/libraries/ios-inspired-
theme/120624/styles.css"/>
```

8. Click on the **Apply Changes** button.

9. Go to **Shared Components**.

10. Click on **Themes**.

11. On the right-hand side of the page, click on **Edit Theme**.

12. Click on the **jQuery Mobile Smartphone** link.

13. In the **Component Defaults** section, select **ios_style_page** in the **Page** listbox:

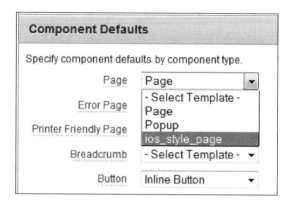

14. Click on **Apply Changes**.

You now have a different theme. Run the page to see how it looks like.

## How it works...

First we made a copy of the original page template. After that, we just added a link to another stylesheet. The stylesheet can be found in the `images` directory at `/i/libraries/ios-inspired-theme/120624/styles.css` and comes shipped with APEX 4.2. Lastly, we changed the default page template so that every page that has the default page template will now show the new style.

## There's more...

If you have access to the APEX installation, take a look at the `libraries` folder which can be found in the `images` folder. You will find amongst others the following libraries:

| Library | Description |
| --- | --- |
| 960-gs | NineSixty grid system to split a screen into 12 or 16 columns to enable responsive design |
| modernizr | Detects HTML 5 and CSS3 features from a browser to enable to modify the CSS settings according to the inabilities of a browser |
| respond-js | Enables the use of media queries on browsers that don't support it (IE 6-8) |
| selectivzr | Utility that emulates CSS3 selectors in IE 6-8 |
| Twitter bootstrap | JavaScript framework that originally came from Twitter |

If you want to use more colors, you can use jQuery mobile Themeroller, accessible via `http://jquerymobile.com/themeroller/index.php`. On this page, you can choose colors for each items on your page. After selecting the desired colors, click on **Download** to download the ZIP file. Unpack it and upload the CSS file via **Shared Components | Cascading Style Sheets**. Refer to the CSS file in the same way as described here in this recipe.

# 4

# Creating Websheet Applications

In this chapter, we will cover:

- ▶ Creating a websheet application
- ▶ Creating a page in a websheet
- ▶ Adding a navigation section to a page
- ▶ Implementing a datagrid
- ▶ Allowing multiple users access to a websheet
- ▶ Creating an enhanced datagrid from a spreadsheet

## Introduction

When Application Express was first introduced as HTML DB at the beginning of the century, it was positioned as a Microsoft Access killer. This was because of the fast and easy way data-centric applications could be created, just like in Access, but centralized and having all the benefits of a multi user, consistent way of manipulating data.

In APEX 4.0, a new type of application is introduced called websheets and developers have already described it as the Excel killer.

Websheets allow multiple users to simultaneously work on the same pieces of data, without directly working on a defined data model. Instead, websheets store data in generic tables that change depending on the design of the websheet.

The biggest innovation in this is that almost every aspect of a websheet application can be altered by users instead of developers. They are easy to use and very flexible. Constraints, lists, and calculations can be added by end users, without having to use the services of a developer.

A websheet application can be published for others to use, with or without privileges to modify data or alter the websheet itself. This multiuser environment erases the need of merging data that is a common problem in spreadsheet programs such as Excel.

All this makes websheets very interesting for use in management environments to quickly have access to data.

# Creating a websheet application

The first task that has to be performed is to create the application itself. In this recipe, we will show you how a basic websheet application can be created.

## Getting ready

Create a user that has enough rights to create and edit websheet applications. The basic information can be entered as follows:

1. From the **Application Builder** overview, navigate to **Administration**.
2. Click on **Manage Users and Groups**.
3. Click on **Create User**.
4. Enter a name (for example, WS_DEV) and an e-mail address in the appropriate fields.
5. Make sure the select list for **Team Development Access** is set to **Yes**.
6. Make sure the radio button for **User is a developer** is set to **Yes**.
7. Enter a password.
8. Click on **Create User**.

## How to do it...

The starting point for creating a new websheet application is the Application Builder. When you open it, you will notice that besides the standard tab for all applications, there is a specific tab for websheet applications. This tab can be clicked to get a report of all websheet applications in the workspace.

1. Click the **Create** button on any of the tabs in the Application Builder.
2. On the first page of the wizard, select **Websheet Application** and click on **Next**.

3. Name the application `Sales` and enter an unused ID for the application number, or leave the proposed number as it is.

4. In the **Home Page** section, enter a text in the **Content** text area.

   **Welcome to the Sales Websheet application**.

   Sections are the blocks that a Websheet application is built up of. To some extent, you can compare them to regions in a 'normal' APEX page.

5. This text can be just plain, but it can also be formatted. To do this, click on the small arrow on the top-right of the content area. If we hover our mouse pointer over it, the alt text will say **Expand Toolbar**.

6. A new area will open up, allowing many layout options for the text. Select the text **Sales Websheet** and click on the **B** button to make it bold.

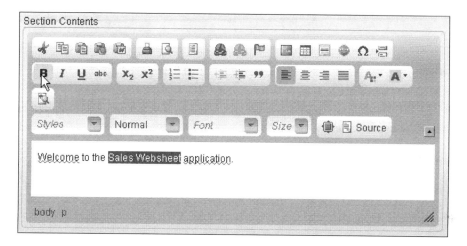

7. Click on **Next**.

8. Click on **Create**.

The basic websheet has now been created. When it is run, we can see that it already looks like an application, despite the fact that we haven't created any pages!

Everything about the websheet can now be managed by the users. The only influence a developer has is some of the basic properties like the logo or authentication.

To change these properties, go to the **Application Builder**, select the websheet application that's called **Sales** and on the following page, select **Edit Properties**.

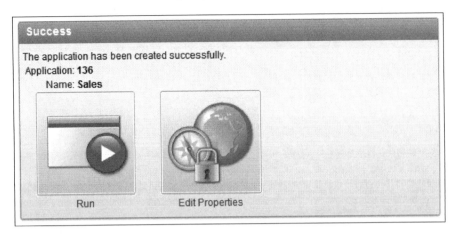

## How it works...

Websheets work a bit different than normal APEX applications. Instead of developers and users, there is a third user level called Websheet Developer. Users with this privilege can create and edit all aspects of the websheet application during runtime, but they cannot use the APEX Application Builder.

Besides this, websheets have three levels of internal users: readers, contributors, and administrators. More on this can be found in the recipe *Allowing multiple users access to a websheet*.

Most of the content is added to the websheet by its users and not by the APEX developer. With that in mind, we will show some of the differences when logging into a websheet application as a normal user or as a user with websheet development rights. More on this can be found in the recipe, *Allowing multiple users access to a websheet*, as well.

## See also

▸  In the next sections, the recipe, *Allowing multiple users access to a websheet*, explains more about collaboration in a websheet application.

# Creating a page in a websheet

Websheets are prepared as a bare skeleton. The APEX developer just creates the application and leaves everything else to the end users. One of the tasks a user can perform is creating a new page. This recipe explains how this is done.

## Getting ready

Make sure there is a websheet application available to use for this recipe.

To gain access to this application, there should be a user available that has websheet developer rights. Log in with that user when asked to run the websheet application.

## How to do it...

Run the websheet application. This will bring up the home page of the websheet application. What immediately catches the eye is the list on the right that offers a host of possible options for the websheet developer.

Some of these options will come up in the next recipes, but for the moment we will concentrate on the second button labeled **New Page**. Click on this button to add a page.

In the next screen, we enter the information we want on this page as shown in the following screenshot:

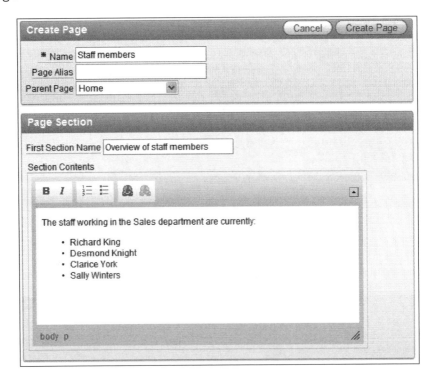

It works just the same as entering the information for the home page like we did in the previous recipe. What's new is that we now have the option to link a **Parent Page**. This will automatically generate two things: on the new page a breadcrumb is created to link to the home page and on the home page a link to the new staff members page is created.

The new staff members page itself will look like the following screenshot:

**Overview of staff members**                                                                edit

The staff working in the Sales department are currently:

- Richard King
- Desmond Knight
- Clarice York
- Sally Winters

Did you notice the **Edit** link in the top-right corner of the page? This allows websheet developers to jump directly to the **Edit** window, thus speeding up the process of configuring the page.

# Adding a navigation section to a page

Sections are the building blocks of websheet pages. Each page in a websheet will contain one or more sections. In the previous recipes, we've seen how creating a new page allows the websheet developer to create the first section.

In this recipe, we will see that there is another type of section and how it can be created.

## Getting ready

As a starting point, we will use the staff members page that was created in the previous recipe.

## How to do it...

1. In the menu on the right side of the page, find the button called **New Section** and click on it. The familiar APEX wizard screen appears offering two options: **Text** and **Navigation**.

   Since we've seen the process of creating a **Text** section in the last two recipes already, we'll choose **Navigation** this time.

   A navigation section is a section that allows users to navigate between pages and sections.

2. So select **Navigate** and click on **Next**.

3. Select **Page Navigation** and click on **Next**.

4. In the next page, set the title to Jump to Home.

5. By clicking the little arrow next to the **Starting Page** field, a pop up appears offering a selection to all available pages as seen in the next screenshot. Select **Home** from the pop up.

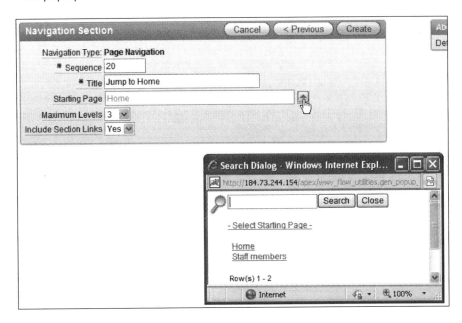

6. Leave the other fields on default and click on the **Create** button.

The screen now returns to the page and allows the websheet developer to inspect the changes that were made.

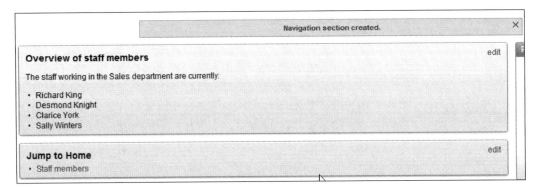

But wait! When we look at the link that has been created, we see that it doesn't navigate to the **Home** page as we would expect.

What really happened is that a link was created to all pages that have the **Home** page as a parent. This becomes clear when we create another page. Let's call it **Sales Overview** and make **Home** its parent. Automatically, a new link to this page will appear in the navigation section on the **Staff members** page.

With this in mind, the title for the navigation section is a bit wrong. So click on the **Edit** button on the section and rename the title to Quick Access.

# Implementing a datagrid

Datagrids are the strong points of websheets. Websheets have been called 'Excel-killers'. If that is true, than datagrids are the weapons.

## Getting ready

Make sure that there is a page available to implement the datagrid on. We can take the **Sales Overview** page from the previous recipe and elaborate on that.

If you didn't create that page yet, do so before starting this recipe.

## How to do it...

Let's say that the company in this example sells only one kind of product. They have no need for an elaborate database, so they would like a simple grid to monitor all sales.

1. When on the **Sales Overview** page, click on the button on the right-hand side called **New Datagrid**.
2. On the first page of the wizard, select the option **From Scratch**.

3. Next, enter the title and columns for the datagrid as shown in the following screenshot:

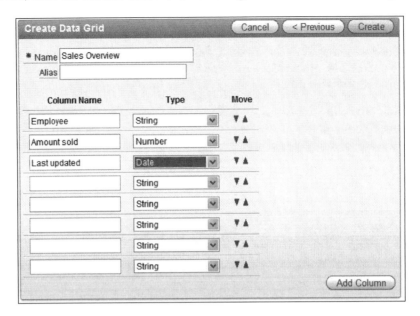

4. Click on **Create**.

What we see now is an empty datagrid. To add data to the grid, click on the **Add Row** button.

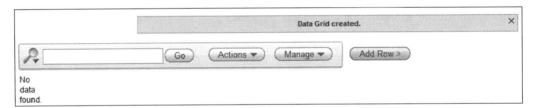

Data can now be entered into the datagrid, row-by-row.

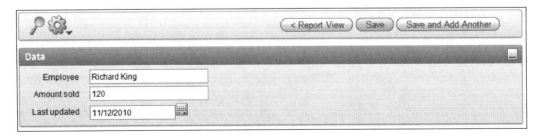

When a row is done, click on **Save** to finish or click on **Save and Add Another** to continue entering data.

After the last row is entered and the page is run, we will see a nice table of data quite similar to an interactive report in Application Express.

Under the **Actions** button, we can find some of the visual attributes to filter and sort the data in the grid.

Everything looks alright, so now we can put the datagrid onto the **Sales Overview** page.

1. Go to the **Sales Overview** page and click on **New Section**.
2. We can see two new options: **Data** and **Chart**. Click **Data** and **Next**.
3. Now select **Sales Overview** from the select list at **Data Grid**, click on **Next** and **Create**.
4. The datagrid is now added as a section to the page.

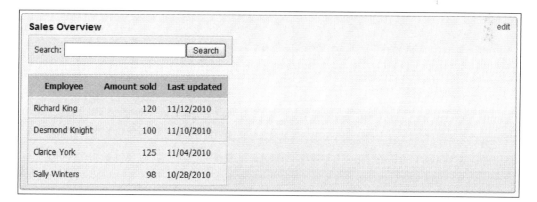

## How it works...

Datagrids look like normal tables in an interactive report. But in the background they are not based on real database tables. APEX keeps the data for datagrids inside metadata tables. That is why we don't have to define tables before creating pages with datagrids. The only drawback is that there are limitations on things such as the number of columns, indexing, and so on because of that.

## See also

▶   The recipe, *Creating an enhanced datagrid from a spreadsheet,* will elaborate on this subject and show some of the advanced features of datagrids.

# Allowing multiple users access to a websheet

In this recipe, we are going to see how access control can be used to allow different types of users to access websheets.

## Getting ready

Before starting this recipe we should have a websheet application containing multiple pages with at least a text section, a navigation section, and a datagrid.

Make sure that there are two APEX users available with websheet access: one named `Richard` and the other named `Sally`. Any other name will do as well, but change the names in the rest of this recipe accordingly.

## How to do it...

First, log in to the websheet application as an APEX administrator. The role of websheet developer is not enough.

When you are logged in, navigate to the **Administration** page and select **Access Control**. Next, click on **Create Entry**.

In the following screen, we can create users that have different roles. These users will be added to the **Access Control List** (**ACL**) for short:

▶   **Reader** is allowed to view content, but cannot edit

▶   **Contributor** is allowed to view and edit content

▶   **Administrator** is allowed to edit the ACL and delete the application

We will create an Administrator, a Contributor, and a Reader, so we can see the difference between the two.

1. In the **Create Entry** screen, enter `Richard` in the name field and select **Contributor** from the **Privilege** radio group.

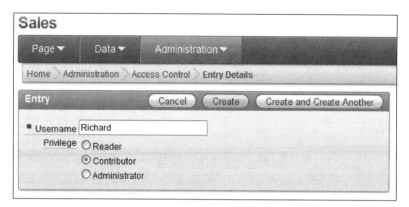

2. Click on **Create and Create Another**.

3. This time enter `Sally` and select **Reader** before clicking on **Create and Create Another**.

4. This last time enter the name of the APEX Administrator that you are logged in with and select **Administrator** before clicking on **Create**.

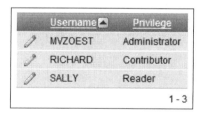

Now there are three users available to work with. Notice that APEX has changed the names to all uppercase.

The next step to be able to use the advantages of the ACL is to edit the application properties to allow use of the access control list.

1. Go to **Edit Properties** of the Sales Websheet application.

2. Scroll down to the **Authorization** section.

3. Set **Access Control List Type** to **Custom**.

4. Click on **Apply Changes**.

Let's see what the differences are between the two users Richard and Sally.

First log in as `Richard`. When we look at the websheet, we can still see the **Edit** links on all the sections and all buttons in the menu on the right are also available. Richard can still navigate to the datagrid on the **Sales Overview** page and edit it.

Now log in as `Sally`. You will immediately notice that the edit links are gone and the right side menu is a lot smaller. Sally can only read the information on the pages and cannot edit anything.

## How it works...

APEX 4.0 has introduced multiple levels of access control. The old-fashioned APEX users are still available, but the introduction of websheets has also brought with it the websheet roles in the form of the access control list.

### Access Control

Once authenticated to an application, access control specifies what users can do within the application. The table below identifies what capabilities different types of users will have based on the authentication being used within this application.

| Category | Capability | Authentication with Access Control List | | | Application Express Account Authentication without Access Control List | | |
|---|---|---|---|---|---|---|---|
| | | Reader | Contributor | Administrator | End User | Developer | Workspace Administrator |
| Administration from within Application Builder | | | | | | | |
| | Create Application | | | | | X | X |
| | Delete Application | | | | | X | X |
| | Update Application Properties | | | | | X | X |
| | Edit Authentication | | | | | X | X |
| | Edit SQL Access and Suggested Objects | | | | | X | X |
| Run and View | | | | | | | |
| | Pages | X | X | X | X | X | X |
| | Data Grids | X | X | X | X | X | X |
| | Reports | X | X | X | X | X | X |
| | Annotations (files, tags, notes) | X | X | X | X | X | X |
| Add / Modify | | | | | | | |
| | Pages | | X | X | | X | X |
| | Sections | | X | X | | X | X |
| | Data Grids | | X | X | | X | X |
| | Data Grid Data | | X | X | | X | X |
| | Reports | | X | X | | X | X |
| | Annotations (files, tags, notes) | | X | X | | X | X |
| | Links | | X | X | | X | X |
| Administration when Running Application | | | | | | | |
| | Access Dashboard | | | X | | | X |
| | Access Monitor Activity | | | X | | | X |
| | Update Application Properties | | | X | | | X |
| | Maintain Access Control List | | | X | | | X |

Make sure that you keep the difference in mind. Properties for APEX users have an influence on the way users can work with websheets.

The access control list, in turn, doesn't have any influence on the way users can work with other APEX applications or the application builder.

# Creating an enhanced datagrid from a spreadsheet

In one of the previous recipes we created a datagrid, by defining all columns by hand. In that recipe we called datagrids a "weapon" for the "Excel-killer", as websheets are called.

Well, if normal datagrids are weapons, then this recipe will show you a thermo-nuclear device.

We will create another datagrid, but this time we will base it on an existing Excel sheet, and therefore, adding many more possibilities.

## How to do it...

The company that we used as an example in the datagrid recipe has decided to add two new products to their portfolio. This means that they have to do a bit more administration. Sales people will be able to sell more types of products and this has to be recorded. Also the company wants to base the bonuses for the sales people on the profit they make and not just on the amount of sales. In short, selling a more expensive product means a higher bonus.

To start with this administration, the company has created an Excel sheet. In this sheet each employee has a row with his or her sales per product and the bonus that is generated by those sales. Product 1 gives a bonus of 10, product 2 a bonus of 20, and product 3 a bonus of 25.

|   | A | B | C | D | E | F |
|---|---|---|---|---|---|---|
| 1 | Employee | Product 1 | Product 2 | Product 3 | Last Updated | Bonus |
| 2 | Richard King | 120 | 10 | 30 | 11-12-2010 | 2150 |
| 3 | Desmond Knight | 100 | 32 | 44 | 10-12-2010 | 2740 |
| 4 | Clarice York | 125 | 50 | 21 | 10-12-2010 | 2775 |
| 5 | Sally Winters | 98 | 22 | 160 | 11-12-2010 | 5420 |
| 6 | | 443 | 114 | 255 | | 13085 |
| 7 | | | | | | |

On the bottom is a row with totals for each column.

To allow employees of the administration department to see and adjust these figures from a web environment, it is decided to put this sheet into a websheet:

1. Click on the **New Datagrid** button on the right menu.
2. Select **Copy** and **Paste** in the wizard and click on **Next**.

3. Name it `Extended Sales Overview` and paste the spreadsheet data directly into the available field. Be sure to only select the five data columns from the Excel sheet and not the computed columns and fields as shown in the screenshot. Keep the checkbox checked.

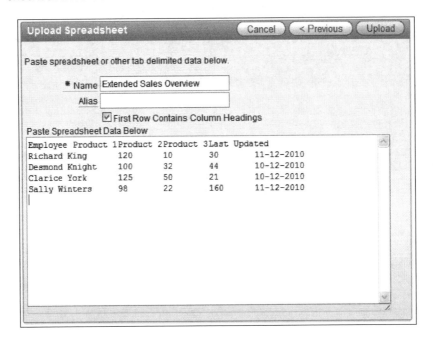

4. Now click on **Upload** and the datagrid is created.

To put this new datagrid into the existing **Sales Overview** page, perform the following steps:

1. Click on **Edit** on the existing Sales Overview datagrid section.

2. Select the delete button and click on **OK** on the following pop up to confirm the deletion.

3. Return to the **Sales Overview** page.

4. Now create a new datagrid section, but this time, select the **Extended Sales Overview** datagrid.

## There's more...

To add the **Bonus** column and **Total** fields to the datagrid, there is still some work to do.

1. Click on the **Edit** link on the **Extended Sales Overview** section.

2. Click on the **Data Grid Name**.

   Now we are back at the interactive report for the datagrid. First, we are adding the **Total** fields under each of the product columns.

3. Select the **Action** button, click on **Format**, and then click on **Aggregate.**

4. Under **Aggregation**, leave the default New Aggregation.

5. In **Function**, select **Sum**.

6. In **Column**, select **Product 1** and click on **Apply**.

7. Repeat these steps for Product 2 and Product 3.

8. When all three columns are done, go to **Actions | Save Report**.

9. Choose **As Default Report Settings** in the **Save** field.

10. Select **Primary** and click on **Apply**.

The settings are now set for all users that can view this datagrid.

To add the **Bonus** column, we have to do something else:

1.  Go to **Actions | Format | Computation**.

2.  Enter Bonus as the column heading.

3.  Use ( B * 10 ) + ( C * 20 ) + ( D * 25 ) as the computation.

4.  Click on **Apply**.

5.  Save the report again by going to **Actions | Save Report**.

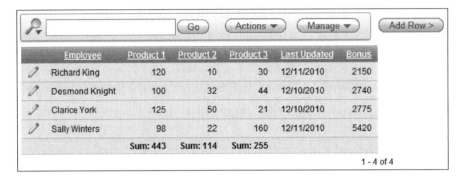

As we can see, the new column is now added.

# 5

# APEX Plug-ins

In this chapter, we will cover:

- ▶ Creating an item type plug-in
- ▶ Creating a region type plug-in
- ▶ Creating a dynamic action plug-in
- ▶ Creating a process type plug-in
- ▶ Creating an authorization plug-in

## Introduction

In APEX 4.0, Oracle introduced the plug-in feature. A plug-in is an extension to the existing functionality of APEX. The idea behind plug-ins is to make life easier for developers. Plug-ins are reusable, and can be exported and imported. In this way it is possible to create a functionality which is available to all APEX developers. And installing and using them without the need of having a knowledge of what's inside the plug-in.

APEX translates settings from the APEX builder to HTML and JavaScript. For example, if you created a text item in the APEX builder, APEX converts this to the following code (simplified):

```
<input type="text" id="P12_NAME" name="P12_NAME" value="your name">
```

When you create an item type plug-in, you actually take over this conversion task of APEX, and you generate the HTML and JavaScript code yourself by using PL/SQL procedures. That offers a lot of flexibility because now you can make this code generic, so that it can be used for more items.

The same goes for region type plug-ins. A region is a container for forms, reports, and so on. The region can be a div or an HTML table. By creating a region type plug-in, you create a region yourself with the possibility to add more functionality to the region.

Plug-ins are very useful because they are reusable in every application. To make a plug-in available, go to **Shared Components | Plug-ins**, and click on the **Export Plug-in** link on the right-hand side of the page. Select the desired plug-in and file format and click on the **Export Plug-in** button. The plug-in can then be imported into another application.

Following are the six types of plug-in:

- Item type plug-ins
- Region type plug-ins
- Dynamic action plug-ins
- Process type plug-ins
- Authorization scheme type plug-ins
- Authentication scheme type plug-ins

In this chapter we will discuss the first five types of plug-ins.

# Creating an item type plug-in

In an item type plug-in you create an item with the possibility to extend its functionality. To demonstrate this, we will make a text field with a tooltip. This functionality is already available in APEX 4.0 by adding the following code to the HTML form element attributes text field in the Element section of the text field:

```
onmouseover="toolTip_enable(event,this,'A tooltip')"
```

But you have to do this for every item that should contain a tooltip. This can be made more easily by creating an item type plug-in with a built-in tooltip. And if you create an item of type plug-in, you will be asked to enter some text for the tooltip.

## Getting ready

For this recipe you can use an existing page, with a region in which you can put some text items.

## How to do it...

Follow these steps:

1. Go to **Shared Components | User Interface | Plug-ins**.

2. Click on the **Create** button.

3. In the **Name** section, enter a name in the **Name** text field. In this case we enter `tooltip`.

4. In the **Internal Name** text field, enter an internal name. It is advised to use the company's domain address reversed to ensure the name is unique when you decide to share this plug-in. So for example you can use `com.packtpub.apex.tooltip`.

5. In the **Source** section, enter the following code in the **PL/SQL Code** text area:

```
function render_simple_tooltip (
p_item                   in apex_plugin.t_page_item
, p_plugin               in apex_plugin.t_plugin
, p_value                in varchar2
, p_is_readonly          in boolean
, p_is_printer_friendly in boolean )
return apex_plugin.t_page_item_render_result
is
l_result            apex_plugin.t_page_item_render_result;
begin
if apex_application.g_debug
then
apex_plugin_util.debug_page_item (
    p_plugin                 => p_plugin
,   p_page_item              => p_item
,   p_value                  => p_value
,   p_is_readonly            => p_is_readonly
,   p_is_printer_friendly => p_is_printer_friendly);
end if;
--
```

```
sys.htp.p('<input type="text" id="'||p_item.name||'" name="'||p_
item.name||'" class="text_field" onmouseover="toolTip_
enable(event,this,'||''''||p_item.attribute_01||''''||')">');
--

return l_result;
end render_simple_tooltip;
```

This function uses the `sys.htp.p` function to put a text item (`<input type="text"`) on the screen. On the text item, the `onmouseover` event calls the function `toolTip_enable()`. This function is an APEX function, and can be used to put a tooltip on an item. The arguments of the function are mandatory.

The function starts with the option to show debug information. This can be very useful when you create a plug-in and it doesn't work. After the debug information, the `htp.p` function puts the text item on the screen, including the call to `tooltip_enable`. You can also see that the call to `tooltip_enable` uses `p_item.attribute_01`. This is a parameter that you can use to pass a value to the plug-in. That is, the following steps in this recipe.

The function ends with the return of `l_result`. This variable is of the type `apex_plugin.t_page_item_render_result`. For the other types of plug-in there are dedicated return types also, for example `t_region_render_result`.

6. Click on the **Create Plug-in** button

7. The next step is to define the parameter (attribute) for this plug-in. In the **Custom Attributes** section, click on the **Add Attribute** button.

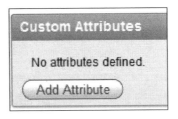

8. In the **Name** section, enter a name in the **Label** text field, for example `tooltip`.

9. Ensure that the **Attribute** text field contains the value **1**.

10. In the **Settings** section, set the **Type** field to **Text**.

11. Click on the **Create** button.

12. In the **Callbacks** section, enter `render_simple_tooltip` into the **Render Function Name** text field.

13. In the **Standard Attributes** section, check the **Is Visible Widget** checkbox.

14. Click on the **Apply Changes** button.

    The plug-in is now ready. The next step is to create an item of type tooltip plug-in.

15. Go to a page with a region where you want to use an item with a tooltip.

16. In the **Items** section, click on the add icon to create a new item.

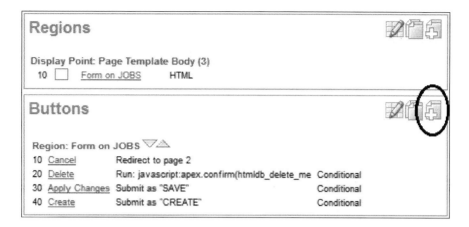

17. Select **Plug-ins**.

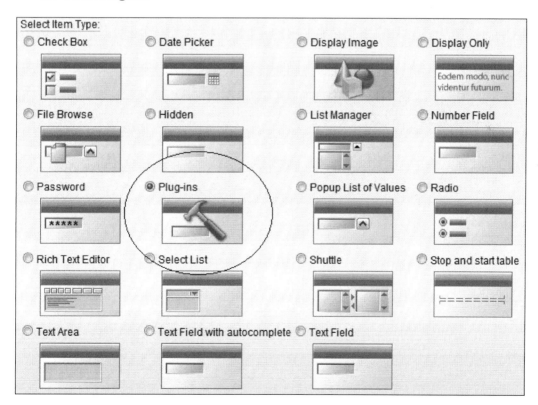

18. Now you will get a list of the available plug-ins. Select the one we just created, that is **tooltip**. Click on **Next**.

19. In the **Item Name** text field, enter a name for the item, for example, `tt_item`.

20. In the **Region** drop-down list, select the region you want to put the item in. Click on **Next**.

21. In the next step you will get a new option. It's the attribute you created with the plug-in. Enter here the tooltip text, for example, `This is tooltip text`. Click on **Next**.

22. In the last step, leave everything as it is and click on the **Create Item** button.

23. You are now ready. Run the page. When you move your mouse pointer over the new item, you will see the tooltip.

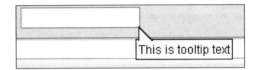

## How it works...

As stated before, this plug-in actually uses the function `htp.p` to put an item on the screen. Together with the call to the JavaScript function, `toolTip_enable` on the `onmouseover` event makes this a text item with a tooltip, replacing the normal text item.

## There's more...

The tooltips shown in this recipe are rather simple. You could make them look better, for example, by using the Beautytips tooltips. Beautytips is an extension to jQuery and can show configurable help balloons. Visit `http://plugins.jquery.com` to download Beautytips. We downloaded Version 0.9.5-rc1 to use in this recipe.

1. Go to **Shared Components** and click on the **Plug-ins** link.

2. Click on the **tooltip** plug-in you just created.

3. In the **Source** section, replace the code with the following code:

```
function render_simple_tooltip (
    p_item                  in apex_plugin.t_page_item,
    p_plugin                in apex_plugin.t_plugin,
    p_value                 in varchar2,
    p_is_readonly           in boolean,
    p_is_printer_friendly in boolean )
    return apex_plugin.t_page_item_render_result
is
    l_result                apex_plugin.t_page_item_render_result;
```

```
begin
  if apex_application.g_debug
  then
    apex_plugin_util.debug_page_item (
          p_plugin                => p_plugin
    ,     p_page_item             => p_item
    ,     p_value                 => p_value
    ,     p_is_readonly           => p_is_readonly
    ,     p_is_printer_friendly   => p_is_printer_friendly);
  end if;
```

The function also starts with the debug option to see what happens when something goes wrong.

```
--Register the JavaScript and CSS library the plug-in
  uses.
  apex_javascript.add_library (
        p_name       => 'jquery.bgiframe.min',
        p_directory  => p_plugin.file_prefix,
        p_version    => null );
  apex_javascript.add_library (
        p_name       => 'jquery.bt.min',
        p_directory  => p_plugin.file_prefix,
        p_version    => null );
  apex_javascript.add_library (
        p_name       => 'jquery.easing.1.3',
        p_directory  => p_plugin.file_prefix,
        p_version    => null );
  apex_javascript.add_library (
        p_name       => 'jquery.hoverintent.minified',
        p_directory  => p_plugin.file_prefix,
        p_version    => null );
  apex_javascript.add_library (
        p_name       => 'excanvas',
        p_directory  => p_plugin.file_prefix,
        p_version    => null );
```

After that you see a number of calls to the function `apex_javascript.add_library`. These libraries are necessary to enable these nice tooltips. Using `apex_javascript.add_library` ensures that a JavaScript library is included in the final HTML of a page only once, regardless of how many plug-in items appear on that page.

```
sys.htp.p('<input type="text" id="'||p_item.name||'"
  class="text_field" title="'||p_item.attribute_01||'">');
  --
```

```
     apex_javascript.add_onload_code (p_code =>
'$("#'||p_item.name||'").bt({
       padding: 20
       , width: 100
       , spikeLength: 40
       , spikeGirth: 40
       , cornerRadius: 50
       , fill: '||''''||'rgba(200, 50, 50, .8)'||''''||'
       , strokeWidth: 4
       , strokeStyle: '||''''||'#E30'||''''||'
       , cssStyles: {color: '||''''||'#FFF'||''''||',
       fontWeight: '||''''||'bold'||''''||'} });');
  --

return l_result;
end render_tooltip;
```

Another difference with the first code is the call to the Beautytips library. In this call you can customize the text balloon with colors and other options. The onmouseover event is not necessary anymore as the call to $().bt in the wwv_flow_javascript.add_onload_code takes over this task. The $().bt function is a jQuery JavaScript function which references the generated HTML of the plug-in item by ID, and converts it dynamically to show a tooltip using the Beautytips plug-in.

You can of course always create extra plug-in item type parameters to support different colors and so on per item.

To add the other libraries, do the following:

1. In the **Files** section, click on the **Upload new file** button.

2. Enter the path and the name of the library. You can use the file button to locate the libraries on your filesystem. Once you have selected the file, click on the **Upload** button.

   The files and their locations can be found in the following table:

| Library | Location |
| --- | --- |
| jquery.bgiframe.min.js | \bt-0.9.5-rc1\other_libs\bgiframe_2.1.1 |
| jquery.bt.min.js | \bt-0.9.5-rc1 |
| jquery.easing.1.3.js | \bt-0.9.5-rc1\other_libs |
| jquery.hoverintent.minified.js | \bt-0.9.5-rc1\other_libs |
| Excanvas.js | \bt-0.9.5-rc1\other_libs\excanvas_r3 |

| File Name ▲ | Mime Type | File Size | File |
|---|---|---|---|
| excanvas.js | application/octet-stream | 26KB | Download |
| jquery.bgiframe.min.js | application/octet-stream | 1KB | Download |
| jquery.bt.min.js | application/octet-stream | 22KB | Download |
| jquery.easing.1.3.js | application/octet-stream | 8KB | Download |
| jquery.hoverIntent.minified.js | application/octet-stream | 2KB | Download |

Upload New File

3. If all libraries have been uploaded, the plug-in is ready. The tooltip now looks quite different, as shown in the following screenshot:

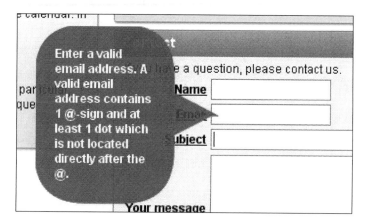

In the plug-in settings, you can enable some item-specific settings. For example, if you want to put a label in front of the text item, check the **Is Visible Widget** checkbox in the **Standard Attributes** section.

For more information on this tooltip, go to `http://plugins.jquery.com/project/bt`.

# Creating a region type plug-in

As you may know, a region is actually a div. With the region type plug-in you can customize this div. And because it is a plug-in, you can reuse it in other pages. You also have the possibility to make the div look better by using JavaScript libraries. In this recipe we will make a carousel with switching panels. The panels can contain images but they can also contain data from a table. We will make use of another jQuery extension, Step Carousel.

## Getting ready

You can download `stepcarousel.js` from `http://www.dynamicdrive.com/dynamicindex4/stepcarousel.htm`. However, in order to get this recipe work in APEX, we needed to make a slight modification in it. So, `stepcarousel.js`, `arrowl.gif`, and `arrow.gif` are included in this book.

## How to do it...

Follow the given steps, to create the plug-in:

1. Go to **Shared Components** and click on the **Plug-ins** link.
2. Click on the **Create** button.
3. In the **Name** section, enter a name for the plug-in in the **Name** field. We will use `Carousel`.
4. In the **Internal Name** text field, enter a unique internal name. It is advised to use your domain reversed, for example `com.packtpub.carousel`.
5. In the **Type** listbox, select **Region**.
6. In the **Source** section, enter the following code in the **PL/SQL Code** text area:

```
function render_stepcarousel (
            p_region                in apex_plugin.t_region,
            p_plugin                in apex_plugin.t_plugin,
            p_is_printer_friendly in boolean )
return apex_plugin.t_region_render_result
is
  cursor c_crl is
    select id
    ,         panel_title
    ,         panel_text
    ,         panel_text_date
    from    app_carousel
    order by id;
    --
    l_code varchar2(32767);
begin
```

The function starts with a number of arguments. These arguments are mandatory, but have a default value. In the declare section there is a cursor with a query on the table APP_CAROUSEL. This table contains several data to appear in the panels in the carousel.

```
--
add the libraries and stylesheets
--
apex_javascript.add_library (
         p_name       => 'stepcarousel',
         p_directory  => p_plugin.file_prefix,
         p_version    => null );
--
--Output the placeholder for the region which is used by
--the Javascript code
```

The actual code starts with the declaration of stepcarousel.js. There is a function, APEX_JAVASCRIPT.ADD_LIBRARY to load this library. This declaration is necessary, but this file needs also to be uploaded in the next step. You don't have to use the extension .js here in the code.

```
--
sys.htp.p('<style type="text/css">');
--
sys.htp.p('.stepcarousel{');
sys.htp.p('position: relative;');
sys.htp.p('border: 10px solid black;');
sys.htp.p('overflow: scroll;');
sys.htp.p('width: '||p_region.attribute_01||'px;');
sys.htp.p('height: '||p_region.attribute_02||'px;');
sys.htp.p('}');
--
sys.htp.p('.stepcarousel .belt{');
sys.htp.p('position: absolute;');
sys.htp.p('left: 0;');
sys.htp.p('top: 0;');
sys.htp.p('}');
sys.htp.p('.stepcarousel .panel{');
sys.htp.p('float: left;');
sys.htp.p('overflow: hidden;');
sys.htp.p('margin: 10px;');
sys.htp.p('width: 250px;');
sys.htp.p('}');
--
sys.htp.p('</style>');
```

After the loading of the JavaScript library, some style elements are put on the screen. The style elements could have been put in a **Cascaded Style Sheet** (**CSS**), but since we want to be able to adjust the size of the carousel, we use two parameters to set the height and width. And the height and the width are part of the style elements.

```
--
sys.htp.p('<div id="mygallery" class="stepcarousel"
  style="overflow:hidden"><div class="belt">');
--
for r_crl in c_crl
loop
  sys.htp.p('<div class="panel">');
  sys.htp.p('<b>'||to_char(r_crl.panel_text_date,'DD-MON-
    YYYY')||'</b>');
  sys.htp.p('<br>');
  sys.htp.p('<b>'||r_crl.panel_title||'</b>');
  sys.htp.p('<hr>');
  sys.htp.p(r_crl.panel_text);
  sys.htp.p('</div>');
end loop;
--
sys.htp.p('</div></div>');
```

The next command in the script is the actual creation of a div. Important here is the name of the div and the class. The Step Carousel searches for these identifiers and replaces the div with the `stepcarousel`. The next step in the function is the fetching of the rows from the query in the cursor. For every line found, the formatted text is placed between the `div` tags. This is done so that Step Carousel recognizes that the text should be placed on the panels.

```
--Add the onload code to show the carousel
--
l_code := 'stepcarousel.setup({
        galleryid: "mygallery"
        ,beltclass: "belt"
        ,panelclass: "panel"
        ,autostep: {enable:true, moveby:1, pause:3000}
        ,panelbehavior: {speed:500, wraparound:true,
          persist:true}
        ,defaultbuttons: {enable: true, moveby: 1,
          leftnav:
          ["'||p_plugin.file_prefix||'arrowl.gif", -5,
          80], rightnav:
          ["'||p_plugin.file_prefix||'arrowr.gif", -20,
          80]}
        ,statusvars: ["statusA", "statusB", "statusC"]
        ,contenttype: ["inline"]})';
```

```
    --
    apex_javascript.add_onload_code (p_code => l_code);
    --
    return null;
end render_stepcarousel;
```

The function ends with the call to `apex_javascript.add_onload_code`. Here starts the actual code for the `stepcarousel` and you can customize the carousel, like the size, rotation speed and so on.

7. In the **Callbacks** section, enter the name of the function in the **Return Function Name** text field. In this case it is `render_stepcarousel`.

8. Click on the **Create Plug-in** button.

9. In the **Files** section, upload the `stepcarousel.js`, `arrowl.gif`, and `arrowr.gif` files.

> For this purpose, the file `stepcarousel.js` has a little modification in it. In the last section (`setup:function`), `document.write` is used to add some style to the `div` tag. Unfortunately, this will not work in APEX, as `document.write` somehow destroys the rest of the output. So, after the call, APEX has nothing left to show, resulting in an empty page. `Document.write` needs to be removed, and the following style elements need to be added in the code of the plug-in:
>
> ```
> sys.htp.p('<div id="mygallery" class="stepcarousel"
> style="overflow:hidden"><div class="belt">');
> ```
>
> In this line of code you see `style='overflow:hidden'`. That is the line that actually had to be included in `stepcarousel.js`. This command hides the scrollbars.

10. After you have uploaded the files, click on the **Apply Changes** button. The plug-in is ready and can now be used in a page.

11. Go to the page where you want this `stepcarousel` to be shown.

12. In the **Regions** section, click on the add icon.

13. In the next step, select **Plug-ins**.

14. Select **Carousel**.

15. Click on **Next**.

16. Enter a title for this region, for example `Newscarousel`. Click on **Next**.

17. In the next step, enter the height and the width of the carousel. To show a carousel with three panels, enter `800` in the **Width** text field. Enter `100` in the **Height** text field. Click on **Next**.

18. Click on the **Create Region** button.

19. The plug-in is ready. Run the page to see the result.

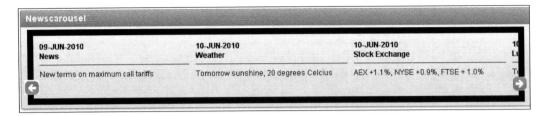

## How it works...

The `stepcarousel` is actually a div. The region type plug-in uses the function `sys.htp.p` to put this div on the screen. In this example, a div is used for the region, but a HTML table can be used also. An APEX region can contain any HTML output, but for the positioning, mostly a HTML table or a div is used, especially when layout is important within the region.

The `apex_javascript.add_onload_code` starts the animation of the carousel. The carousel switches panels every 3 seconds. This can be adjusted (**Pause**: 3000).

## See also

▶  For more information on this jQuery extension, go to http://www.dynamicdrive.com/dynamicindex4/stepcarousel.htm.

# Creating a dynamic action plug-in

A dynamic action is a piece of code that can handle page events (`onchange`, `onclick`, and so on). It is actually the APEX implementation of JavaScript event handling. For example, you can show or hide an item or a region at a specific moment. And that moment can be, for example, when a user clicks on an item with the mouse, or when a user enters some text in an item. These moments are called events. There are several events which we already described in the *Controlling the display of regions and items with Dynamic Actions* recipe in *Chapter 1, Creating a Basic APEX Application*.

A dynamic action plug-in offers the same functionality, but you can customize the appearance of the affected objects. In this recipe we will show you how you can make a dynamic action plug-in which changes the color of a text item when a user enters some text in another text item.

## Getting ready

No preparations needed, except that you should have an existing page with a region where you can put the items from this recipe.

## How to do it...

Follow these steps:

1. In the **Application Builder**, go to **Shared Components | Plug-ins**.

2. Click on the **Create** button.

3. In the **Name** section, enter a name for the plug-in, for example, `setcolor`.

4. In the **Internal Name** text field, enter a unique name, for example, `com.packtpub.setcolor`. In the **Type** listbox, select **Dynamic Action**.

5. In the **Category** listbox, select **Miscellaneous** (use this category to easily find the plug-in back in the categorized action listbox, explained later on in the recipe).

6. In the **Source** section, enter the following code into the **PL/SQL Code** text field:

```
function render_setcolor (
         p_dynamic_action in apex_plugin.t_dynamic_action,
         p_plugin         in apex_plugin.t_plugin )
return apex_plugin.t_dynamic_action_render_result
is
   l_result apex_plugin.t_dynamic_action_render_result;
begin
   l_result.javascript_function :=
     'function(pAction){this.affectedElements.css("color",
     this.action.attribute01);}';
   l_result.attribute_01        :=
     p_dynamic_action.attribute_01;
   --
   return l_result;
end render_setcolor;
```

This piece of code starts with the declaration of the function with its parameters. The return value should be of type `apex_plugin.t_dynamic_action_render_result`. This return type contains the call to the built-in JavaScript function `this.affectedElements.css()` which can change the style attributes of an object in the web page, in this case a text item. The value of the color is set by the parameter `p_dynamic_action.attribute_01`.

7. In the **Callbacks** section, enter `render_setcolor` into the **Render Function Name** text field.

8. In the **Standard Attributes** section, check the **For Item(s)** and the **Affected Element Required** checkbox.

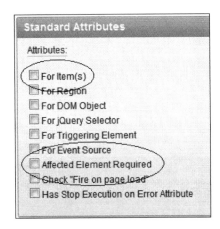

9. Click on the **Create Plug-in** button.

10. In the **Custom Attributes** section, click on the **Add Attribute** button.

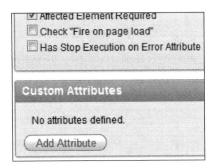

11. In the **Name** section, enter color into the **Label** text field.

12. Click on the **Create** button.

13. Click on the **Apply Changes** button.

14. The plug-in is ready and now we will create two text items, one for triggering the event, and one that is going to be the affected item.

15. Go to an existing page where you want to put this.

16. In the **Items** section, click on the add icon.

17. Select **Text Field**.

18. Enter a name in the text field, for example, PX_EVENT (replace X by the page ID)

19. Click on **Next** three times.

20. Click on the **Create Item** button to end the **Create Item** wizard.

21. Again in the **Items** section, click on the add icon.

22. Select **Text Field**.

23. Enter a name in the text field, for example, PX_TEXT (replace X by the page ID).

24. Click on **Next** three times.

25. Click on **Create Item**.

26. The two items are ready now. The last thing we have to do is to create the dynamic action.

27. In the **Dynamic Actions** section in the lower-left corner, click on the add icon.

28. Select **Advanced**.

29. Enter a name for the dynamic action, for example, set_color. Click on **Next**.

30. In the **Item(s)** text field, enter the name of the event item, PX_EVENT (replace X by the page ID).

31. In the **Condition** listbox, select **equal to**.

32. In the **Value** text area, enter SEMINAR. Click on **Next**.

33. In the **Action** listbox, select our newly created plug-in, **setcolor[Plug-in]**.

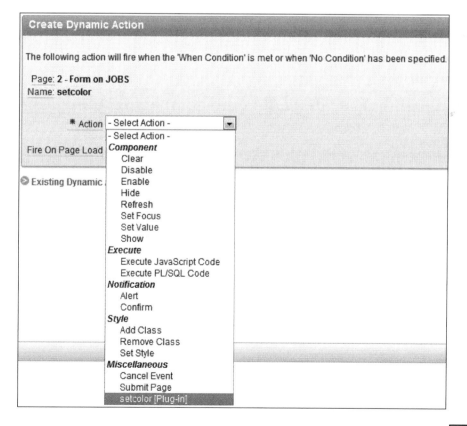

34. In the **Color** text field, enter a color, for example, `blue`. Click on **Next**.

35. In the **False Action** listbox, again select the new plug-in, **setcolor[Plug-in]**.

36. In the **Color** text field, enter another color, `green`. Click on **Next**.

37. In the **Selection Type** listbox, select **Item(s)**.

38. Click on the item **PX_TEXT** (replace **X** by the page ID) and click on the single right arrow in the middle of the shuttle. Click on the **Create Dynamic Action** button.

You are ready now. Run the page and see what happens when you enter SEMINAR in the **Event** text field.

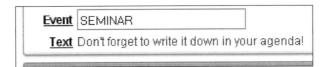

## How it works...

This dynamic action plug-in works just as the normal dynamic actions, except that there is a new action. Instead of show or hide, we now give the affected object a certain color, simply by changing the style of the object. We could have used some other styles, for example, font-weight instead of color. In that case, don't use the color names (`blue` and `green`), but use bold and normal.

# Creating a process type plug-in

A process type plug-in extends the functionality of a page process. This can be anything, but it is typically used for APEX built-ins or Internet functionalities like e-mail sender or Twitter update. The benefit of this is that the process type plug-ins can be reused. We will create a process type plug-in which changes the language by using the `apex_util.set_session_lang` built-in. There are more ways to change the session language, but in this recipe we will use this built-in in a page process to demonstrate how it works.

## Getting ready

Make sure you have an existing web page with a region.

## How to do it...

Follow these steps:

1. Go to **Shared Components** and click on **Plug-ins**.

2. Click on the **Create** button.

3. In the **Name** section, enter `set_language` in the **Name** text field.

4. In the **Internal Name** text field, enter a unique name, for example, `com.packtpub.set_language`.

5. In the **Type** listbox, select **Process**.

6. In the **PL/SQL Code** text area, enter the following code:

```
function set_language (
            p_process in apex_plugin.t_process,
            p_plugin  in apex_plugin.t_plugin )
   return apex_plugin.t_process_exec_result
is
  --Dynamic Attribute mapping
  l_language      varchar2(50)  := p_process.attribute_01;
  l_result        apex_plugin.t_process_exec_result;
begin
  --Set session language
  apex_util.set_session_lang(l_language);
  --Set success message
  l_result.success_message := 'Session language switched to
    '||l_language;
  return l_result;
end set_language;
```

The function starts with two arguments, which are necessary, but have a default value. The return type is `apex_plugin.t_process_exec_result`. The actual switch Is done by `apex_util.set_session_lang`.

7. In the **Callbacks** section, enter `set_language` in the **Execution Function Name**.

8. Click on the **Create Plug-in** button.

9. In the **Custom Attributes** section, click on the **Add Attribute** button.

10. In the **Name** section, enter `language` in the Label text field.

11. Click on the **Create** button. The process type plug-in is ready. Now we will create a text item and a button to start the process.

12. Go to your application and click on the page you want to edit.

13. In the **Processes** section, click on the add icon.

14. Select **Plug-ins**.

15. Select the plug-in we just created, **set_language**.

16. Enter a name for this plug-in, for example `setlang`. Click on **Next**.

17. In the **Language** text field, enter `&PX_LANGUAGE` (replace `X` by the page ID).

18. Click on the **Create Process** button.

19. In the **Items** section, click on the add icon.

20. Select the **Select List** option.

21. Enter PX_LANGUAGE (replace X by the page ID) in the **Item Name** text field.

22. In the **Region** listbox, select the region you want to put this item on. Click on **Next** two times.

23. In the **Create Item** section, set the **Page Action when Value Changed** listbox to **Submit Page**. Click on **Next**.

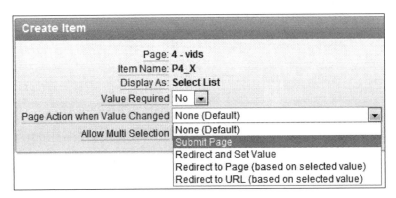

24. Click on the **Create or edit static List of Values** link.

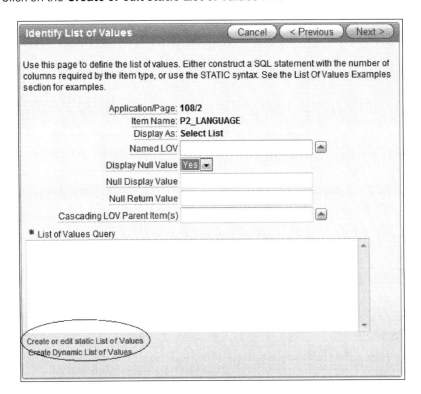

25. In the pop-up window, enter the following languages in both columns:

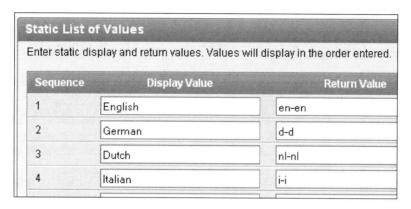

26. Click on the **Apply** button.
27. Click on **Next**.
28. Click on the **Create Item** button.

The process type plug-in and the page are ready now. Run the page and test the plug-in.

The only thing this plug-in does is a call to apex_util.set_session_lang with a language abbreviation.

## See also

▸    For a list of country and language codes, go to `http://download.oracle.com/docs/cd/B19306_01/server.102/b14225/applocaledata.htm#i634428`.

# Creating an authorization plug-in

In Version 4.1, the authorization plug-in was introduced. The advantages of plug-ins are mostly reusability and declarative setup. To demonstrate the use of an authorization plug-in, we will create a page and a tab that will only be displayed when the logged user has the correct privilege, that is ADMIN. This privilege is stored in the APP_USERS table. When the user logs in and he or she has no correct privilege (ADMIN), the tab will not be displayed. On top of that, when the user tries to access that page by modifying the URL (with the concerned page number), an error message will be displayed.

## Getting ready

Make sure you have access to an existing application and the APP_USERS table and the APP_COUNTRIES table.

## How to do it...

Follow the given steps to create the plug-in:

1.  Go to **Shared Components**.

2.  In the **User Interface** section, click on **Plug-ins**.

3.  Click on **Create**.

4.  In the **Name** text field, enter is_admin.

5.  In the **Internal Name** text field, enter com.packtpub.is.admin.

6.  In the **Type** listbox, select **Authorization Scheme Type**.

7.  In the **PL/SQL Code** text area, enter the following code:

```
function is_admin
            (p_authorization in apex_plugin.t_authorization
            ,p_plugin       in apex_plugin.t_plugin)
return apex_plugin.t_authorization_exec_result
is
  cursor c_usr  (b_role in varchar2) is
    select 1
    from   app_users
    where  username = p_authorization.username
    and    role = b_role;
  --
  r_usr       c_usr%rowtype;
  l_usr_found boolean;
  l_role      varchar2(4000) := p_authorization.attribute_01;
  l_result    apex_plugin.t_authorization_exec_result;
begin
  open c_usr(l_role);
  fetch c_usr into r_usr;
  l_usr_found := c_usr%found;
  close c_usr;
  --
  if l_usr_found
  then
    l_result.is_authorized := true;
  else
    l_result.is_authorized := false;
  end if;
  --
  return l_result;
end is_admin;
[9672_5_1.txt]
```

8. In the **Callbacks** section, enter `is_admin` in the **Execution Function Name** text field.

9. Click on **Create Plug-in**.

10. In the **Custom Attributes** section, click on the **Add Attribute** button.

11. In the **Label** text field, enter `Role`.

12. Click on **Create**.

Next, we will create the authorization scheme in the following steps:

1. Go to **Shared Components**.

2. In the **Security** section, click on **Authorization Schemes**.

3. Click on **Create**.

4. Click on **Next**.

5. In the **Name** text field, enter `is_admin`.

6. In the **Scheme Type** listbox, select **is_admin [Plug-in]**.

7. In the **Role** text field, enter `ADMIN`.

8. In the **Identify error message displayed when scheme violated (Value Required)** text area, enter `Only administrators have access to this page`.

9. Click on **Create Authorization Scheme**.

Now we have created the plug-in and the authorization scheme. We will create the form and the tab in the following steps:

1. In the **Application Builder**, click on the **Create Page** button.

2. Click on the **Form** icon.

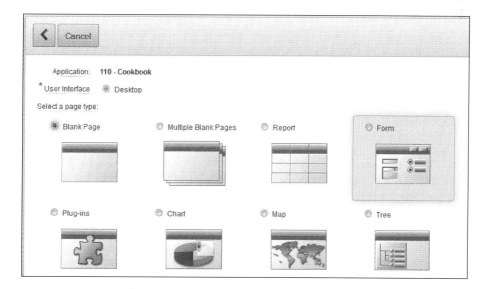

3. Click on the **Form on a table with Report** icon.

4. Enter a page name and a region title. Click on **Next**.

5. In the **Table / View Name** listbox, select **APP_COUNTRIES**. Click on **Next**.

6. Select **Use an existing tab set and create a new tab within the existing tab set**.

7. In the **Tab Set** listbox, select an existing tab set.

8. In the **New Tab Label** text field, enter the name of the new tab, that is `Maintain Countries`. Click on **Next**.

9. Click on **Next**.

10. Click on **Next**.

11. Enter the **Page Name** and the **Region Title** for the form, that is `Maintain Countries`.

12. Click on **Next**.

13. Select **Select Primary Key column(s)**.

14. In the **Primary Key Column 1** listbox, select **ID**.

15. Click on **Next**.

16. Click on **Existing Sequence**.

17. In the **Sequence** listbox list, select **CTR_SEQ**. Click on **Next**.

18. In the next step, transfer all available columns to the right-hand side panel. Click on **Next**.

19. Click on **Next**.

20. Click on **Create**.

21. Click on Edit Page.

22. In the **Page Rendering** section, click on the **Authorization** link.

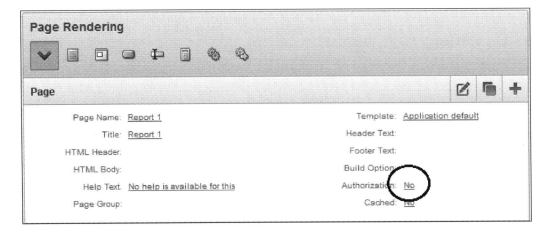

23. In the **Authorization Scheme** listbox, select **IS_ADMIN**.

24. Click on **Apply Changes**.

25. Now the authorization step is only done for the report, not for the form, so you still have to do that in the same way as described in the previous steps.

26. Go to **Shared Components**.

27. In the **Navigation** section, click on **Tabs**.

28. Click on the **Maintain Countries** tab.

29. In the **Authorization** section select **IS_ADMIN** in the **Authorization Scheme** listbox.

30. Click on **Apply Changes**.

Run the application. When logged in with the ADMIN role, the user will see the **Maintain Countries** tab, and the user can click on the tab to access the page. The user can even access the page by modifying the URL. However, if the user hasn't got the necessary privilege, the tab will not be visible at all, and when trying to access the page via the URL, the user will get an error message.

# How it works...

In the plug-in, the query checks whether the user with the ADMIN role appears in the APP_USERS table. If so, `true` is returned, otherwise, `false` is returned.

To make use of the plug-in, it needs to have the following parameters:

| Name | Type |
| --- | --- |
| p_authorization | apex_plugin.t_authorization |
| p_plugin | apex_plugin.t_plugin |

And the return value needs to be of type `apex_plugin.t_authorization_exec_result`.

The t_authorization type contains the following attributes:

| Attribute | Datatype | Description |
|---|---|---|
| id | NUMBER | ID |
| name | VARCHAR2(255) | Name of the authorization scheme |
| username | VARCHAR2(255) | Username of the current user |
| attribute_01 | VARCHAR2(32767) | Attribute value 1 |
| attribute_02 | VARCHAR2(32767) | Attribute value 2 |
| ... | ... | ... |
| attribute_15 | VARCHAR2(32767) | Attribute value 15 |

## There's more...

The authorization scheme has a default evaluation point of once per session. This means that if you change the role in the APP_USERS table, the user will only see the change when he or she first logs out and in. You can change the evaluation point to once per page view, which means that a change in the APP_USERS table will be in effect when the user re-queries the page. You can change the evaluation point in the following way:

1. Go to **Shared Components**.
2. Click on the concerned authorization scheme, in this case **is_admin**.
3. In the **Evaluation Point** section, click on the **Once per page view** radio button.

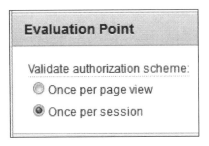

# 6

# Creating Multilingual APEX Applications

In this chapter, we will cover the following topics:

- ► Creating a translatable application
- ► Using XLIFF files
- ► Switching languages
- ► Translating data in an application

## Introduction

The consequence of publishing applications on the web is that anyone from anywhere in the world (and beyond since they have the Internet on the International Space Station) can view your work. When your target audience is in one country, a single language is often enough. But what can you do when you want to serve your website to many international visitors in their native tongue?

Application Express offers built-in functionality to translate applications, without having to rebuild the application completely.

This chapter is about how we can fully translate an application using those built-ins and adding something of ourselves to easily switch between languages.

# Creating a translatable application

An application needs to be altered before translations will work. It has to know for instance that it is going to be translated, by setting some properties.

This recipe will show how an application can be prepared for translations.

## Getting ready

To start with this recipe we will need a new application. We will use the EMP and DEPT tables to build a straightforward application with minimal effort.

1. In **Application Builder**, click on **Create** to start making a new application.

2. Select **Database** as the Application Type and click on **Next**.

3. Select **From Scratch** and click on **Next**.

4. Name the application HR Multilingual. Leave the Application ID and other options on their default values and click on **Next**.

5. Select the Page Type: **Report and Form**.

6. Enter **EMP** as the **Table Name**.

7. Select the implementation classic and click on **Add Page**.

8. Repeat these steps to add a report and form for the DEPT table.

9. Click on **Create** to finalize the application using Theme 1 or click on **Next** and follow the wizard to select another theme. When you do that, remember to keep the language as English.

We now have an application with five pages: one **Login** page and a **Report** and **Form** page for both the EMP and DEPT tables.

When we run the application, we will see the application in English as can be expected. We are now ready to implement the functionality that is necessary to make this a multilingual application.

## How to do it...

Now that we have an application at our disposal, we can start to prepare it for translations. The first step that we have to take is that we have to tell the application how it will know what language to use. This is going to require a special application item.

1. First navigate to the **Application Overview** and click on the button that is labeled **Edit Application Properties**.

2. Go to the tab **Globalization**.

3. Set the property **Application Language Derived From** to **Item Preference (use item containing preference)**.

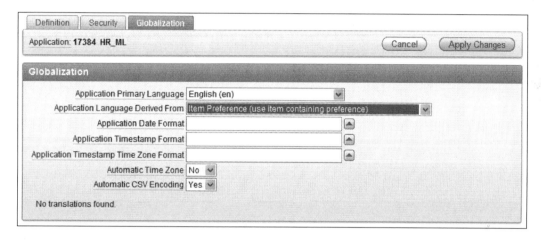

APEX now knows that it can derive the language to show the page in from a special application item. But this item still has to be created. To do this, follow the next steps:

1. Go to **Shared Components**.

2. Under **Logic** click on **Application Items**.

3. Click on the **Create** button.

4. Enter the name FSP_LANGUAGE_PREFERENCE for the item and leave all other properties on their default value.

5. Click on **Create** to finish.

The item is called FSP_LANGUAGE_PREFERENCE, because APEX recognizes that name as an item reserved for application languages. When a page is rendered, APEX checks the FSP_LANGUAGE_PREFERENCE item to see in what language the page has to be shown.

There is a snag in this process. Because of the way Application Express builds up its page, a change in the FSP_LANGUAGE_PREFERENCE item is not immediately visible. Whenever the language is changed, the page has to be reloaded to show the result.

To make this happen, we will add an application process that will handle the reloading of the page:

1.  Return to **Shared Components**.

2.  Under **Logic** click on **Application Processes**.

3.  Click on the **Create** button.

4.  Enter the name set_language.

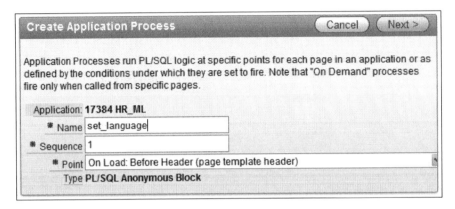

5.  Select **On Load: Before Header (page template header)** at the **Point** property to trigger the process as soon as possible on the page.

6.  Click on **Next**.

7.  In the Process Text, enter the following PL/SQL code:

```
begin
owa_util.redirect_url('f?p='||:APP_ID||':'||:APP_PAGE_
ID||':'||:APP_SESSION);
end;
```

8.  In the **Error Message** box, enter **Process cannot be executed** and click on **Next**.

We choose to start this process when a page is called using a special Request. This will be defined with the following steps:

1.  As the **Condition Type**, select **Request = Expression 1**.

2.  In the textarea that appears enter LANG (all uppercase).

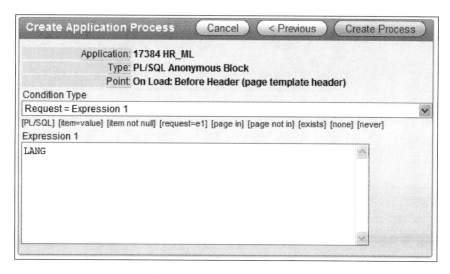

3. Click on **Create Process** to finish.

When we now review the list of application processes, we can see the new process has been added to the list.

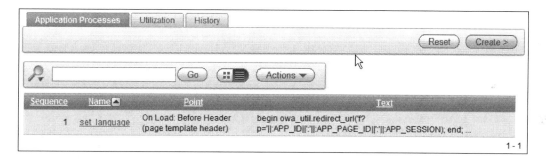

The application is now ready to be translated. Everything is in place to run it in any language imaginable.

To call the application in another language, change the URL of your application to the following:

```
http://yourdomain:port/pls/apex/f?p=&APP_ID.:&PAGE_ID.:&SESSION_
ID.:LANG:NO::FSP_LANGUAGE_PREFERENCE:nl
```

This example will call the chosen page in the application and show it in the Dutch language instead of in English. To select another language change the property `nl` at the end of the URL to your desired language code.

## See also

Now that we have a translatable application, we can start on the translation itself. The application is still only available in English, so we will have to create a translated version of the application in another language.

This will be shown in the recipe, *Using XLIFF files*.

Next to that we can only call the application in other languages by changing the FSP_LANGUAGE_PREFERENCE item in the URL. We should create a more user-friendly way to navigate to different languages.

This topic will be covered in the recipe, *Switching languages*.

Item preference is not the only way of telling an application how to get it's language. A new option in APEX is **Session**. The recipe, *Translating data in an application,* will show how to use this. It will also show an example of translating the data in an application.

# Using XLIFF files

One of the world's most recognized standards in localization is the XLIFF format. XLIFF is the abbreviation for **XML Localization Interchange File Format**. As the name explains, it's an XML standard and it has been adopted by Application Express as the format in which different language files can be exported from and imported into APEX applications.

This recipe will show how we can use XLIFF to quickly translate an application from its default language to a new language.

## Getting ready

Start with the translatable application that we have built in the first recipe of this chapter. By doing that, we have a good and clean starting point for the first translation.

## How to do it...

1. Navigate to **Shared Components**.

   At the bottom of the page we can see a section called **Globalization**. This section holds all options that are needed to translate the current application.

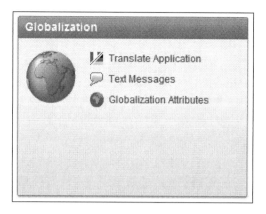

2.  Click on the link that is labeled **Translate Application**.

    This will open up a new page with several options to use when translating an application. In fact, it's a list of all steps necessary to fully translate the application in APEX.

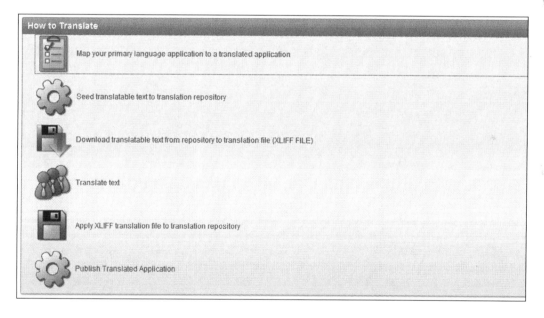

3.  Click on the first link **Map your primary language application to a translated application**. This will tell APEX the new language that is going to be used.

4.  Click on the **Create** button.

5.  Enter a new application ID that is not yet used by your APEX environment.

6.  Select the language code that you want to translate to. In this example, we will use 'Dutch (Netherlands) (nl)'.

7. Click on **Create**.

   The fundament for the new translation is now in place and we can proceed to the next step.

8. Return to the application translation home by clicking on the **Translate** link in the breadcrumb.

9. Click on the second step called **Seed Translatable Text** to translation repository.

10. Select the **Language Mapping** that we just created.

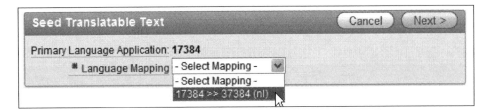

11. Click on **Next**.

12. Click on **Seed Translatable Text**.

This will create entries in the APEX repository for every translatable text in the application. These entries will be used later to generate the XLIFF files.

After the seeding process is completed, APEX shows an overview with summaries of all relevant figures. Click on **Done** to close this screen.

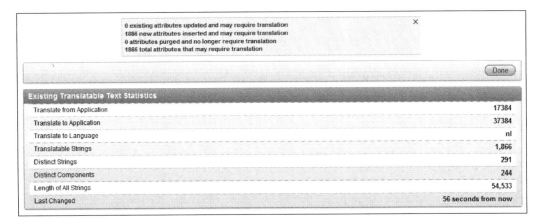

1. Return to the application translation home again by clicking on the **Translate** link in the breadcrumb.

2. Click on the third step called **Download translatable text from repository to translation file (XLIFF FILE)**.

   The following screen offers two options; download an XLIFF file for the complete application or download a file for a specific page. We will use the second option to get a feeling of what is required to use an XLIFF file.

3. In the bottom section called **Download XLIFF file for Application Page** use the first select list to select the application we are working on.

4. In the second select list **Page**, select **101 Login**.

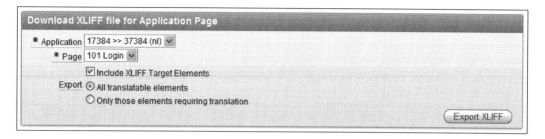

5. Click on the button **Export XLIFF**.

6. Use the dialogs to save the file to a location on the hard drive.

   The XLIFF file has now been downloaded and is ready to be edited. This is the fourth step in the translation process.

7. Use your file browser program to locate the downloaded .xlf file and open it for editing in your favorite text editor.

8. Scroll down to the bottom and find the entries with Username and Password. Change the text between the target tags to the following:

   ```
   <source>Username</source>
   <target>Gebruikersnaam</target>

   <source>Password</source>
   <target>Wachtwoord</target>
   ```

By changing these two entries, we will at least be able to see the changes. Feel free to change all other translations as well to see the effect on the login page, but this is not necessary for this recipe.

We will now upload the altered file back into APEX.

1. Save the XLIFF file and return to the APEX application translation home.

2. Click on the fifth step called **Apply XLIFF translation file to translation repository**.

3. Click on the button labeled **Upload XLIFF**.

4. Enter the title **en_nl_translation** and use the **Browse** button to find the .xlf file that we have just edited.

5. Click on **Upload XLIFF File**.

6. Click on the title of the XLIFF file we just uploaded.

7. In the next screen, select the translation mapping to apply the XLIFF file to.

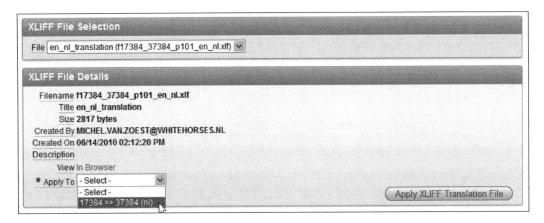

8. Click on **Apply XLIFF Translation File** to finish connecting the file to the mapping.

9. In the next screen, select the translation mapping again in the select list labeled **Publish Application Translation**. Note that this is equal to Step 6 in the list on the Application Translation Home.

10. Click on **Publish Application**.

We are done with the translation of all APEX texts in this application.

## How it works...

All translatable text is saved in the Application Express Repository. It's possible to directly alter these entries by navigating to a special page.

1. Go to **Shared Components**.

2. Go to **Translate Application**.

3. In the bottom section called **Translation Utilities**, click on the item **Manually Edit Translation Repository**.

From there, we can select the right mapping and if desired a single page. Because this is an interactive report, we can use filters and other features to find the desired text to translate.

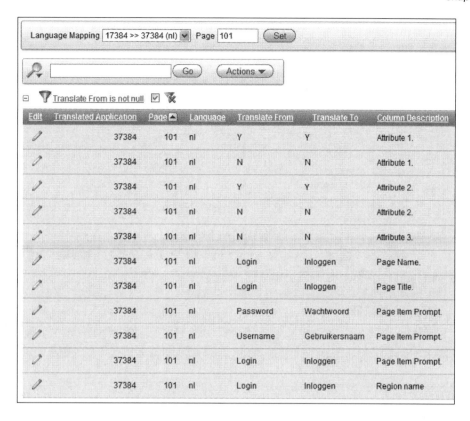

The quickest way to translate a lot of text is still using the XLIFF file. Because this is an international standard, an XLIFF file can be handled by any translation service.

An XLIFF file is always built the same way: a header and a body. The first part of the header shows some information about the file, the original application, and the translation target application. Because this is commented, it will not be used by a processing application:

```
<?xml version="1.0" encoding="UTF-8"?>
<!--
   ******************
   ** Source    :   17384
   ** Source Lang:  en
   ** Target    :   37384
   ** Target Lang:  nl
   ** Filename:     f17384_37384_en_nl.xlf
   ** Generated By: MICHEL.VAN.ZOEST@WHITEHORSES.NL
   ** Date:         15-JUN-2010 14:05:34
   ******************
-->
```

The second part of the header shows the version of the XLIFF standard that is used. The latest specification version is 1.2, but APEX still uses 1.0 by default.

```
<xliff version="1.0">
```

The third part of the header holds some more information about the file, the source language, and the target language. This information is used by APEX when importing the file.

```
<file original="f17384_37384_en_nl.xlf" source-language="en" target-
language="nl" datatype="html">
<header></header>
```

After the header the body starts.

```
<body>
```

The following part is repeated for every text in the APEX repository: an identification for the item that holds the text, a source in the original language, and a target in the new language.

```
<trans-unit id="S-2-27846723888160713-17384">
<source>Logout</source>
<target>Uitloggen</target>
</trans-unit>
```

Finally, the file is closed.

```
</body>
</file>
</xliff>
```

There is one thing that you will always have to keep in mind when using XLIFF files for translating an application. Every time something is changed in the application, you will have to repeat the process of seeding, exporting, translating, and importing. Otherwise, not all changes will be visible in the translated version of the application.

So when the translating itself is done by an external company, it would be wise to send them the XLIFF file after the application in the default language is completely done. This could save a lot of money.

# Switching languages

In the past two recipes, we have changed a standard application so that it can be translated and we performed the translation itself. In this recipe, we will add something that will make switching between languages much easier for users.

## Getting ready

To start this recipe, we will need an application that has been translated like the application we created in the past two recipes.

# How to do it...

The best place to create a language switch is a place that is visible at all times. In this case, we will use the navigation bar. Since this bar is in the header of our application, it is visible on all pages and ideal for our purposes.

1. Navigate to the **Shared Components**.

2. In the **Navigation Section** find the **Navigation Bar Entries** and click on it.

3. There should already be an entry called **Logout** in place.

4. Click on the **Create** button.

5. Confirm that the option **From Scratch** is selected and click on **Next**.

6. Select **Navigation to URL** and click on **Next.**

7. Enter English as **Entry Label** and click on **Next**.

8. In the next page, enter the following for the properties:

   ❑ **Target is a**: **Page in this application**

   ❑ **Page**: **&APP_PAGE_ID.** (do not forget the dot at the end)

   ❑ **Request**: LANG

   ❑ **Set these items**: FSP_LANGUAGE_PREFERENCE

   ❑ **With these values**: en

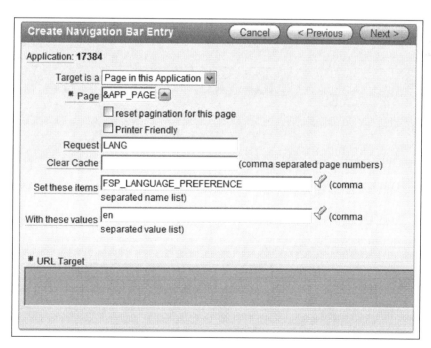

9. Click on **Next**.

10. Click on **Create**.

We have now created a link in the navigation bar that will direct users to the English part of the application. To create a link to the Dutch version of the application, repeat these steps but change **Entry Label** to **Nederlands** and set **With these values** to **nl** instead of **en**.

Remember to run the XLIFF translation steps again to make sure the new text is available in both languages.

When we now run the application, we can see that two entries are available in the navigation bar.

Clicking on **Nederlands** will show the application in Dutch and clicking on **English** will change it back to the English language.

# Translating data in an application

Besides the application labels, there is more to translate in an application, for instance, data.

In this recipe, we will see an example of this. To accomplish this, we will use a built-in way of translating the session language that is new in APEX.

## Getting ready

Start by creating some new database objects. Remember that this is a crude setup. In a production environment, this should be more elaborate.

First, we will create a copy of the EMP table, but with a change. The JOB column will now be called JOB_NO and it's content will reference to a EMP_JOB_TITLES table.

```
create table EMP_LANG
(
   empno     NUMBER(4) not null,
   ename     VARCHAR2(10),
   job_no    NUMBER,

   mgr       NUMBER(4),
   hiredate  DATE,
   sal       NUMBER(7,2),
   comm      NUMBER(7,2),
   deptno    NUMBER(2)
);
[emp_lang.sql]
```

Also create the EMP_JOB_TITLES table. This table contains a LANGUAGE column that will hold the language in which the job_title is entered for that row.

This also means that job_no is not a unique column in this table, but job_no in combination with language is the unique key.

```
create table EMP_JOB_TITLES
(
   job_no     NUMBER,
   job_title  VARCHAR2(32),
   language   VARCHAR2(10)
);
[emp_job_titles.sql]
```

Next, it will need data. First the EMP_JOB_TITLES. This script will fill the table with the original five job titles from the EMP table with language en and add five translations in Dutch for the same titles.

```
insert into EMP_JOB_TITLES (job_no, job_title, language)
values (1, 'PRESIDENT', 'en');
insert into EMP_JOB_TITLES (job_no, job_title, language)
values (2, 'MANAGER', 'en');
insert into EMP_JOB_TITLES (job_no, job_title, language)
values (3, 'ANALYST', 'en');
insert into EMP_JOB_TITLES (job_no, job_title, language)
values (4, 'CLERK', 'en');
```

```
insert into EMP_JOB_TITLES (job_no, job_title, language)
values (5, 'SALESMAN', 'en');
insert into EMP_JOB_TITLES (job_no, job_title, language)
values (1, 'Directeur', 'nl');
insert into EMP_JOB_TITLES (job_no, job_title, language)
values (2, 'Manager', 'nl');
insert into EMP_JOB_TITLES (job_no, job_title, language)
values (3, 'Analist', 'nl');
insert into EMP_JOB_TITLES (job_no, job_title, language)
values (4, 'Klerk', 'nl');
insert into EMP_JOB_TITLES (job_no, job_title, language)
values (5, 'Verkoper', 'nl');
[emp_job_titles_data.sql]
```

For the EMP_LANG table, copy the data from the EMP table, but replace the contents of the JOB column with the reference number as it was entered in the EMP_JOB_TITLES table (for example; PRESIDENT will become 1, CLERK will become 4).

Some examples of this data are:

```
insert into EMP_LANG (empno, ename, job_no, mgr, hiredate, sal, comm,
deptno)
values (7839, 'KING', 1, null, to_date('17-11-1981', 'dd-mm-yyyy'),
5000, null, 10);
insert into EMP_LANG (empno, ename, job_no, mgr, hiredate, sal, comm,
deptno)
values (7698, 'BLAKE', 2, 7839, to_date('01-05-1981', 'dd-mm-yyyy'),
2850, null, 30);
[emp_lang_data.sql]
```

The emp_lang_data.sql script contains 12 more rows.

## How to do it...

When there is a datamodel available that allows data to be saved in multiple languages, the hardest part is writing smart queries to get this data out in the right language for the user. We will create a page based on such a query for our simple datamodel.

The first step is getting the application ready. To use the **Session** option, take the following steps.

1. Go to the **Application Properties**.
2. Go to the **Globalization** tab.
3. In the select list **Application Language Derived From** select **Session**.
4. Click on **Apply Changes**.

Next step is to create a page based on a language-driven query.

5.  On the application overview, click on **Create Page**.

6.  Select **Report** and click on **Next**.

7.  Select **Classic Report** and click on **Next**.

8.  Enter a number and name for the page and click on **Next**.

9.  Select **Do Not Use Tabs** and click on **Next**.

10. Enter the query that will drive the page.

```
select emp.empno
, emp.ename
, job.job_title
, emp.hiredate
, emp.sal
from emp_lang emp
, emp_job_titles job
where emp.job_no = job.job_no
and upper(job.language) = upper(apex_util.get_session_lang)
```

11. Click on **Next** a few times until the **Finish** button appears and click on it.

To test the changes, run the page by altering the URL to accept a `p_lang` parameter like the following:

```
http://server:port/apex/f?p=app_id:page_id:session&p_lang=en
```

| Empno | Ename  | Job Title | Hiredate  | Sal  |
|-------|--------|-----------|-----------|------|
| 7369  | SMITH  | CLERK     | 17-DEC-80 | 1900 |
| 7499  | ALLEN  | SALESMAN  | 20-FEB-81 | 1600 |
| 7521  | WARD   | SALESMAN  | 22-FEB-81 | 1250 |
| 7566  | JONES  | MANAGER   | 02-APR-81 | 2975 |
| 7654  | MARTIN | SALESMAN  | 28-SEP-81 | 1250 |
| 7698  | BLAKE  | MANAGER   | 01-MAY-81 | 2850 |
| 7782  | CLARK  | MANAGER   | 09-JUN-81 | 2450 |
| 7788  | SCOTT  | ANALYST   | 09-DEC-82 | 3200 |
| 7839  | KING   | PRESIDENT | 17-NOV-81 | 5000 |
| 7844  | TURNER | SALESMAN  | 08-SEP-81 | 1500 |
| 7876  | ADAMS  | CLERK     | 12-JAN-83 | 1100 |
| 7900  | JAMES  | CLERK     | 03-DEC-81 | 950  |
| 7902  | FORD   | ANALYST   | 03-DEC-81 | 3000 |
| 7934  | MILLER | CLERK     | 23-JAN-82 | 1300 |

For the Dutch language, enter the following URL:

```
http://server:port/apex/f?p=app_id:page_id:session&p_lang=nl
```

| Empno | Ename | Job Title | Hiredate | Sal |
|-------|--------|-----------|----------|------|
| 7369 | SMITH | Klerk | 17-12-80 | 1900 |
| 7499 | ALLEN | Verkoper | 20-02-81 | 1600 |
| 7521 | WARD | Verkoper | 22-02-81 | 1250 |
| 7566 | JONES | Manager | 02-04-81 | 2975 |
| 7654 | MARTIN | Verkoper | 28-09-81 | 1250 |
| 7698 | BLAKE | Manager | 01-05-81 | 2850 |
| 7782 | CLARK | Manager | 09-06-81 | 2450 |
| 7788 | SCOTT | Analist | 09-12-82 | 3200 |
| 7839 | KING | Directeur | 17-11-81 | 5000 |
| 7844 | TURNER | Verkoper | 08-09-81 | 1500 |
| 7876 | ADAMS | Klerk | 12-01-83 | 1100 |
| 7900 | JAMES | Klerk | 03-12-81 | 950 |
| 7902 | FORD | Analist | 03-12-81 | 3000 |
| 7934 | MILLER | Klerk | 23-01-82 | 1300 |

## How it works...

Using the **Session** option for globalization, allows developers to take advantage of some additional built-in functions and procedures.

1. `apex_util.set_session_lang(p_lang in varchar2)`

   ❏ This procedure will set the language for the session to the value in the parameter

2. `apex_util.get_session_lang`

   ❏ This function will get the current session language. It can also be called using the variable `v('BROWSER_LANGUAGE')`

3. `apex_util.reset_session_lang`

   ❏ This procedure will clear the session language

In this recipe we took advantage of the `apex_util.get_session_lang` procedure to retrieve the correct job titles in our report. It doesn't take a lot of imagination to see the possibilities of this kind of construction. We have now seen how to put translatable data into a separate table and making it unique by combining an ID column like the JOB_NO column in our example to a LANGUAGE column.

Of course this can be used for any kind of data. Just remember to keep a keen eye on the performance of your application.

# 7
# APEX APIs

In this chapter, we will cover the following topics:

- ▶ Updating a table with the hidden primary key
- ▶ Reading a checkbox programmatically
- ▶ Creating help functionality with `apex_application.help`
- ▶ Counting clicks with `apex_util.count_clicks`
- ▶ Setting default item settings with `apex_ui_default_update`
- ▶ Creating a background process with `apex_plsql_job`

## Introduction

APEX comes with a set of Application Programming Interfaces (APIs). These APIs help the APEX developer to programmatically change the settings you would normally do in the APEX builder. The APIs offer a lot of flexibility and speed in developing web applications. Especially when you have to do a lot of repeating actions in the APEX builder, the APIs can be very useful.

In this chapter, we will show you how to use some of the APIs. For more information, refer to the APEX API reference which is included in your APEX download.

# Updating a table with the hidden primary key

The `APEX_ITEM` API is a PL/SQL package that you can use to programmatically put items on the screen. The package also contains a function to put hidden items on the screen. Hidden items are items that are placed in a webpage but are not visible. However, they can contain a value. In this way, you can make each row in a report unique. We will make an updatable report which makes use of the `APEX_ITEM` API.

## Getting ready

Make sure you have access to the table APP_EVENTS.

## How to do it...

First, we will make a classic report based on the APP_EVENTS table.

1. In the **Application Builder**, click on the **Create Page** button.
2. Select **Report**.
3. Select **Classic report**.
4. Enter a name for the page and click on **Next**.
5. Select **Do not use tabs** and click on **Next**.
6. In the text area, enter the following query:

```
select apex_item.hidden(1,id)||apex_item.text(2,event) appevent
,       apex_item.date_popup(3,rownum,event_date,'dd-mm-yyyy')
event_date
,       apex_item.text(4,location) location
,       apex_item.text(5,event_type) event_type
from    app_events;
[9672_07_01.txt]
```

7. Click on **Next**.
8. You can enter a region name. After that, click on **Next**.

9.  Click on **Finish**. The report has been created and we are now going to edit it.

10. Click on the **Edit Page** icon.

11. Click on the **Report** link in the **Regions** section to edit the report attributes.

12. Click on the Edit icon (the pencil) to edit the first column.

13. In the **Column Attributes** section, select **Standard Report Column** in the **Display As** listbox.

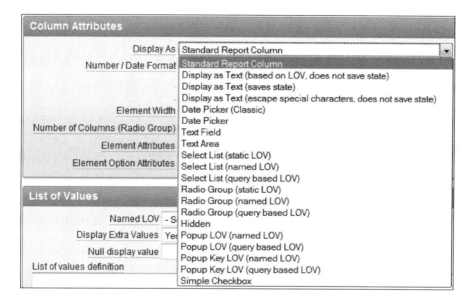

14. Click on the **Apply changes** button.

15. Repeat these steps for the other three columns and click on the **Apply changes** button to return to the page definition.

Now we will make a button and a page process to enable the saving of data.

1. In the **Buttons** section, click on the Add icon.

2. Select a region for the button and click on **Next**.

3. Select **Create a button in a region position** and click on **Next**.

4. Enter a name for the button, for example, Save. Enter a label for the button. You can enter here Save as well. Click on **Next**.

5. Select **Bottom of region** and click on **Next**.

6. In the **Action** listbox, select **Submit Page.** Click on the **Create** button.

7. In the **Processes** section, click on the Add icon.

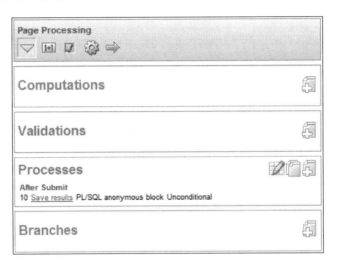

8. Select **PL/SQL**.

9. Enter a name for the page process. You can enter here save_results. Click on **Next**.

10. In the text area, enter the following code:

```
begin
for i in 1..apex_application.g_f01.count
loop
update app_events
set    event      = apex_application.g_f02(i)
,      event_date = to_date(apex_application.g_f03(i),
                                'dd-mm-yyyy')
,      location   = apex_application.g_f04(i)
,      event_type = apex_application.g_f05(i)
```

```
where   id          = to_number(apex_application.g_f01(i));
end loop;
end;
[9672_07_2.txt]
```

11. Click on the **Create** button.

12. The page is ready. Run it and try to change some values in the page. Then try to save it by clicking on the **Save** button.

## How it works...

With `APEX_ITEM` you can put an item on the screen. The first parameter in the function (hidden, text, or date_popup) is the index which you can use to find the item back. Let's say you use the following command to put an item on the screen:

`APEX_ITEM.TEXT(2,'COLUMN_NAME')`

When submitted, the values of the APEX items will be stored in the PL/SQL array `APEX_APPLICATION.G_F0X` where X is the number of your page. Then you can find this item back with:

`APEX_APPLICATION.G_F02(i).`

Where i is the row indicator in case you are working with a multi row tabular form.

Furthermore, you can use the first variable to do some aggregate functions like count. Use it in the following way:

`APEX_APPLICATION.G_F01.COUNT.`

Note that the example in this recipe only handles existing rows.

# Reading a checkbox programmatically

In the previous recipe, we saw that we can use `APEX_ITEM` and `APEX_APPLICATION` to programmatically display and control items. We can also create and manipulate a checkbox. In this recipe, we will show you how to use the `APEX_ITEM.CHECKBOX` function and how to avoid problems. We will use the previous recipe and extend it with a checkbox.

A checkbox is a special kind of item on a webpage. It can either be checked or unchecked. But APEX doesn't know the unchecked state and therefore it replaces the unchecked value with null. Since `APEX_APPLICATION` is an array, null values will not be stored in `APEX_APPLICATION`. But if you try to look up the value of a certain row, you might get a no data found error.

## Getting ready

Make sure you have a working events page from the previous recipe. Add a column to the table `APP_EVENTS` by entering the following in SQL plus:

```
Alter table app_events
Add oracle_event varchar2(1);
[9672_07_03.txt]
```

## How to do it...

We will make a change to the page from the previous recipe.

1. Go to the page you created in the previous recipe.

2. In the **Regions** section, click on the **Report region** link.

3. Replace the region source with the following code:

```
select apex_item.hidden(1,id)||apex_item.text(2,event) appevent
,       apex_item.date_popup(3,rownum,event_date,'dd-mm-yyyy')
event_date
,       apex_item.text(4,location) location
,       apex_item.text(5,event_type) event_type
,       apex_item.checkbox(6,id,decode(nvl(oracle_
event,'N'),'Y','CHECKED',null)) oracle_event
from    app_events
[9672_07_04.txt]
```

The difference with the query in the previous recipe is that there is one extra column: `APEX_ITEM.CHECKBOX`. The third argument is the decode, which sets the checkbox to be checked if the value is `Y`. If the value of `ORACLE_EVENT` is N or empty, the checkbox is unchecked. However, in APEX, you cannot speak of an unchecked status. The checkbox is either checked or null. This is an HTML restriction. And this is exactly the point you need to pay attention to. However, besides the checked status, a checkbox can also get a value and in this query the checkbox gets the value of the ID column of the `APP_EVENTS` table. We will use that later on in the recipe.

1. Click on the **Apply changes** button.

2. Click on the **Report** link in the **Regions** section.

3. Click on the Edit icon (the pencil) next to the column **ORACLE_EVENT**.

4. In the **Column Attributes** section, select **Standard report column** in the **Display as select** list.

5. Click on the **Apply changes** button.

6. Click on the **Apply changes** button again.

7. In the **Processes** section in the middle of the screen, click on the **SAVE_RESULTS** link.

8. Replace the code in the **Process** text area with the following:

```
declare
  type         t_event is table of varchar2(10) index by
                                        binary_integer;
  v_event      t_event;
  l_index      number(3);
  l_oracle_event varchar2(10);
begin
  -- use a pl/sql table to put the 'Y' in the
  -- right index
  for a in 1..apex_application.g_f06.count
  loop
    if apex_application.g_f06.exists(a)
    then
      l_index := to_number(apex_application.g_f06(a));
      v_event(l_index) := 'Y';
    end if;
  end loop;
  --
  -- Loop through the records
  for i in 1..apex_application.g_f01.count
  loop
    -- if the pl/sql table contains a value for this
    -- row, oracle_event has to be set to 'Y'. Otherwise
    -- leave oracle_event to null
    if v_event.exists(to_number(apex_application.g_f01(i)))
    then
      l_oracle_event :=
            v_event(to_number(apex_application.g_f01(i)));
    else
      l_oracle_event := null;
    end if;
    --
    update app_events
    set    event       = apex_application.g_f02(i)
    ,      event_date  = to_date(apex_application.g_f03(i),
                                    'dd-mm-yyyy')
    ,      location    = apex_application.g_f04(i)
    ,      event_type  = apex_application.g_f05(i)
    ,      oracle_event = l_oracle_event
    where  id          = to_number(apex_application.g_f01(i));
  end loop;
end;
[9672_07_05.txt]
```

This code is different from the code in the previous recipe. You can see that the ORACLE_EVENT is added to the update statement. Furthermore, you can see that a PL/SQL table (V_EVENT) is used to store the checked values. APEX_ITEM.CHECKBOX only stores the checked values. This means that when the checkboxes of rows 1, 3 and 5 are checked, the array for the checkbox, apex_application.g_f06, contains only three values. But when you try to read the value of the fifth row, you will get an error message. Contrary to, let's say event (with the apex_application.g_f03 array), you cannot get the value of the checkbox of a certain row.

To make this clear, have a look at the following table. You can see that the arrays for the ID and the EVENT column contain the correct values for each row. But the array for the checkbox shows the checked state for the first three rows where it should be checked for the rows 1, 3, and 5.

| Index value | Value of ID column Array | Value of EVENT column array | Value of Checkbox array |
|---|---|---|---|
| 1 | 2 | ODTUG... | Checked (1) |
| 2 | 3 | OBUG... | Checked (3) |
| 3 | 4 | OOW... | Checked (5) |
| 4 | 5 | Dinner... | |
| 5 | 6 | Knowledge session... | |

To avoid this, we use a PL/SQL table (V_EVENT) that only stores a value for the rows that contain a checked checkbox. We already saw that in the query each checkbox gets the value of the ID column. This value is used as index for the PL/SQL table V_EVENT. Later on in the code, where APEX loops through the array for the ID column, APEX checks whether V_EVENT contains a value for that particular index (ID). If so, the column ORACLE_EVENT should be updated with Y.

1. Click on the **Apply changes** button.

2. The page is ready. Run it, check some checkboxes, and see if it works.

# Creating help functionality with apex_application.help

To support a user-friendly interface, applications can be enhanced with a help functionality. In APEX, you can easily build a context sensitive help. You can place a help link in the navigation bar so that it is available on every page in the application.

## Getting ready

Make sure you have an existing application with some pages where you can show some help.

## How to do it...

First, let's create the help page.

1. In the **Application Builder**, click on the **Create Page** button.
2. Select **Blank page**.
3. Enter a page number and an alias. Click on **Next**.
4. Enter a name for the help page. Click on **Next**.
5. Select **No tabs** and click on **Next**.
6. Click on **Finish**.

   The page has now been created. Click on the Edit page icon to continue.

7. In the **Regions** section, click on the Add icon.
8. Select **PL/SQL Dynamic content**.
9. Enter a title. Click on **Next**.
10. In the PL/SQL source text area, enter the following code:

```
APEX_APPLICATION.HELP(
p_flow_id => :APP_ID,
p_flow_step_id => :REQUEST,
p_before_region_html => '<p><br/><table bgcolor="#33BED8"
width="100%"><tr><td><b>',
p_after_prompt_html  => '</b></p>  ');
[9672_07_06.txt]
```

This piece of code calls the APEX built-in `APEX_APPLICATION.HELP`, which shows the help. This help is customizable by using parameters. You can find an overview of the parameters at the end of this recipe. In the previous example, you can see that the parameter `P_BEFORE_REGION_HTML` and `P_AFTER_PROMPT_HTML` are used to display a help with a header with a background color `#33BED8` (blue).

You can also see the parameters `P_FLOW_ID` and `P_FLOW_STEP_ID`. Those are the two parameters to indicate the application and the page where the call comes from. To pass these parameters, `:APP_ID` and `:REQUEST` are used.

11. Click on the **Create region** button.

    The region has now been created and the help page is ready now. Next, we will enter some help text and create a link in the navigation bar.

12. Go to a page where you want to enter the help text.

13. In the **Page** section, click on the link next to **Page Name**.

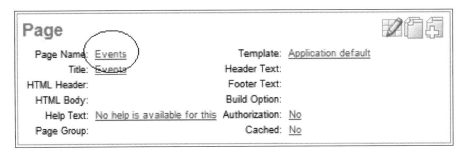

14. Click on the **Show all** tab.

15. Go to the **Help** section and enter some help text in the text area.

16. Click on the **Apply changes** button.

17. If you have items on the page click on the item and go to the help text section.

18. Enter some help text in the text area.

19. Click on the **Apply changes** button.

20. Repeat these steps for the other items on the page.

21. Go to **Shared Components | Navigation Bar Entries** (navigation section in the upper-right corner).

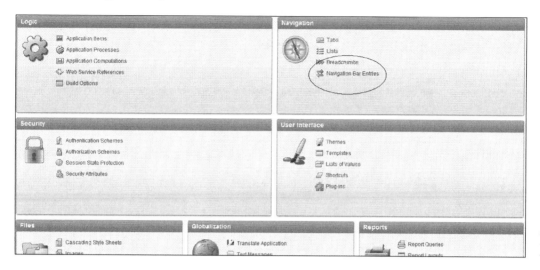

22. Click on the **Create** button.
23. Select **From scratch** and click on **Next**.
24. Select **Navigation to URL** and click on **Next**.
25. Enter help in the entry label text field and click on **Next**.
26. In the target listbox, select **URL**.
27. In the URL target text area, enter the following:

```
javascript:popupURL('f?p=&APP_ID.:<PAGE>:&SESSION.:&APP_PAGE_
ID.');
[9672_07_07.txt]
```

Where <PAGE> is the page number of the help page you just created.

28. Click on **Next**.
29. Click on the **Create** button.

The help functionality is ready now. To offer a complete help, check that help text is entered at every page and every item.

When you run a page you will see that the navigation bar contains a help link. Clicking on this link will show you a pop-up window with the help text.

---

**Help page**

Use this page to add, modify or delete employees.

**Form on EMP**

**Empno**

  The employee's ID

**Ename**

  The name of the employee.

**Job**

  The job title of the employee.

**Mgr**

  The employee ID of the manager of this employee.

**Hiredate**

  Date hired.

**Sal**

  The employee's salary.

**Comm**

  The employee's commission. This field is only applicable if the employee is a Salesman.

**Deptno**

  The ID of the department the employee works for.

---

## How it works...

In this example, we make use of the APEX_APPLICATION.HELP built-in. The built-in collects the help information and shows it in a pop-up window. The call to APEX_APPLICATION.HELP comes from within a PL/SQL dynamic region. It gets the information from the help link. The help link in the navigation bar contains the URL to the help page and contains the session ID and the page ID so that these two variables can be passed to the call to APEX_APPLICATION.HELP.

You can also use a region of type Help to get the same result. However, with the built-in, you can customize with colors and other formatting options.

## There's more...

The `APEX_APPLICATION.HELP` function has the following parameters:

| Parameter | Meaning |
|---|---|
| P_REQUEST | Not used. |
| P_FLOW_ID | The ID of the application. |
| P_FLOW_STEP_ID | The ID of the page. |
| P_SHOW_ITEM_HELP | Show item help. Default `Yes`. |
| P_SHOW_REGIONS | Show region headers. Default `Yes`. |
| P_BEFORE_PAGE_HTML | Use HTML code between page level help text and item level help text. |
| P_AFTER_PAGE_HTML | Use HTML code at the end of the page. |
| P_BEFORE_REGION_HTML | Use HTML code before every region section. Ignored if `P_SHOW_REGIONS` is `No`. |
| P_AFTER_REGION_HTML | Use HTML code after every region section. Ignored if `P_SHOW_REGIONS` is `No`. |
| P_BEFORE_PROMPT_HTML | Use HTML code before every item label for item level help. Ignored if `P_SHOW_ITEM_HELP` is `No`. |
| P_AFTER_PROMPT_HTML | Use HTML code after every item label for item level help. Ignored if `P_SHOW_ITEM_HELP` is `No`. |
| P_BEFORE_ITEM_HTML | Use HTML code before every item help text for item level help. Ignored if `P_SHOW_ITEM_HELP` is `No`. |
| P_AFTER_ITEM_HTML | Use HTML code after every item help text for item level help. Ignored if `P_SHOW_ITEM_HELP` is `No`. |

# Counting clicks with apex_util.count_click

Sometimes you want to keep statistics on your web application, for example, to measure the level of interest in the application. Or you may want to log when a user clicks a certain link in the application. In that case, you could use the `APEX_UTIL.COUNT_CLICK` function. We will show you how to use this function in the following recipe.

## Getting ready

We will create a section on a page, for example Page 1, with the latest news. Just a few words of the news article is displayed. Below the text is a link, **[read more]**, which redirects the user to the complete news article. Make sure you have a page where you can create a news section.

## How to do it...

1. In the **Application Builder**, go to the page where you want to put the news section on.

2. In the **Regions** section, click on the Add icon.

3. Select **PL/SQL dynamic content**.

4. Enter a title for the region, for example, news. Click on **Next**.

5. In the PL/SQL source text area, enter the following code:

```
declare
cursor c_nws is
select id
,       title
,       date_published
,       substr(text,1,300)||'...' text
from    app_news;
--
l_url VARCHAR2(255);
l_cat VARCHAR2(30);
l_workspace_id VARCHAR2(30);
```

```
begin
for r_nws in c_nws
loop
l_url := 'http://host:port/apex/f?p=&APP_ID.:2:&APP_
SESSION.::NO::P2_ID:'||r_nws.id;
l_workspace_id := TO_CHAR(APEX_UTIL.FIND_SECURITY_GROUP_ID('WS'));
l_cat := 'news';
--
htp.print('<h1>'||r_nws.title||'</h1>');
htp.print(r_nws.date_published);
htp.print(r_nws.text);
htp.print('<br>');
htp.print('<a href="http://host:port/apex/z?p_url=' || l_url
|| '&p_cat=' || l_cat || '&p_workspace=' || l_workspace_id ||
'">[read more]</a>');
end loop;
end;
[9672_07_08.txt]
```

In the preceding code there is a cursor with a query on the `APP_NEWS` table. The code loops through the records found and displays the first 300 characters. This is done using the `htp.print` function. After that, a link with the text **[read more]** will be displayed. Again, this is done using the `htp.print` function. However, in the link you can find the APEX function, which is used to count the clicks. In the code you see the following link:

```
http://host:port/apex/z?p_url=...
```

Where `host` is the name of the host where APEX resides and `port` is the port number used by APEX. Furthermore, you see `z?p_url=`. Z is the shortcut for `APEX_UTIL.COUNT_CLICK`. Next to the function call you can see a number of parameters which can be used to distinguish the different links. The most important parameters are `p_url`, which passes the URL APEX should navigate to, and `p_cat`, which passes the category (you can choose any name). In this case, the URL is a link to another page in the application. We use the `&APP_ID` and `&SESSION_ID` to dynamically determine the application ID and session ID. The ID of the page as well as the other parameters you might possibly need must be entered by yourself. In this case, the news article ID is passed in the URL. WS is the name of the workspace.

6. Click on **Next**.

7. Click on **Create region**.

The region is now ready. Run the page and hover with the mouse over the **[read more]** link below a news article. In the bottom status bar of your browser you will see the link to the news article. You will see that this link starts with the call to z, or the APEX_UTIL.COUNT_CLICK function. Try to click on a link. At first sight nothing special happens except that APEX redirects to the page where the news article will be shown. However, use SQL*Plus or an IDE like SQL developer and query on the APEX_WORKSPACE_CLICKS view. This view is accessible for all Oracle users so you should be able to query it. You can use the following query:

```
select  workspace
,       category
,       apex_user
,       to_char(clickdate,'DD-MM-YYYY HH24:MI:SS')
,       click_id
,       clicker_ip
,       workspace_id
from    apex_workspace_clicks
order by clickdate desc;
[9672_07_09.txt]
```

This query retrieves all rows from the view and displays the data in date descending order. The date is shown together with the timestamp to be able to see exactly when a link has been clicked.

## How it works...

The APEX_UTIL.COUNT_CLICK function is actually a function which can be called either via the URL or via a call in a PL/SQL procedure. You can also use z as a shortcut. The function actually inserts a line in the apex_workspace_clicks view. The function has more parameters:

| Parameter | Meaning |
|---|---|
| P_url | The URL to which to navigate |
| P_cat | A category to distinguish between different links |
| P_id | Secondary id to associate with the click |
| P_user | The application user ID |
| P_workspace | The workspace name |

## There's more...

You can also use a PL/SQL procedure to directly call the `count_clicks` function:

```
declare
  p_name varchar2(100) := 'apx_usr';
begin
  apex_util.count_click(
    p_url         => 'http://host:port/apex/f?p=<app>:<page>:
                      &SESSION_ID.',
    p_cat         => p_name,
    p_id          => null,
    p_user        => owa_util.get_cgi_env('REMOTE_ADDR'),
    p_company     => apex_util.find_security_group_
id('YOURWORKSPACE'));
end;
[9672_07_10.txt]
```

Where `<app>` is the ID of your application and `<page>` is the id of the page. Make a page process and use this code. Use a button to call this page process. APEX will redirect to the link in `p_url` and insert a line in `APEX_WORKSPACE_CLICKS`.

If you use a list to use as a menu, you can use the built-in count click mechanism:

1. Go to **Shared Components** and click on the **Lists** link in the **Navigation** section.

2. Click on an existing list. You will get an overview of links included in this list. Click on a link.

3. Click on the **Click Counting** tab.

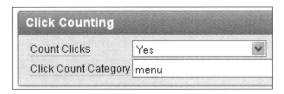

4. In the **Count Clicks** listbox, select **Yes**.

5. In the **Click Count Category** text field, enter a category name. You can choose any name, as long as it is unique within the application so that you can find it back in the `APEX_WORKSPACE_CLICKS` view. This view shows a row for each call to `APEX_UTIL.COUNT_CLICK`. You can view the workspace, the workspace ID, the category, the date and time of the moment the user clicked, the APEX user, and the IP address.

# Setting default item settings with apex_ui_default_update

When you create a form or a report, most of the time this is done with the help of a wizard. It is very easy for the most common things, but if you want a different width of a text item, other than the default width, you have to do this afterwards. When you have a lot of items on your screen this could be very cumbersome. In this recipe, we will show you how to set the default width of columns with the APEX_UI_DEFAULT_UPDATE.UPD_ITEM_DISPLAY_WIDTH procedure. We will set the default width of column EVENT in table APP_EVENTS to 200.

## Getting ready

Before you can use this function, the table needs to be included in the APEX dictionary. The view APEX_UI_DEFAULTS_COLUMNS holds the columns and their default width. You can add your table to this dictionary view by doing the following:

1. In APEX, go to **SQL workshop.**

2. Click on **Utilities**.

3. Click on **User interface defaults**.

4. Click on the **Manage table dictionary** button.

5. Click on the **Synchronize** button on the right-hand side of the screen.

6. You will see a small report which shows the objects with defaults and the objects without defaults. Click on the **Synchronize defaults** button. When APEX is ready, you will see a success message. All the tables in the schema that is linked to your workspace are now in the APEX dictionary.

7. You can also synchronize in SQL plus. Log in as the table owner and issue the following command:

```
exec apex_ui_default_update.synch_table('APP_EVENTS');
[9672_07_11.txt]
```

The only difference is that in the APEX builder, all tables will be included at once and in SQL plus you have to do this for every table separately (OK, you could write a script).

If you ignore these steps, the table with the columns you wish to set the default width for might not be in the APEX dictionary, and the steps in the next paragraph will lead to a **ORA-20001: UI Default update failed - there is no associated table** error message.

## How to do it...

1. Go to SQL plus or an IDE where you can enter SQL commands. Log in to the schema where your tables for the APEX application reside.

2. Enter the following command:

```
begin
apex_ui_default_update.upd_item_display_width(
p_table_name     => 'APP_EVENTS'
,p_column_name   => 'EVENT'
,p_display_width => 200);
end;
/
[9672_07_12.txt]
```

   This small procedure calls the APEX_UI_DEFAULT_UPDATE.UPD_ITEM_DISPLAY_WIDTH function and sets the display width of column EVENT in table APP_EVENTS to 200.

3. To demonstrate the default width of the EVENT column, go to the **Application Builder**, go to your application, and click on the **Create Page** button.

4. Select **Form**.

5. Select **Form on a table or view**.

6. Select the table or view owner and click on **Next**.

7. In the **Table/view name** text field, enter the name of the table, in this case APP_EVENTS. Click on **Next**.

8. Change the page number or the page name or the region title or change nothing at all and click on **Next**.

9. Select **Do not use tabs** and click on **Next**.

10. In the **Primary key** listbox, select the primary key column of the APP_EVENTS table. In this case it is ID, so select **ID** and click on **Next**.

11. Select **Existing sequence**. In the **Sequence** listbox, select the sequence used for this column. In this case, select APP_AET_SEQ and click on **Next**.

12. Select **All columns** and click on **Next**.

13. If you want, you can change the button labels. When you're done, click on **Next**.

14. Enter the page numbers where this page should navigate to after clicking on the buttons. You can also use the current page number. Click on **Next**.

15. Click on **Finish**.

16. Run the page and you will see that the **Event** text item has a width of **200**.

## How it works...

The call to the function actually updates the APEX dictionary view. You can see that when you do a query on APEX_UI_DEFAULTS_COLUMNS where table_name is APP_EVENTS and column name is EVENT:

```
select  table_name
,       column_name
,       label
,       display_width
,       display_in_form
from    apex_ui_defaults_columns
where   table_name  = 'APP_EVENTS'
and     column_name = 'EVENT';
[9672_07_13.txt]
```

The result is as follows:

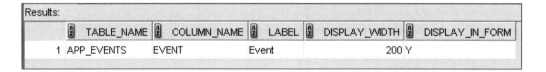

Results:

| | TABLE_NAME | COLUMN_NAME | LABEL | DISPLAY_WIDTH | DISPLAY_IN_FORM |
|---|---|---|---|---|---|
| 1 | APP_EVENTS | EVENT | Event | 200 | Y |

The DISPLAY_WIDTH is adjusted to **200**.

## There's more...

The APEX_UI_DEFAULT_UPDATE package contains more functions to set default values of tables or columns, for example form region title, item format mask, and labels.

# Creating a background process with apex_plsql_job

APEX supports running background processes. This can be useful, for example, when you want to postpone all reports printing to evening hours or you want to e-mail some information to a large number of e-mail addresses. After submitting the job, the user can continue working with the application and is able to monitor the job. This recipe will show you how to submit a background process. We will create a button on a report page which shows an overview of all upcoming events. When the user clicks the button, a background process is submitted which starts a procedure that sends the overview to a number of e-mail addresses.

## Getting ready

Make sure you have a report of all upcoming events. If you don't have it, create one through the following steps:

1. In the **Application Builder**, click on the **Create page** button.
2. Click on **Report**.
3. Click on **Classic report**.
4. Enter a page number or a page name. Click on **Next**.
5. Select **Do not use tabs** and click on **Next**.
6. Enter the following query:

```
select id
,       title
,       date_published
,       text
from    app_news;
[9672_07_14.txt]
```

7. Click on **Next**.
8. Click again on **Next**.
9. Click on **Finish**. The report is ready now and you can choose to run it or edit it.

## How to do it...

We will now edit the report. We will create a button and a PL/SQL page process.

1. Click on the Edit page icon.
2. In the **Buttons** section, click on the Add icon.
3. Select a region for the button. In this case, there is only one region which is already selected. Click on **Next**.
4. Select **Create a button in a region position**. Click on **Next**.
5. Enter a name for the button, for example `Mail events`. Click on **Next**.
6. Click on **Next**.
7. Click on **Create button**.
8. In the **Processes** section, click on the add icon.
9. Select **PL/SQL**.
10. Enter a name for the page process, for example, `Sendevents`. Click on **Next**.

11. In the text area, enter the following code:

```
declare
l_sql VARCHAR2(4000);
l_job NUMBER;
begin
l_sql := 'begin'||
'  -- here goes your code to send emails'||
'  app_mail.send_mail;'||
'end;';
l_job := apex_plsql_job.submit_process(p_sql    => l_sql
,p_status => 'Send mail job started');
end;
[9672_07_15.txt]
```

12. Click on **Next**.

13. Now you can enter a success message and a failure message, if desired. Click on **Next**.

14. In the **When button pressed** listbox, select **mail_events**. Click on the **Create Process** button.

15. You are ready now to test it. Run the page and click on the **Mail events** button.

## How it works...

When the user clicks on the button, the page process is started. The page process submits a job using the APEX_PLSQL_JOB.SUBMIT_PROCESS function.

## There's more...

You can monitor the job using some other functions in the APEX_PLSQL_JOB package. There is the TIME_ELAPSE function which shows you how long the job already is running and you can use UPDATE_JOB_STATUS to set the status of the job.

# 8

# Using Web Services

In this chapter, we will cover:

- ▸ Creating a SOAP web service reference
- ▸ Creating a REST web service reference
- ▸ Building a page based on a web service reference
- ▸ Publishing a RESTful web service

# Introduction

Data-centric applications can have many different architectures. In some of these architectures, the data is not even in the database itself. In these cases, a possible scenario can be that the data is collected by calling web services.

Essentially, a web service provider offers a way for external applications to unlock its data, but not give away total access to its database (or other data sources).

A call to a web service will have to satisfy certain standards as set by the **World Wide Web consortium** (**W3C**). Since the fourth version of Application Express, it provides the possibility to natively call two of these standards: **Simple Object Access Protocol** (**SOAP**) and **Representational State Transfer** (**REST**). But by using a little more PL/SQL and XML DB, it's possible to use any type of web service in APEX.

In this chapter we are going to create some examples of how to use web services in APEX.

# Creating a SOAP web service reference

As explained in the introduction of this chapter, SOAP stands for Simple Object Access Protocol. It is a standard that defines how the message that calls the web service should be defined and how the answer is returned. Both messages are in XML.

SOAP web services can be defined in so called **Web Service Description Language** (**WSDL**) documents. By reading a WSDL, an application knows what web services are available, how to call them, and what response it can expect back. APEX uses the information in a WSDL document to generate the SOAP messages, without the developer having to do any programming.

In this recipe we are going to show how we can call an SOAP web service using built-in functionality of Application Express.

## Getting ready

Have an APEX application ready. It doesn't have to be empty, as long as we can add new pages.

Also make sure that if you are working on an Oracle 11g database, that the host of each web service that we are going to use is entered into the **Access Control List** (**ACL**) for the APEX user.

The ACL is a structure to allow access to network services. In earlier versions, the database access was essentially granted to all services or none. In 11g, this has been changed, so it is now possible to allow fine grained access to selected network services.

To allow the APEX user access to a network service like a web service, we can use the following script (for 4.2, replace APEX_040000 by APEX_040200):

```
begin
  dbms_network_acl_admin.create_acl (acl         => 'acl_user.xml'
  ,description => 'Description'
  ,principal   => 'APEX_040000'
  ,is_grant    => true
  ,privilege   => 'connect'
  ,start_date  => null
  ,end_date    => null);
  --
  DBMS_NETWORK_ACL_ADMIN.ADD_PRIVILEGE(acl         =>
    'acl_user.xml'
  ,principal => 'APEX_040000'
  ,is_grant  => true
```

```
    ,privilege => 'resolve');
    --
    DBMS_NETWORK_ACL_ADMIN.ASSIGN_ACL(acl   => 'acl_user.xml'
    ,host => 'name of website or host, i.e. soap.amazon.com');
    --
    commit;
  end;
  [9672_08_01.txt]
```

This piece of code will do three things.

- ▸ First, it will create a new entry in the ACL for the APEX_040000 user to allow this user to connect to network and/or internet resources.
- ▸ Second, it will add a privilege for the same user to resolve addresses.
- ▸ And third, it will assign a certain hostname to the ACL entry.

So these three together will allow the APEX_040000 user to resolve a network address and connect to it.

The ACL entries can be inspected as a DBA user by querying the database using the query:

```
select * from dba_network_acls;
```

Their associated privileges can be found again as a DBA user by using the query:

```
select * from dba_network_acl_privileges;
```

Instead of a single URL for the host, a wildcard (*) can be entered. But be careful when doing this, because this will allow any APEX user to connect to any network and internet address from any APEX application or PL/SQL code.

## How to do it...

In this recipe we are going to create a page and a report based on a web service using the information from a WSDL document:

1. Navigate to the **Web Service Reference** overview by going to **Shared Components | Web Service References**.
2. Click on the **Create** button.

3. We are now in the wizard that will guide us through the creation process. On the first screen, choose **Based on WSDL** and click on **Next**.

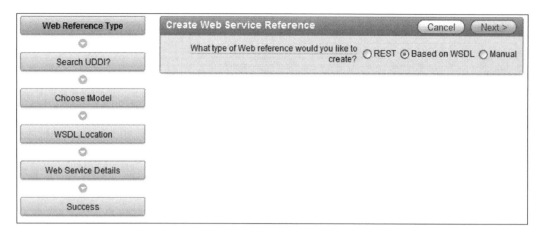

4. Select **No** when asked if we want to search a UDDI registry and click on **Next.**

5. For the WSDL location, enter `http://ws.cdyne.com/WeatherWS/Weather.asmx?wsdl`.

6. Click on **Next**.

7. In the following screen, change the name to `CDYNE Weather`. Leave everything else on its default value and click on **Create Reference.**

We can see that APEX has gathered some information about the web service by calling the WSDL document. It has found the name of the web service, its endpoint, and more importantly the available operations to use. Later in the recipe we will use the `GetCityWeatherByZIP` operation.

After creating the web service reference, APEX gives us the option to inspect it or continue directly to build a page using the reference:

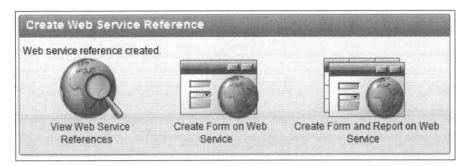

1.   Click on **Create Form on Web Service** to continue.

2.   From the available references in the pulldown on the next page, select **CDYNE Weather**.

3.   A new select list appears with the available operations. Select **GetCityWeather ByZIP** and click on **Next**.

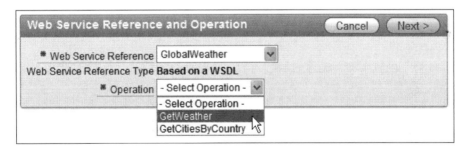

4.   Application Express will now show a list of default properties. When necessary change the page number, else leave the values at their default and click on **Next**.

     The next screen will allow us to create items that can be used in the web service call. These have been generated based on the information from the WSDL. If the page number has changed, then rename the items accordingly. In this case, there is only one parameter, the input parameter, to hold the ZIP code for our web service request.

5.   Change **Item Label** to `Zipcode` and click on **Next**.

6. The next screen follows the same principle, but for output parameters. APEX has generated 15 items. One for each possible item in the response. This screen might look a little strange, but that should be fixed in a later version of Application Express. Click on **Next**.

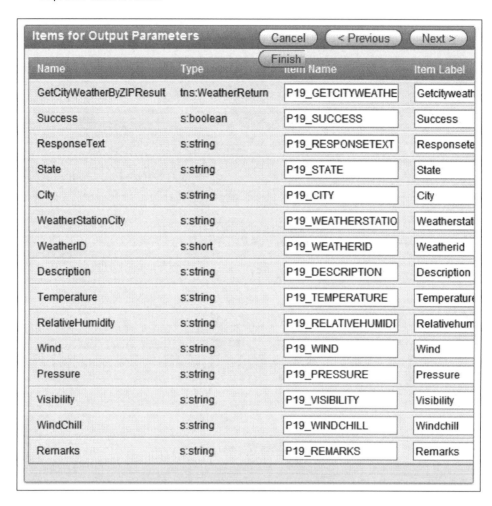

| Items for Output Parameters | | | | |
|---|---|---|---|---|
| Name | Type | Item Name | | Item Label |
| GetCityWeatherByZIPResult | tns:WeatherReturn | P19_GETCITYWEATHE | | Getcityweath |
| Success | s:boolean | P19_SUCCESS | | Success |
| ResponseText | s:string | P19_RESPONSETEXT | | Responsete |
| State | s:string | P19_STATE | | State |
| City | s:string | P19_CITY | | City |
| WeatherStationCity | s:string | P19_WEATHERSTATIO | | Weatherstat |
| WeatherID | s:short | P19_WEATHERID | | Weatherid |
| Description | s:string | P19_DESCRIPTION | | Description |
| Temperature | s:string | P19_TEMPERATURE | | Temperature |
| RelativeHumidity | s:string | P19_RELATIVEHUMIDI | | Relativehum |
| Wind | s:string | P19_WIND | | Wind |
| Pressure | s:string | P19_PRESSURE | | Pressure |
| Visibility | s:string | P19_VISIBILITY | | Visibility |
| WindChill | s:string | P19_WINDCHILL | | Windchill |
| Remarks | s:string | P19_REMARKS | | Remarks |

(Buttons: Cancel, < Previous, Next >, Finish)

7. Select the tab that you want to use or create a new tab and click on **Next**.
8. Click on **Create Form** and run the page.

You will see that APEX has created a straightforward page that will allow us to enter the required input parameter for the web service. It has also created text fields for all the output parameters.

| GetCityWeatherByZIP | Submit |
| --- | --- |
| Zipcode | |
| Getcityweatherbyzipresult | |
| Success | |
| Responsetext | |
| State | |
| City | |
| Weatherstationcity | |
| Weatherid | |
| Description | |
| Temperature | |
| Relativehumidity | |
| Wind | |
| Pressure | |
| Visibility | |
| Windchill | |
| Remarks | |

Try the web service by entering an American ZIP code into the appropriate field (for the non-Americans, everybody remembers 90210 don't we?) and click on **Submit**. This will result in the web service returning an XML file with weather information for the chosen city. APEX automatically translates this data and enters it into the right fields on the screen.

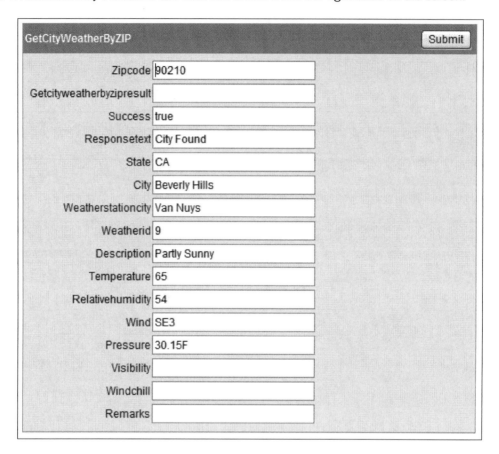

## How it works...

When we call a web service from an APEX application, `request` and `response` are XML files. Thanks to the built-in functionality, we don't always have to worry about the structure of these files. In a straightforward example like this, all translations to and from XML are done under the hood.

## See also

▶ In the recipe, *Building a page based on a web service reference*, we will see an example that utilizes the built-in XML DB functionality to extract data from the XML response of a web service.

# Creating a REST web service reference

A **Representational State Transfer** (**REST**) web service service is another kind of web service standard. REST does not necessarily use WSDL or SOAP messaging, but can be called directly by using methods like `POST` and `GET` and other HTTP operations. So we can call a REST service directly from a URL unlike SOAP. This makes testing a lot easier.

APEX developers can use REST web services and the wizard interface offers many possibilities for creating the call.

In this recipe, we are going to use the opportunities that APEX offers us to create a page based on a public REST web service; the popular photo application Flickr.

## Getting ready

Before starting this tutorial, create a Flickr account at `http://www.flickr.com` and request an API key.

## How to do it...

1. Go to **Shared Components** and click on **Web Service References**.
2. Click on the **Create** button.
3. Select the radio button next to **REST** and press **Next**.

   In the **Name** field, enter `Flickr REST service`.
4. In the URL field, enter `http://www.flickr.com/services/rest/`.
5. Leave the rest on default and click on **Next**.

In the input parameters, we are going to enter three parameters.

1. Name the first as `method` and click on **Add Parameter**.
2. Name the second as `api_key` and click on **Add Parameter**.
3. Name the last as `user_id` and click on **Next**.
4. In the **XPath to Output Parameters** text field, enter `/rsp`.
5. Click on **Create** to save the web service call.

Now we are ready to test if everything is okay.

1. Navigate back to the list of web service references.

2. Make sure the **Report View** is selected by pressing the corresponding button in the toolbar above the list.

3. Now click on the **Test** button for our Flickr REST service.

4. To make this work, enter values for the three input parameters we created earlier:

   ❑ method: `flickr.people.getPublicPhotos`

   ❑ api_key: This is your Flickr API Key

   ❑ user_id: This is your Flickr user id (or use mine: `52012402@N05`)

5. Now click on the **Test** button.

   After a little wait, a response is returned as an XML file, containing all publicly available pictures for the selected user:

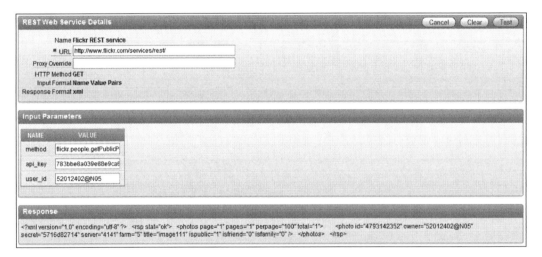

## How it works...

There are a lot of other differences between REST and SOAP. Both of them have advantages. Some of these for REST are as follows:

- It is lightweight without a lot of extra XML markup
- It has human-readable results
- It's easy to build without any toolkits

The main advantages of SOAP are as follows:

- Easier to consume (most of the time)
- Contract driven
- There are a lot of development tools available

The industry lately seems to be in favor of using REST for internet services. A lot of the larger companies (such as Twitter, Google, and Amazon) have chosen this standard for their web services. SOAP still seems to be the standard for enterprise applications. But choosing REST or SOAP in a project is completely dependent on the specifications of that project.

## There's more...

With the information from this recipe, it is possible to create a page to enter the required parameters and to display the response in a more readable format. We will do so in the next recipe.

# Building a page on a web service reference

Creating a standard looking page on a web service reference is one thing. Making it more user-friendly is another. In this recipe we are going to take a look at some of the possibilities for fine-tuning the look of the page created in the previous recipe.

## Getting ready

Make sure that the Flickr REST web service reference from the previous recipe is available.

## How to do it...

Because the REST service we created earlier responds with an XML message, we can use output parameters to hold the returned data. To add these parameters, navigate to the **Shared Components | Web Service References** and select **Flickr REST service**.

1.  Find the **REST Output Parameters** section and click on **Add Output Parameter.**
2.  In the **Name** field, enter `photo_id`.
3.  In the **Path** field, enter `/photos/photo/@id`.
4.  Add another parameter with values `title` and `/photos/photo/@title`.
5.  Add a third parameter using values `secret` and `/photos/photo/@secret`.

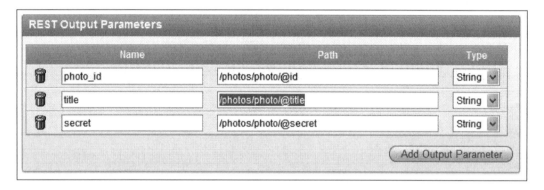

6.  Click on **Apply Changes** at the top of the screen.

We are now going to create a Form and Report based on these new parameters:

1.  Go to the **Application Builder**.
2.  Click on the **Create Page** button.
3.  Select **Form** and click on **Next**.
4.  Select **Form** and **Report** on web service and click on **Next**.
5.  Select the Flickr REST service and the operation **doREST** and click on **Next.**
6.  Keep all defaults and click on **Next**.
7.  Check all boxes next to the **Result** parameters to select them all and click on **Next**.
8.  Create a new tab for this page and click on **Next** until we reach the confirmation page.
9.  Click on **Create Form and Report**.

Now we can run the page to see the result. In the input fields, use the same values that we used in the previous recipe to compare the outcome.

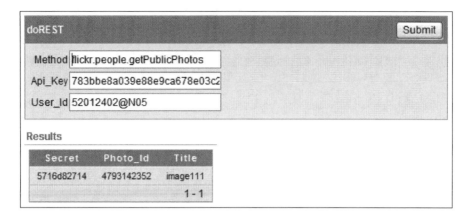

Keep in mind that this will only work correctly if the response contains a single record, else APEX will throw an error. For this to be corrected, we have to change the generated query that extracts the data out of the XML response. We will do that later in this recipe.

To make this page a little more user-friendly, we will make some changes to the way the fields are displayed. First of all, not all input parameters need to be shown. **Method** and **Api_Key** will always be the same, so we will make hidden parameters of them:

1. Go to **Application Builder** and open the page we created for this web service call.
2. Under **Region | Body | doREST**, find the item for **Method**.
3. Right-click the **Method** item and click on **Edit**.
4. Change **Display as** to **Hidden** using the select list.
5. Change **Default Value** to **flickr.people.getPublicPhotos**.
6. Click on **Apply Changes**.
7. Now find the **Api_Key** item and click on **Edit**.
8. Again change **Display as** to **Hidden**.
9. Change **Default Value** to your Flickr Api_Key.
10. Click on **Apply Changes**.

If we run the page now, we can see only the **User_id** field is left on the screen. The other values will be sent to the web service call without the user having to input them.

The report could also use a little makeover. Let's make the **Photo_Id** column a clickable link to the Flickr page for the photo:

1. Find the **Results** region and expand all report columns.

2. Right-click on the **Photo_Id** column and click on **Edit**.

3. Scroll down to the **Column Link** section.

4. Change **Link Text** to **#photo_id#**.

5. Change **Target** to **URL**.

6. Change **URL** to `http://www.flickr.com/photos/&P17_USER_ID./#photo_id#`. If the **User_Id** item is named differently in your situation, change that part of the URL accordingly.

7. Click on **Apply Changes** and run the page again.

Clicking on the data in the **Photo_Id** column will redirect to the Flickr page for the photo:

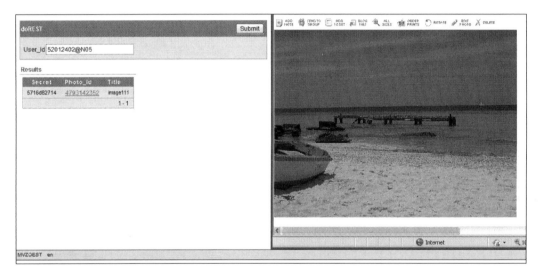

## How it works...

The extraction of data from the XML response is done by making use of the XML DB functionality of the Oracle database. Most of the time we won't see a lot of this when we are creating simple request/response pages. In this recipe we've seen a hint of this when we extracted data using paths such as `/photos/photo/@id`. This path is directly related to the structure of the XML response. In the next section we will see a more elaborate way to extract date from this XML.

## There's more...

Remember that we promised to solve the problem of users that have more than one photo attached? We're going to do that now.

To understand the problem, we need to look at the XML response that we are getting from Flickr. The following is an example from a user that has two photos available to show.

```xml
<?xml version="1.0" encoding="utf-8" ?>
<rsp stat="ok">
  <photos page="1" pages="1" perpage="100" total="2">
  <photo id="5155098679" owner="52012402@N05" secret="3f51a3dc69"
    server="4042" farm="5" title="image074" ispublic="1"
    isfriend="0" isfamily="0" />
  <photo id="4793142352" owner="52012402@N05" secret="5716d82714"
    server="4141" farm="5" title="image111" ispublic="1"
    isfriend="0" isfamily="0" />
  </photos>
</rsp>
[9672_08_03.xml]
```

As we can see, the XML has three nodes: `rsp`, `photos`, and `photo`. And that is exactly the problem here. Because the generated code from APEX says that there is a single photo node, it will fail when a second photo is found. For that to be corrected, we have to explain APEX to look at a level higher and loop through everything that is found underneath that level:

1. Go to the **Edit Page** screen, right-click on the **Results** region and click on **Edit**.

2. Change the query to the following:
```sql
select extractValue(value(t),'*/@page') "page"
  , extractValue(value(ti),'*/@secret') "secret"
  , extractValue(value(ti),'*/@id') "photo_id"
  , extractValue(value(ti),'*/@title') "title"
from wwv_flow_collections c
  , table(xmlsequence(extract(c.xmltype001,'*/photos'))) t
  , table(xmlsequence(extract(value(t),'*/photo'))) ti
where c.collection_name = 'P17_DOREST_RESULTS'
[9672_08_04.sql]
```

3. Now run the page again and use a `User_Id` item with more than one photo in the profile:

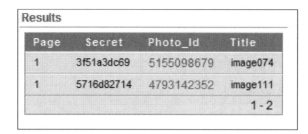

Further, we can also change the page so that the image itself is shown as a thumbnail on this page itself and have the link on the page direct to the photo immediately.

4. Return to the query for the **Results** region.

5. Change the query to the following:

```
select extractValue(value(t),'*/@page') "page"
   , extractValue(value(ti),'*/@secret') "secret"
   , extractValue(value(ti),'*/@id') "photo_id"
   , extractValue(value(ti),'*/@farm') "farm"
   , extractValue(value(ti),'*/@server') "server"
   , extractValue(value(ti),'*/@title') "title"
   , '<img
     src="http://farm'||extractValue(value(ti),'*/@farm')||'.sta
     tic.flickr.com/'||extractValue(value(ti),'*/@server')||'/'|
     |extractValue(value(ti),'*/@id')||'_'||extractValue(value(t
     i),'*/@secret')||'_s.jpg">' "image"
from wwv_flow_collections c
   , table(xmlsequence(extract(c.xmltype001,'*/photos'))) t
   , table(xmlsequence(extract(value(t),'*/photo'))) ti
where c.collection_name = 'P17_DOREST_RESULTS'
```

As we can see there are some new columns that will be selected. We need those later to create the direct link to the large image. The last column with the image alias is actually some HTML code to generate an `<img>` tag for a Flickr image with size `s`, which is the size of a thumbnail.

6. Now go the **Report Attributes** tab and click on the pencil icon next to the image column.

7. Under column attributes, change **Display as** to **Standard Report Column** and click on **Apply Changes**.

The thumbnail is now set up. Now let's change the link:

1.  Click on the pencil icon next to the **Photo_Id** column.
2.  Scroll down to the **Column Link** section and change the URL to
    `http://farm#farm#.static.flickr.com/#server#/#photo_`
    `id#_#secret#_b.jpg`.
3.  Click on **Apply Changes**.

As we are tidying up, we can also remove the columns that are not interesting from view:

1.  Uncheck the checkboxes under the **Show** column for page, secret, farm, and server.
2.  Click on **Apply Changes**.
3.  Run the page to see the final results.

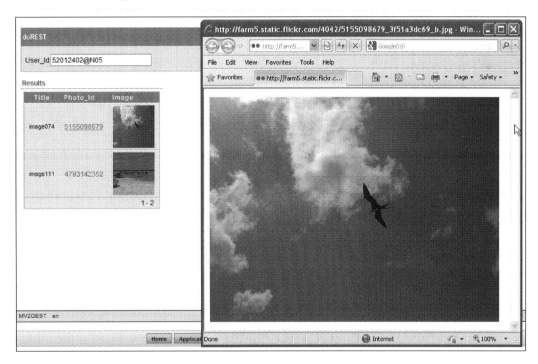

With this knowledge in hand, we can turn our APEX application into an online photo album, for example.

# Publishing a RESTful web service

REST is a type of web service architecture. In recent years, it has gained a lot of popularity. This is due to the fact that RESTful web services follow a protocol that is relatively simple and easy to implement.

In this recipe we will show how it is possible in Application Express to publish the contents of a report as a RESTful web service.

## Getting ready

To follow this recipe, APEX Listener 2.0 (or higher) and APEX 4.2 (or higher) should be used.

First, we have to make sure that RESTful access is allowed to the APEX instance. This has to be set in the APEX Administration Services:

1. Log in to the APEX Administration environment.
2. Click on **Manage Instance**.
3. Find the link to **Security** in the section called **Instance Settings** and click on it.
4. Go to the **RESTful Access** section.
5. Set **Allow RESTful Access** to **Yes**.

6. Click on **Apply Changes**

Furthermore, we'll need a report that we can use as the source for our RESTful web service. For this recipe, we'll assume a simple database application (app 109) with a single report page (page 1), based on the following query:

```
select emp.*
, dept.dname
from emp
, dept
where  dept.deptno = emp.deptno
[9672_08_100.txt]
```

## How to do it...

We are now going to expose this report to the world, by enabling RESTful access to it. The following steps explain how to do this. First we need to make the page holding the report public:

1. Go to **Application Builder** and open the application.
2. Click on the page holding the report.
3. In the tree view, right-click on the page name and click on **Edit**.
4. In the **Security** section, find the attribute named **Authentication**. Change its value to **Page Is Public**.

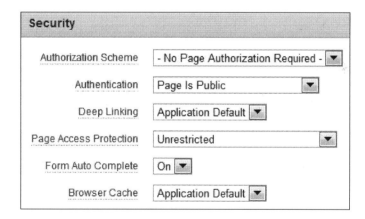

5. Click on **Apply Changes**.

Now the page is available to the public. The next part explains how to make the report itself available as a RESTful web service:

1. On the report page, right-click on the report region and click on **Edit**.

2. Find the **Attributes** region.

3. In the field **Static ID**, enter `1092` or any other value.

4. Select the value **Yes** in the select list for **Enable RESTful Access**.

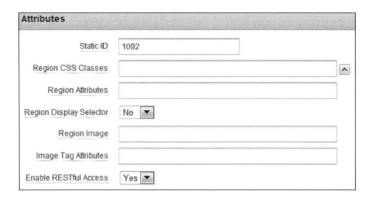

5. Click on **Apply Changes**.

And that is all there is to it. The report is now available as a RESTful web service.

## There's more...

To retrieve data from the web service, we first need to know how to call it. To get this information, it is possible to invoke a service.

The URL for this service is `http://<server>:<port>/apex/apex_rest.getServiceDescription?app=109`, where `109` is the ID for the application that we built in this recipe.

The response for this service call is a description of all available RESTful web services in this application. In this case, just the one we have built:

```
<?xml version="1.0"?>
<urn:getServiceDescriptionResponse
    xmlns:urn="urn:oasis:names:tc:wsrp:v1:types">

    <urn:requiresRegistration>false</urn:requiresRegistration>
    <urn:offeredPortlets>

        <urn:PortletDescription>
```

```
        <urn:portletHandle>1092</urn:portletHandle>
        <urn:markupTypes>
           <urn:mimeType>application/xml</urn:mimeType>
           <urn:mimeType>application/json</urn:mimeType>
        </urn:markupTypes>
        <urn:groupID>1</urn:groupID>
        <urn:description/>
        <urn:title>Employees</urn:title>
        <urn:keywords/>
      </urn:PortletDescription>
    </urn:offeredPortlets>
  </urn:getServiceDescriptionResponse>
```

The important parts are the tags for `portletHandle` and `groupID`. They represent the static ID that was entered previously and the page ID. These ID can be used to invoke the RESTful web service itself.

The URL to do so is built up like this: `http://<server>:<port>/apex/apex_rest.getReport?app=109&page=1&reportid=1092`.

Calling this URL will result in a response similar to the following:

```
<?xml version="1.0"?>
<ROWSET>
  <ROW>
    <EMPNO>7782</EMPNO>
    <ENAME>CLARK</ENAME>
    <JOB>MANAGER</JOB>
    <MGR>7839</MGR>
    <HIREDATE>09-JUN-81</HIREDATE>
    <SAL>2450</SAL>
    <DEPTNO>10</DEPTNO>
    <DNAME>ACCOUNTING</DNAME>
  </ROW>
  <ROW>
    <EMPNO>7839</EMPNO>
    <ENAME>KING</ENAME>
    <JOB>PRESIDENT</JOB>
    <HIREDATE>17-NOV-81</HIREDATE>
    <SAL>5000</SAL>
    <DEPTNO>10</DEPTNO>
    <DNAME>ACCOUNTING</DNAME>
  </ROW>
</ROWSET>
```

## See also

> ► Using this information, it is possible to build a web service reference from any environment like another APEX application. See other recipes in this chapter for more information.

# 9
# Publishing from APEX

In this chapter, we will cover:

- ▶ Exporting to a comma-separated file
- ▶ Creating a PDF report
- ▶ Creating a report query
- ▶ Creating a report layout using Oracle BI publisher
- ▶ Linking the report layout to the report query
- ▶ Calling a report from a page

## Introduction

Using APEX it is possible to create reports that can be displayed on the screen. However, as a user, you would also like to print the report on paper or at least get the output in some kind of digital format such as PDF or Microsoft Excel. APEX supports a number of formats your reports can be exported to. This needs a little setup work. Furthermore, you can use your output in BI Publisher. In this chapter, we will show you how to export reports and how to interact with BI Publisher.

# Exporting to a comma-separated file

APEX offers a standard built-in to export data to a **Comma-separated Value** (**CSV**) file. A CSV file is readable by Microsoft Excel or OpenOffice Calc. Each row contains the data of a record in a table and each value in the row is separated by a comma and represents the value of a column of the table. When **Export to CSV** is enabled, a link is shown just below the region with the data. We will show you how to add this link.

## Getting ready

You should have a working application with at least one standard report. If you don't have a report, create one. You can find a recipe for creating a simple report in *Chapter 1, Creating a Basic APEX Application*.

## How to do it...

First, we will adapt the report and then we will put a link on the report.

1. Go to the **Report** page.

2. In the **Regions** section, click on the **Report** link.

3. In the **Report Export** section, select **Yes** in the **Enable CSV output** listbox:

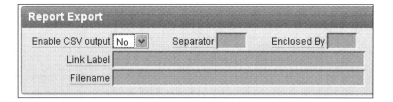

4. In the **Link Label** text field, enter `Export to csv`. This text appears as a link below the region.

5. In the **Filename** field, you can enter a filename. By default, the filename is the name of the region with the extension `.csv`.

6. Click on the **Apply changes** button.

7. The link should now appear when you run the report:

When you click on the link, you will get a pop-up window asking whether you want to open the file with the program of your choice or download it to your computer.

## How it works...

The link on the screen points to the same page but with an extra argument in the URL:

```
http://localhost:8000/apex/f?p=114:12:2184716804402017:FLOW_EXCEL_
OUTPUT_R435417443089863248_en
```

At the end of the URL, you see `FLOW_EXCEL_OUTPUT_R435417443089863248_en`. The large number after `FLOW_EXCEL_OUTPUT_R` is the region ID. You can find it in the view `APEX_APPLICATION_PAGE_REGIONS`. So, with the help of that view, you can make your own link. You just need the application ID and the page ID. So, for example, if you have an application with the application ID 114 and a report with the page ID 12, and you want to add an "export to csv" link in your report, enter the following:

```
select 'http://localhost:8000/apex/f?p='||application_id||':'||page_
id||':&SESSION.:FLOW_EXCEL_OUTPUT_R'||region_id||'_en'
from    apex_application_page_regions
where   upper(source_type) = 'REPORT'
and     application_id = 114
and     page_id = 12;
[9672_09_01.sql]
```

(This is provided that APEX is installed on your local machine and that it is set to port 8000). The result will be something like this:

```
http://localhost:8000/apex/f?p=114:12:2184716804402017:FLOW_EXCEL_
OUTPUT_R435417443089863248_en
```

This link also works even if you have set **Enable CSV output** to **No**.

If you have an interactive report, you have also the possibility to export to CSV. Click on the **Actions** button and select **Download**:

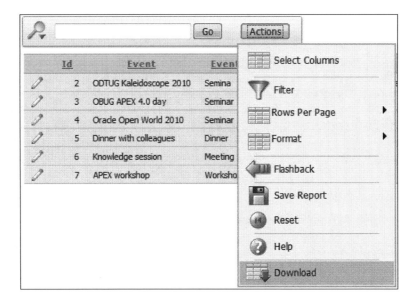

In the **Download** section you can click on the CSV icon to export the report to CSV format. To see the link, just hover over the **CSV** icon. In the status bar at the bottom of your screen you will see something like the following:

```
http://localhost:8000/apex/f?p=108:15:2184716804402017:CSV:
```

So here it's even simpler to generate a download to CSV link.

# Creating a PDF report

In APEX it is possible to export the data to **Portable Document Format** (**PDF**) format. The PDF format is created by Adobe and is widely accepted as a standard. To be able to export to PDF format, you need a report server like BI Publisher, a Java application server like Tomcat or Oracle's WebLogic with Apache FOP, or a standard XSL-FO processing engine. We will discuss the interaction with Oracle BI Publisher.

# Getting ready

First you need to install Oracle BI Publisher. You can download it from `Oracle.com`. We downloaded Version 10.1.3.4.1 for Windows.

 Don't make the install path too long, otherwise the installer will fail.

After downloading and unpacking, run `setup.exe` and follow the steps in the installer. After installing, try to run BI Publisher. You can find the relevant settings such as the BI Publisher admin screen URL with the username and password and the commands to start and stop BI Publisher in the file `BI_Publisher_readme.txt`, which you can find in `<drive:>\ Orahome_1`, where `<drive:>` is your local hard drive. By default, the URL is `http:// localhost:9704/xmlpserver` if you installed BI Publisher on your own computer. If you installed BI Publisher on another computer, localhost must be replaced by the name of the other host. For this recipe, we will use the default hostname `localhost` and port `9704`.

If the installation went OK, you should see something like the following screenshot:

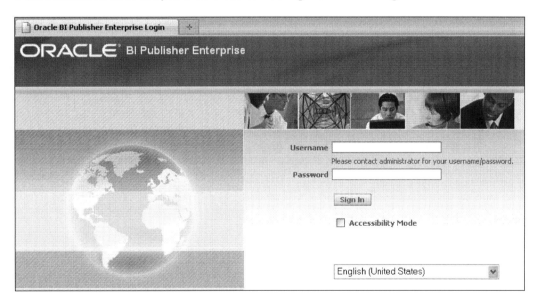

The next step is to configure APEX for BI Publisher. Therefore, you have to log in to the internal workspace as administrator:

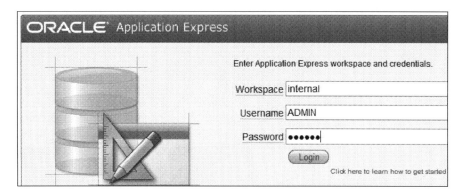

1. If you don't know the password, ask your administrator. If the password is unknown, you can change it using the `apxchpwd.sql` script, which you can find in the APEX directory. You need to execute this script as the SYS user.

2. After successful login, select **Manage Instance**.

3. In the instance settings section, click on the **Instance settings** link.

4. In the **Report Printing** section, select **Advanced (requires Oracle BI Publisher)** in the **Print server** radio button.

5. In the **Print Server Host Address** field, enter the name of the host where BI Publisher is installed. In our case, this is the local machine, so enter here `localhost`.

6. In the **Print Server Port** field, enter **9704**. That is the default port number of BI Publisher. In the **Print Server Script** field, enter `/xmlpserver/convert`.

7. Click on the **Apply changes** button. APEX is now configured for interaction with BI Publisher.

You should have an application with at least one report.

## How to do it...

Now we will make a link below a report region which enables the user to export the report to PDF format.

1. Go to the **Report** page.

2. In the **Regions** section, click on the **Report** link.

3. Click on the **Print Attributes** tab:

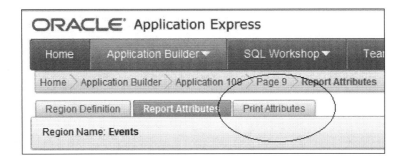

4. In the **Printing** section, select **Yes** in the enable **Report Printing** listbox.

5. In the **Link Label** field, enter a name for the link.

6. In the **Output Format** listbox, select **PDF**.

7. Click on the **Apply Changes** button.

8. The link is ready now. In the **Regions** section, you will see that there is a **Print** link behind the **Report** region.

9. Click on **Run** to run the report.

10. You will see a link below the report region. Click on this link:

11. The result will be a pop-up window where the user can choose to save the report in PDF format or open the report using Adobe Reader. In the last case, you will see something like this:

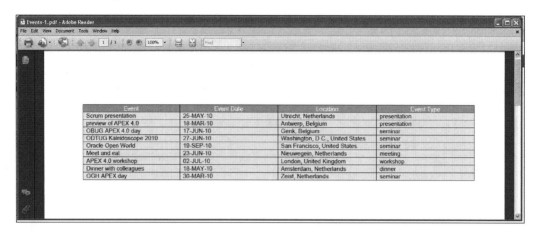

## How it works...

When using the print link, APEX converts the data to an XML format and sends it to the BI Publisher engine. The convert script then converts it to PDF format and sends it back to APEX.

## There's more...

The output shown is rather simple. Using BI Publisher and templates you can make more advanced and nice looking reports.

# Creating a report query

The report in the previous recipe was rather simple. You see a table with headers and data and that's it! Nothing more, nothing less. But we want a nice, good looking report with headers and footers. Fortunately, APEX offers a way to design reports with a custom layout using Microsoft Word and Oracle BI Publisher. The first step is to define the query the report should be based on. We will do that in this recipe.

## Getting ready

Make sure you have access to the APP_CUSTOMERS table.

## How to do it...

1. Go to **Shared Components**.

2. In the **Report** section, click on the **Report queries** link.

3. Click on the **Create** button.

4. In the **Report Query Name** field, enter a name for the query. Enter `rq_customers`. Click on **Next**.

5. In the **SQL query** textarea, enter the following query:

```
Select cust_first_name
,           cust_last_name
,           cust_street_address1
,           cust_postal_code || ' ' || cust_city "city"
,           cust_state
From app_customers
[9672_09_02.sql]
```

6. Click on **Next**.

7. In the next step, we must download the XML definition of this query. We will use that in the next recipe. Select **XML data** and click on the **Download** button. Select **Save file** and click on **OK**. Remember the location where you saved the file. We need the file when we want to create a layout in Microsoft Word:

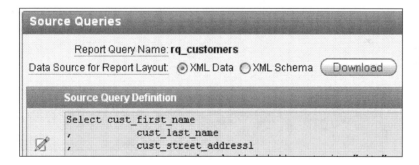

8. Go back to the APEX application builder and click on **Create report query**.

9. At this point, you can test the report by clicking on the **Test Report** button. You will see the same simple layout.

10. Click on the **Finish** button.

11. The report query is ready now. We can use the definition in the next recipe.

## How it works...

Oracle APEX creates an XML file from the query. In Microsoft Word, using the BI Publisher Desktop add-in, we can use this XML definition to create a custom layout.

# Creating a report layout using Oracle BI Publisher

In this recipe, we will show you how to work with templates. We will create a report which presents data from the APP_CUSTOMERS table.

## Getting ready

Make sure you have installed Oracle BI Publisher desktop. BI Publisher desktop is packed with BI Publisher Enterprise. You can find it in `<local hard drive>:\OraHome_1\xmlp\XMLP\Tools`, assuming that you have installed Oracle BI Publisher in `\OraHome_1`. During installation, all Microsoft applications such as Word and Outlook need to be closed.

After installation, Microsoft Word is enriched with a BI Publisher add-on. How the plug-in looks depends on the version of Word:

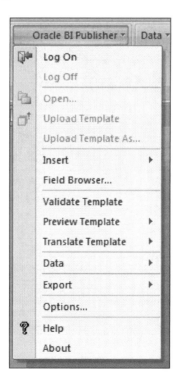

## How to do it...

1.  Open **Microsoft Word**.

2.  Select **Add-ons**.

3.  Click on the **Oracle BI Publisher** tab and select **Data** – **Load sample XML data**:

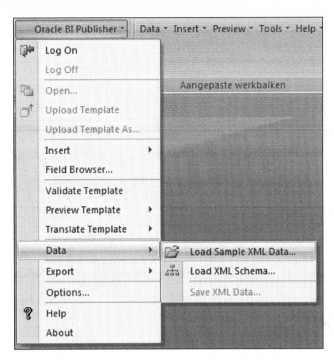

4.  In the pop-up window, select the file that you just created in APEX. Click to open the file.

5.  It seems that nothing happens. That is OK.

6.  Click on the **Oracle BI Publisher** tab again and select **Insert –Table wizard**.

7. A pop-up window with a wizard appears:

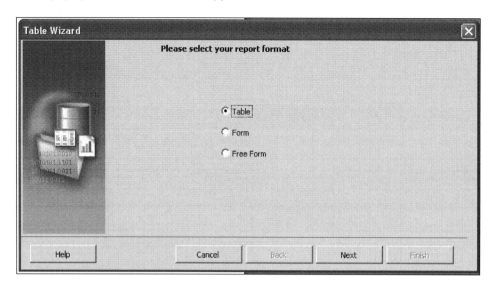

8. Select **Table** and click on **Next**.

9. Click on **Next** again.

10. We want to select all columns, so click the button with the double arrows.

11. Click on **Next**.

12. If desired, you can group the report in the next step. If you don't want to group, just click on **Next**.

13. In the next step, you can enter the sort order. Select the column that you want to use to order the data (or leave the **Sort By** listbox empty) and click on **Next**.

14. In the last step, you can enter a different name for the labels. Click on **Finish**.

15. The wizard is ready now and if everything went ok, you will see a table with a header and five columns.

16. You can also add a header and a footer to the document to make it complete:

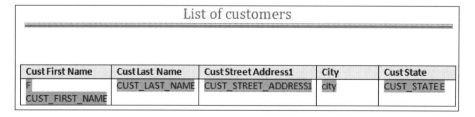

17. Save the report by clicking on the **Save** button. In the pop-up window that appears, select **RTF** in the **Save as** listbox. In the **filename** field, enter a name for the report, for example, `customers_layout.rtf`. Select the desired map and click on **Save**.

18. Close Microsoft Word. The layout is ready and saved in the `.rtf` file.

## How it works...

Take a closer look at the `.rtf` file in Microsoft Word. In the second row of the table that you see, you can see the names of the columns of the report query. Just before the first column, you see an "F". Behind the last column, you see an "E". These are actually control fields. "F" stands for "for each" and "E" stands for "end". This is very important, because APEX recognizes these fields. On running the report, APEX loops through the records and replaces the columns by the values of the query.

# Linking the report layout to the report query

Now that we have created a layout in Word we want to use it for our report. In this paragraph, we will show you how to upload the `.rtf` file and link the layout to a report query.

## Getting ready

1. Make sure that you selected **Advanced** in the **Print server** settings. You can set these fields in the internal workspace logging in as admin.

2. After successful login, click on **Manage Instance**.

3. In the **Instance settings** section, click on the **Instance settings** link.

4. In the **Report printing** section, select **Advanced (requires Oracle BI Publisher)** in the **Print server** radio button.

5. Click on the **Apply changes** button.

6. This step is necessary as otherwise you won't see the **Named columns (RTF)** option in the **Report Layout Type** radio group.

## How to do it...

1. Go to **Shared Components | Report layouts**.

2. Click on the **Create** button.

3. Select **Named columns (RTF)**. Click on **Next**:

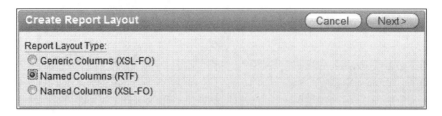

4. In the **Layout Name** text field, enter a name for the report, for example, cmr_layout.

5. Click the **Browse** button to upload the RTF file.

6. In the pop-up screen, select the file customers_layout from the map where you saved it and click on **Open**.

7. Click on the **Create layout** button.

8. The layout is ready. Now we must link this layout to the report query that we created in the previous recipe.

9. Go to **Shared Components | Report queries**.

10. Click on the icon of the report query **rq_customers**.

11. In the **Report Layout** listbox, select **cmr_layout**.

12. You can now click on the **Test Report** button in the **Source Queries** section to see how the report and the layout look like. Otherwise, click on the **Apply changes** button.

13. The report query and the report layout are ready now.

## How it works...

We made a query and a layout. And now we bring them together. We uploaded the report layout that we made in Microsoft Word and modified the settings of the report query so that it should use the uploaded layout. The query should contain at least the same columns that are used in the Microsoft Word layout, no matter in what order they are. You can use more columns in the query, but if they are not in the layout file, you will not see them on the report. On the other hand, if your layout file contains a column that is not in the query, the report will show an empty column.

And just to make it more complex, if you use another column in your query and you give it an alias that is the name of one of the columns in the layout file, APEX will show a report with data from that other column.

# Calling a report from a page

In the previous paragraphs, we made a report query and a report layout. Since we want to call this report from a page within our application, we have to add something to the webpage like a button or a link. We will show you how to do this in this recipe.

## Getting ready

In the previous recipes, you have created a report query and a report layout. Make sure they work as desired. You should also have a webpage based on the APP_CUSTOMERS table.

## How to do it...

1. Go to the page based on the APP_CUSTOMERS table.

2. In the **Buttons** section, click on the **Add** icon to create a new button.

3. Select the appropriate region and click on **Next**.

4. Select **Create button in a region position** and click on **Next**.

5. Enter a name and a label for the button and click on **Next**.

6. Click on **Next** again.

7. In the **Action** select list, select **Download Printable Report Query** (after selecting this option, the **Report Query** select list appears below the **Execute Validations** select list):

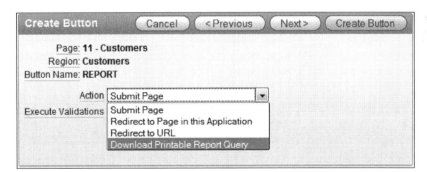

8. In the **Report Query** select list, select **rq_customers**.

9. Click on the **Create** button.

10. The button is ready. You can run the page now and click on the button to see what happens:

## List of customers

| Cust First Name | Cust Last Name | Cust Street Address1 | City | Cust State |
|---|---|---|---|---|
| John | Dulles | 45020 Aviation Drive | 20166 Sterling | VA |
| William | Hartsfield | 6000 North Terminal Parkway | 30320 Atlanta | GA |
| Edward | Logan | 1 Harborside Drive | 02128 East | MA |

## How it works...

Like the link for CSV export, the button in this page uses a URL to call the report. It looks like the following:

```
http://localhost:8000/apex/f?p=114:0:&SESSION.:PRINT_REPORT=rq_
customers
```

You could copy this link and paste it in the address bar of your browser, provided you have a valid session ID that has to replace the `&SESSION.` variable. The `0` in the URL, just behind the application ID of `114`, is an indicator that this is an internal application process. Normally, a page number should be entered at this place. The last part of the URL is the `PRINT_REPORT` argument. Here you can pass the name of the report query you would like to see. In this case, it is `rq_customers`.

# 10
# APEX Environment

In this chapter, we will cover:

- ▶ Setting up a development environment using subscriptions
- ▶ Debugging an APEX application
- ▶ Debugging an APEX application remotely
- ▶ Deploying an application with SQL Developer
- ▶ Setting up version control with APEX and SVN
- ▶ Setting up a production environment using an Apache proxy
- ▶ Setting up the APEX Listener on Tomcat
- ▶ Creating an error handler
- ▶ Using packaged applications

## Introduction

When starting with APEX development, it's important to choose the right architecture. It should be straightforward, allow flexibility, and should not need much maintenance.

This chapter will contain recipes that will show how to set up and use a development environment, how to use version control, and how to deploy Application Express on a web container with APEX Listener.

# Setting up a development environment using subscriptions

The architecture of a single APEX application is simple. You create a workspace, then you create an application, and then you build pages inside that application.

But what if we anticipate more than one application in our workspace? It's possible that a company has a single corporate style for all of its web applications. If we had to create templates for this style in every single APEX application we create, we would lose a lot of time which could otherwise be spent on creating functionalities for the application itself.

In this recipe we will see how we can set up a development environment that can reuse as many elements as possible and still be flexible.

Application Express uses a feature called **subscriptions**. This allows developers to inherit a number of properties from one application to another. By using these subscriptions we don't have to build something like a template twice, but instead, we create it once in a parent application and then use that same template in a child application by subscribing to it.

Now whenever a change is made to the layout of the template in the parent application, all we have to do is update the subscriptions to roll out the changes to all of its child applications.

But this is not limited to templates. It can also be used for CSS files, authentication, JavaScript, and many more parts of the parent application.

In a very simple graph, the architecture would look similar to the following:

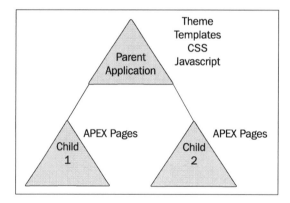

Developers can go as far with this architecture as they want. For example, if a company has a layout that is used for all web applications, but the financial department needs to add an extra region containing legal statements to some of its pages for legal purposes, we can add another layer of child applications. So the company has a standard layout and the financial department subscribes to this standard to comply with company policies. They themselves create a standard layout for the required legal regions. The applications created by the financial department then subscribe to this new legal standard.

This would change the architecture to something like the following:

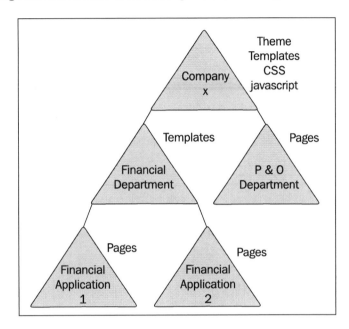

And this can go as far and deep as the developers want.

 Keep in mind however that pushing a master subscription will only update the first level of subscriptions. So if you want to apply a change in the master subscription more than one level down, you have to publish the change on every level.

## How to do it...

First we have to create an application to be used as the parent:

1. Navigate to the **Application Builder** and click on the **Create >** button.

2. Select **Database** and click on **Next**.

3. Select **From Scratch** and click on **Next**.

4. Name the application Company Parent and click on **Next**.

5. Add a single blank page, name it Main, and then click on **Next**.

6. Select **One Level of Tabs** and click on **Next** until we reach the **Theme selection** screen.

7. Select **Theme 1** and click on **Next.**

8. Finally click on **Create** to finish.

Now when we an almost empty application (except for the **Main** page), so let's adjust something in a template to see what happens:

1. Navigate to **Shared Components** and then to **Templates**.

2. In the list of templates, locate the one called **One Level Tabs - Right Sidebar (optional / table-based)** under the **Page** templates and open it.

3. In the **Definition** section, find the **Body** section. In this section, change the first `<div>` area with the ID header to the following:

```
<div id="header">
  <div id="logo"><h2>Company X</h2><a href="#HOME_
LINK#">#LOGO##REGION_POSITION_06#</a></div>
  #REGION_POSITION_07#
  <div id="navbar">
    #NAVIGATION_BAR#
    <div class="app-user">#WELCOME_USER#</div>
    #REGION_POSITION_08#
  </div>
</div>
[9672_10_1.txt]
```

4. Click on **Apply Changes**.

5. Now run the Company Parent application.

You will see that the header for the **Main** page has been changed. It now contains the text **Company X**, as shown in the following screenshot:

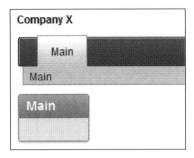

Now let's create a child application that will subscribe to this template:

1. Navigate to **Application Builder** and click on the **Create** button.

2. Select **Database** and click on **Next**.

3. Select **From Scratch** and click on **Next**.

4. Name the application Company Child and click on **Next**.

5. Add a single blank page, name it **Main**, and then click on **Next**.

6. Select **One Level of Tabs** and click on **Next** until we reach the **Theme selection** screen.

7. To show the contrast with the **Company Parent** application, select **Theme 2**, click on **Next**, and then on **Create**.

When we run this new application, we can see that it's mainly blue and does not contain the name Company X in the header:

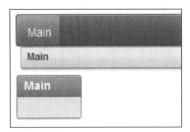

Now we are going to subscribe to the template we changed in the first part of this recipe, so we can see how this works:

1. Navigate to **Shared Components | Templates** in the **Company Child** application.

2. Click on the **One Level Tabs - Right Sidebar (optional / table-based)** template to open it.

3.  In the **Subscription** section, click on the button next to the field labeled **Reference Master Template From**.

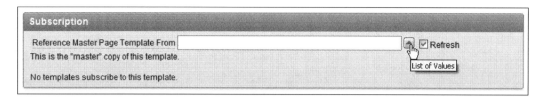

4.  In the pop up that opens, find the entry for **One Level Tabs - Right Sidebar (optional / table-based)** that corresponds to the Application ID of our **Company Parent** application.

5.  Click on **Apply Changes**.

When we now return to the template, we can see that the **Subscription** section has changed.

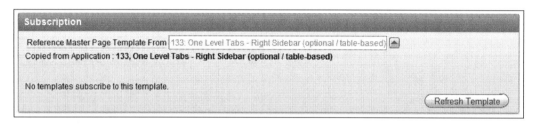

We can see that the template is now copied from our **Company Parent** application (in this screenshot the Application ID is **133**), and a button called **Refresh Template** has been added. This button pulls in all changes made to the master copy of the template; in fact, it is the opposite of the publish process which we will see later on in this recipe.

If we run the **Main** page in the **Company Child** application, we can see that it looks exactly like the **Main** page of the **Company Parent** application. At least, the parts that belong to our **One Level Tabs** region template. This proves that the copy process for the template works.

Let's return to our **Company Parent** application to find out if the publishing works as well.

1.  Return to the **Company Parent** application, navigate to **Shared Components | Template**, and click on the **One Level Tabs - Right Sidebar (optional / table-based)** template again.

2.  Let's assume that the CEO of Company X has a new marketing strategy and wants to let the world know how good the company is. In the **Body** section change the header div to the following:

    ```
    <div id="header">
       <div id="logo"><h1>The best company in the world!</h1><a
    href="#HOME_LINK#">#LOGO##REGION_POSITION_06#</a></div>
    ```

```
#REGION_POSITION_07#
<div id="navbar">
  #NAVIGATION_BAR#
  <div class="app-user">#WELCOME_USER#</div>
  #REGION_POSITION_08#
</div>
</div>
[9672_10_2.txt]
```

3. Click on **Apply Changes**.

4. Run the **Company Parent** application as well as the **Company Child** application to see the difference.

5. Return to the **Company Parent** application, navigate to **Shared Components | Template**, and click on the **One Level Tabs - Right Sidebar (optional / table-based)** template again.

   In the **Subscription** section we can see that there is a list of templates that reference this:

   In the screenshot there is the reference from our **Company Child** application with Application ID **134**.

6. Click on the button **Publish Template** to apply the changes to the referencing templates.

7. Click on **Refresh All** to complete the publishing:

When we now run the **Company Child** application we can see the result. This application now automatically looks like its parent.

# Debugging an APEX application

An essential part of the development process of almost any software project is debugging. A good debug method allows developers to exactly pinpoint problems in the application.

Application Express offers some built-in functionalities to debug applications, pages, and even items. This recipe will explain how to set up debugging on an application and how to interpret the reports that APEX generates.

## Getting ready

The only thing we need to start on this recipe is a (working) application. We will use a simple application, based on the EMP table.

Create a new application with a form and report (based on an interactive report) on the EMP table. That is enough to get through this recipe.

## How to do it...

First of all, debugging has to be enabled for the application. By default, this option is disabled.

To enable debugging, perform the following steps.

1. In the **Application Builder** select the application that we are going to debug.

2. Locate the button labeled **Edit Application Properties** near the top of the main region and click on it.

3. Find the area called **Properties** and change the value of the select list called **Debugging** from **No** to **Yes**.

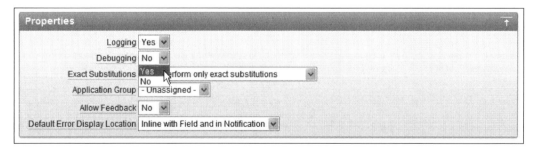

4. Click on **Apply Changes**.

Now the application is ready to be debugged.

1.  Start the application.

2.  In the Developer toolbar at the bottom of the screen, click on the button labeled **Debug**. If the steps in the first part of this recipe have gone well, the label will change to **No Debug**. Else, an error message will appear and we have to check if debugging on the application is really set to **Yes**:

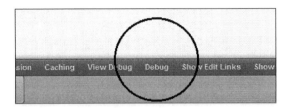

3.  Perform some actions on the application such as navigating or performing a search.

4.  When you navigate to a different page, the **Debug** option will turn off automatically. If you want to re-enable it, simply click on the button in the Developer toolbar again. To avoid this behavior we can also call the application using the value YES for the debug parameter in the URL. The debug parameter can be found on the fifth parameter position. Buttons and links calling URLs inside the application will have to hold the substitution as well. A URL with this substitution will look like the following:

    ```
    f?p=APP_ID:APP_PAGE_ID:APP_SESSION::YES:::
    ```

    Instead of YES or NO, you can also enter a debug level, such as LEVELn, where *n* is a number from 1 to 9 and indicates when to debug. LEVEL4 is the default level if debugging is enabled.

5.  Click on the button labeled **View Debug** in the **Toolbar**. This will open up a new window with a list of actions that have been performed during the time that **Debug** was enabled.

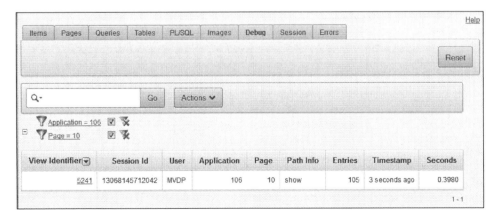

By default the current page is selected. To see debug information for other pages, deselect the filter for **Page**.

The list in the screenshot shows a timestamp for when the page was called, how many actions took place while loading the page (under the **Entries** column), and how many seconds it took to fully load the page.

1.  Click one of the links in the column **View Identifier** to see the debug information for the loading of that page.

2.  Review the report that is now shown. The following screenshot shows an example of a **Save** action on the **Edit** page of the **EMP** application. Results may look different when another action or page has been selected:

This report is made up of three regions of interest. The top region shows information about the currently selected page. Most of it is also shown in the main overview from the previous screenshot, but **Maximum Execution Time** is new. This tells us the time it took the longest process to complete, so we can quickly identify where a performance problem might exist.

In this same perspective of quickly identifying problems, the **Graph** section can be seen. Processes taking a lot of time to load will get a higher graph bar. When hovering over a bar with the cursor, the relevant process can be identified.

The main part of the screen is occupied by a report. This report shows all processes that are executed during the load of the currently selected page.

The first column shows the elapsed time after processing the current line. The second column shows the time that a particular process took.

The total report can be used to know three things: what happened, when did it happen, and how long did it take.

We can see some NLS parameters being set in lines such as `NLS: CSV charset=WE8MSWIN1252` or `alter session set nls_language="AMERICAN"`.

Because we selected a `SAVE` operation to debug, we can also find a couple of lines for this as well (variable names and values may vary):

```
Session State: Saved Item "P2_ENAME" New Value="SCOTT"
Session State: Saved Item "P2_SAL" New Value="3200"
```

Now we will change the **Edit** page and try to find out if we can find this alteration in the debug information:

1. Navigate to the **Application Builder** and select page **2** to edit.
2. In the **Edit Emp** region, add a hidden item.
3. Name it `DEBUG_TESTING` and click on **Next**.
4. Set **Value Protected** to **No** and click on **Next**.
5. The **Source Type** will be **SQL Query (return single value)**.
6. In **Item Source Value** enter the query `select sysdate from dual`.
7. Click on **Create Item**.

Now when we run the application and enable **Debug** on the pages, the information for this new item should be seen in the debug report.

To check this, click on the **View Debug** button again and find the latest entry for page **2**. When browsing down the debug report, you will find a line with the text `Item: DEBUG_TESTING NATIVE_HIDDEN` to show that the new item was indeed created at runtime with the rest of the page. In the same fashion, any item loaded in a page can be found and analyzed.

## There's more...

Besides the debug messages that APEX generates itself, it's also possible to create our own custom messages inside PL/SQL processes:

1. Navigate to Page **1** of this application.
2. Expand the **Before Header** node.

3. Right-click on **Processes** and click on **Create**.

4. Select **PL/SQL** and click on **Next**.

5. Enter the name `show_custom_debug` and click on **Next**.

6. Enter the following code in the **PL/SQL Process** area and click on **Create Process**:

```
wwv_flow.debug('My Custom Debug Message');
```

7. Run the page and click on the **Debug** button in the Developer toolbar.

8. Click on the **View Debug** button.

   In the **Debug** screen we can now see two entries in our custom code. The first is the process itself that is being called. The second is our custom debug message itself.

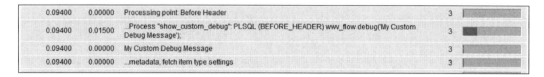

| 0.09400 | 0.00000 | Processing point: Before Header | | 3 | |
| 0.09400 | 0.01500 | Process "show_custom_debug": PLSQL (BEFORE_HEADER) wwv_flow.debug('My Custom Debug Message'); | | 3 | |
| 0.09400 | 0.00000 | My Custom Debug Message | | 3 | |
| 0.09400 | 0.00000 | ...metadata, fetch item type settings | | 3 | |

Using this it's possible to quickly find certain pieces of code using these custom messages as a sort of bookmarks. But more advanced debugging is also possible, for example, by showing the value of a variable.

9. Go back to the page and edit the **show_custom_debug** process.

10. Change the PL/SQL code to the following:

```
wwv_flow.debug('My Custom Debug Message for: '||:APP_USER);
```

   This will add the username of the current logged in user to the message.

11. Click on **Apply Changes**.

12. Run the page and click on the **Debug** button in the Developer toolbar.

13. Click on the **View Debug** button.

When we open the **Debug** window now and look for our message, we can see that it has indeed changed and now shows the username:

| 0.12500 | 0.01600 | ...Process "show_custom_debug": PLSQL (BEFORE_HEADER) wwv_flow.debug('My Custom Debug Message for: '||APP_USER); | | 3 | |
| 0.12500 | 0.00000 | My Custom Debug Message for: MVZOEST | | 3 | |

# Debugging an APEX application remotely

When developing an application you may want to see what actually happens on page processing or running some PL/SQL code. Especially PL/SQL code that is stored in the database and called from a page within APEX, is hard to debug. However, Oracle SQL Developer offers a way to debug PL/SQL code that is called from APEX. We will show you how to do that.

## Getting ready

Make sure you have the latest version of SQL Developer, which can be found on http://www.oracle.com/technetwork/index.html. And that you have an application with a page that calls a PL/SQL procedure in the database. In this recipe we take the Twitter search from *Chapter 1, Creating a Basic APEX Application*. We will call the app_search_user procedure.

Furthermore, you need to grant some privileges:

```
grant debug any procedure to <user>;
grant debug connect session to <user>;
[9672_10_10.txt]
```

Where <user> is the user that needs the privileges. If you use the embedded PL/SQL gateway, use ANONYMOUS, otherwise use APEX_PUBLIC_USER.

If you are running APEX on Oracle 11g database, you also need to create an **Access Control List (ACL)** and its privileges:

```
begin
  dbms_network_acl_admin.create_acl (acl          => 'acl_anm.xml'
                                    ,description => 'Description'
                                    ,principal   => 'ANONYMOUS'
                                    ,is_grant    => true
                                    ,privilege   => 'connect'
                                    ,start_date  => null
                                    ,end_date    => null);
  --
  DBMS_NETWORK_ACL_ADMIN.ADD_PRIVILEGE(acl          => 'acl_anm.xml'
                                      ,principal => 'ANONYMOUS'
                                      ,is_grant  => true
                                      ,privilege => 'resolve');
  --
  DBMS_NETWORK_ACL_ADMIN.ASSIGN_ACL(acl  => 'acl_anm.xml'
                                    ,host => '127.0.0.1'
```

```
                                        ,lower_port => 4000
                                        ,upper_port => 4000);
   --
   commit;
end;
/

begin
   dbms_network_acl_admin.create_acl (acl         => 'acl_db.xml'
                                     ,description => 'Description'
                                     ,principal   => '<dbusr>'
                                     ,is_grant    => true
                                     ,privilege   => 'connect'
                                     ,start_date  => null
                                     ,end_date    => null);
   --
   DBMS_NETWORK_ACL_ADMIN.ADD_PRIVILEGE(acl         => 'acl_db.xml'
                                       ,principal => '<dbusr>'
                                       ,is_grant  => true
                                       ,privilege => 'resolve');
   --
   DBMS_NETWORK_ACL_ADMIN.ASSIGN_ACL(acl  => 'acl_db.xml'
                                    ,host => '*');
   --
   commit;
end;
/
```

The code creates an ACL for the ANONYMOUS user and the database user who is the owner of the procedure, marked with <dbusr>. Replace it with your own database user (schema owner). The ACL for the ANONYMOUS user gives that user the privilege to connect to the localhost at port 4000—the port we will use for the remote debug session. To keep it simple, we create an ACL for the owner of the procedure with the privilege to connect to any host.

## How to do it...

The following steps will allow us to debug an APEX application remotely.

1. Start **Oracle SQL Developer**.

2. Right-click on the database connection where the procedure is stored.

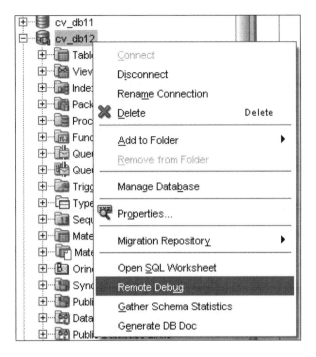

3. Select **Remote Debug**.

4. A pop up is shown with three text fields: **Port**, **Timeout**, and **Local address**.

5. Choose a port number that is not yet assigned to any process and is not blocked by a firewall. You will need this port number later.

6. Enter a number in seconds in the **Timeout** field to indicate how long the debug session must be kept open before it automatically closes. Enter 0 to leave the session open without closing. You can leave the **Local address** field empty:

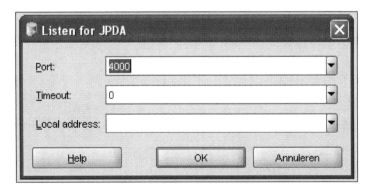

7. Click on **OK** to start the debug session.

8. Click on the open database connection and go to the **APP_SEARCH_USER** procedure.

9. Right-click on the procedure and select **Edit**. The procedure is now open for edits.

10. Set some breakpoints by clicking on the line number in the gutter.

11. When you are ready, click on the Compile for Debug icon.

The procedure is now ready to be compiled. We now will create a page in APEX with a text item and a button and when the button is pressed; APEX will start the debug session:

1. In APEX, navigate to the **Application Builder** and select the application that you want to edit.

2. Click on the **Create Page** button.

3. Select **Blank Page**.

4. Click on **Next**.

5. Enter a name and a title for the page. For example `Check Twittername` and click on **Next**.

6. Click on **Next** again and then click on **Finish**.

7. Click on the Edit Page icon.

8. In the **Regions** section, click on the Add icon to create a new region.

9. Select **HTML** and then click on **Next**.

10. Enter a title for the region, for example `check`. Click on the **Create** button.

11. In the **Items** section, click on the Add icon to create a new item.

12. Select **Text**.

13. Select **Text Field** and then click on **Next**.

14. Enter a name for the item, for example `P_TWITTERNAME` and click on **Next**.

15. Click on **Next** again.

16. In the **Buttons** section, click on the Add icon to create a new button.

17. Click on **Next** two times.

18. Enter a name for the button, for example `Check name` and click on **Next**.

19. Click on **Next** two times.

20. Click on **Create** button.

21. Click on the **Create Item** button.

22. In the **Validations** section, click on the Add icon to create a new validation.

23. Select **Item Level Validation** and click on **Next**.

24. Select the item **P_TWITTERNAME** and click on **Next**.

25. Select **PL/SQL**.

26. Select **Function returning error text** and click on **Next**.

27. Enter a name for the validation, for example `chk_twt` and click on **Next**.

28. In the **Validation** textarea, enter the following code:

```
dbms_debug_jdwp.connect_tcp('127.0.0.1',4000);
declare
  l_result varchar2(100);
begin
  app_search_user('TWITTERUSER','password',:P_TWITTERNAME,l_
result);
  if l_result = 'user found'
  then
    return null;
  else
    return 'false';
  end if;
end;
dbms_debug_jdwp.disconnect;
[9672_10_12.txt]
```

The code starts with the call to DBMS_DEBUG_JDWP.CONNECT_TCP to initiate the connection to the debug session. The call takes two arguments: the local address and the port number we need to enter when starting the debug session in SQL Developer. After that, the code calls the procedure APP_SEARCH_USER with the arguments: Twitter username, password, search argument, and the result. The search argument is kept in the item P_TWITTERNAME. If the result of the call is positive (the entered Twitter name exists), a null value is returned, otherwise the text `false` is returned. The code ends with the call to dbms_debug_jdwp. disconnect, which disconnects the session.

1. In the **Error Message** textarea, enter an error message, such as `User not found` and click on **Next**.

2. In the **When Button Pressed** listbox, select the **CHECK_NAME** button.

3. Click on the **Create** button.

The page is ready. Run the page, enter some text in the **Twittername** field and click on **Check Name**. The debug session is started and APEX gives control to SQL Developer. You can go to SQL Developer to debug the code.

In the debug mode, you have several ways to run the code, such as step over, step into, and resume to next breakpoint. At the bottom of the screen, you can click the **Data** tab to see the several variables and arguments that show their value at that moment. When you reach the end of the code after step over, step into, or resume, SQL Developer stops and gives the control back to APEX. APEX resumes like it would normally do.

## How it works...

Actually, this is not really an APEX feature. You can make use of the `dbms_debug_jdwp.connect_tcp` and `dbms_debug_jdwp.disconnect` in SQL*Plus as well. When using the Embedded PL/SQL Gateway, you just have to make sure that the `ANONYMOUS` user has the right privileges, just like any other user that tries to remotely debug in SQL*Plus. When you are using another setup with Apache/MOD_PLSQL for example, it will connect to the database using `APEX_PUBLIC_USER`. In that case, the privileges should be granted to that user instead.

## There's more...

There are also external tools available for remote debugging, such as **Logger**—a PL/SQL logging utility created by Tyler Muth and Martin Giffy D'Souza. You can find the latest version at `https://github.com/tmuth/Logger---A-PL-SQL-Logging-Utility`.

# Deploying an application with SQL Developer

In most situations, an application is developed in a development environment on a development database. When the application is ready, it is deployed to the test environment so that it can be tested. Finally, when the test results are fine, the application is deployed to the production environment. To deploy an application, you can use Oracle SQL Developer.

## Getting ready

You need to have Oracle SQL Developer installed on your computer. Preferably the latest version. You can download Oracle SQL Developer via `http://otn.oracle.com`.

Also, you need to have two different environments to deploy the application from one environment to another.

Furthermore, you need to have an application that is ready to be deployed.

And last, make sure that you have a connection in SQL Developer using the right database user. If you use the embedded PL/SQL gateway, use `ANONYMOUS`, otherwise use `APEX_PUBLIC_USER`.

## How to do it...

Perform the following steps:

1. Open Oracle SQL Developer and connect to the desired database.

2. Click on the **+** sign besides the database connection to open the connection. You may be asked to enter your username and password.

3. In the list of objects, you will see **Application Express**. Click on it to open. After that, you will see the applications you made. Click on the application you want to deploy.

4. Right-click on the application and from the pop-up menu, select **Deploy application**:

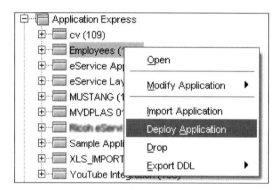

5. In the listbox, select the appropriate connection:

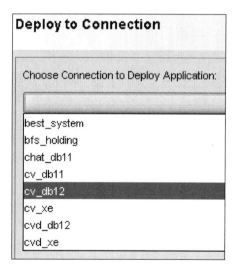

After choosing the connection, you can change some options such as the application name or the build status. Also, you can choose to assign an application ID yourself or let APEX generate an ID for you. If you enter an ID that already belongs to an existing application, you must check the **Overwrite** checkbox. However, if you overwrite an application, you cannot use the same alias.

6. Click on **Next**:

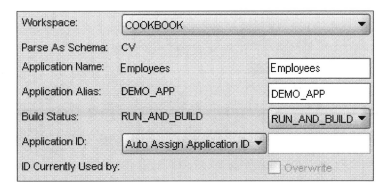

7. Then click on **Finish**.

   The application will be deployed. When APEX is finished, you will get a message and you can continue.

8. In APEX, go to the **Application Builder** to see the changes.

# Setting up version control with APEX and SVN

An important part of any software engineering project is **versioning**. By keeping different versions of the software in a backup, we can revert back to a previous state of the application when problems arise.

Using a versioning tool has always been a bit of a challenge in Oracle software development. Mainly because most of the time PL/SQL code is kept inside the database. Application Express is no exception to this.

So how can we get a secure and easy-to-use repository of your APEX application? In this recipe we are going to show you by using **Subversion** (**SVN**). This is a version control system that is developed under the Apache License, which makes it open source. More information can be found at `http://subversion.apache.org/`.

## Getting ready

First of all make sure you have an SVN server available that you can use for this recipe. If you don't, you can download some software from `http://subversion.apache.org/`. For this example, we have installed VisualSVN Server Standard Edition 2.1.3. Using this software we create a repository called `apex_book` and create a default SVN directory structure underneath this. The URL to this repository is now `https://yourhost/svn/apex_book`.

Optionally, we can add some security to this repository by adding users and groups and granting access to the repository to them; but we will skip this for our recipe.

Next to the server, we will need an SVN client that can connect to the repository. For this purpose we have selected TortoiseSVN because of its nifty right-click menu integration in Windows Explorer; but feel free to use any other software that serves the same purpose.

When you have both installed and configured, check out the `apex_book` repository. On your local system you should now have three subdirectories under the `apex_book` main directory: `branches`, `tags`, and `trunk`.

## How to do it...

There are two challenges when trying to apply versioning to an APEX application. The first one is that not all pieces that APEX uses are in one place. In a standard setup, images, JavaScript, and CSS files are on the filesystem, while the code for the pages themselves are in the database. In theory, all files can exist in the database of course, but we will ignore that possibility for this recipe.

The second challenge is that checking out files in the versioning system doesn't always lock them to prevent others from altering them. But in this recipe we'll work out a system that provides a smooth way to save the application files and keep them safe.

The first part will be the files that actually exist on the filesystem: JavaScript, CSS, and images (and perhaps some other files as well).

To save these into the repository is the easiest part of the job.

Copy the `theme` directory of your application and its contents, including any subdirectory into the `trunk` directory:

Notice that a question mark icon is placed in front of the directory. This indicates that it hasn't been added to the repository yet. To do this, perform the following steps:

1. Right-click on the `company_theme` directory.

2. Enter the menu for TortoiseSVN and click on **Add**.

3. The pop-up menu shows all files that will be added into the repository. Click on **OK** to continue.

After a short wait (depending on how many files are added), a summary is shown. We'll see that the icon for the newly added files have changed to a **+** sign.

Also, the icon for the `trunk` and `apex_book` directories have changed to an exclamation mark, to indicate that there are pending changes:

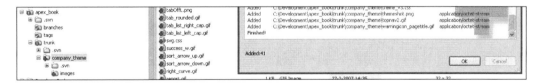

4. To secure these changes to the repository, right-click on the `apex_book` directory and click on **SVN Commit**.

5. A list of pending changes is shown in a pop-up menu. Click on **OK** to continue.

6. After the commit is completed, click on **OK** to finish.

On the filesystem all icons will have changed to indicate they are up-to-date. All files and directories are now available to anyone that is allowed into the repository.

When someone else has changed something, we would want to get those changes onto our local filesystem:

1. Right-click on the `apex_book` directory and click on **SVN Update**.
2. Click on **OK** to finish.

This same process of commit and update applies to the parts that are in APEX and on the database as well. The only extra work that we have to do is get all the code on the filesystem.

Because it's a bit too much to show how to export all of the pieces of an APEX application, we will stick to a selection. Later in the book we will see how this works in more detail.

First, we have to think how small the chunks of the application need to be. We can export the entire workspace in a single file or we can do it application-by-application, page-by-page, or a selection of other pieces.

1. Navigate to the **Application Builder**.
2. Click on the **Export** button.
3. Choose **Database Application**:

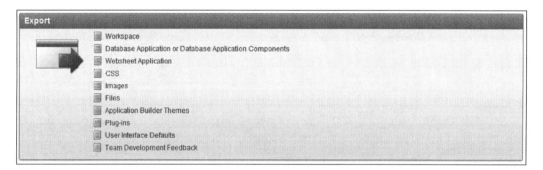

4. Select one of the applications.
5. When we want to export the entire application, click on the button labeled **Export Application** and follow the steps.
6. When we want to go deeper and export a single page, click on the link **Export Page** from the **Tasks** list to the right-hand side of the screen and follow the steps.

Both these exports will create one or more SQL files on the filesystem. To commit these to the repository, we take the same steps that we did for the `theme` directory.

These steps can be repeated for anything that is available in the APEX environment. Keep in mind that the smaller we make the parts, the more flexible we are in sharing the workload among the development team. But also, the more work it is to keep everything checked in and up-to-date. Every development team has to find a balance between flexibility and amount of work. Good practice to help with that is to provide SVN substitutions in the code, pages, and items, so you can actually see which revision is currently running.

# Setting up a production environment using an Apache proxy

In a production environment it's possible to choose many different architectures. One of the architectures that is widely used is one where the URL is rewritten by an Apache proxy server, so it's friendlier to be called by the user.

Normally an APEX URL looks something like `http://<servername>:<port>/apex/ f?p=123:1:32413124434::NO:::::` or anything else involving a lot of numbers, colons, and random characters. Not very easy to understand and very hard to remember.

What we want to deliver to our visitors is an easy-to-remember URL that will redirect to the underlying APEX page.

In this recipe we will explain how to use rewrite in the configuration of an Apache Proxy server, so an APEX application can be called by a friendly URL.

## Getting ready

Using a simple machine (can be a virtual machine) we have to set up an Apache web server. The software is available at `http://httpd.apache.org`, but when the server runs a Linux operating system, Apache is already there:

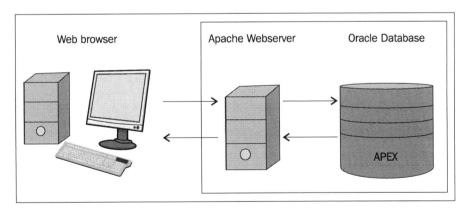

## How to do it...

When we investigate the installation directory of Apache, we can find a directory called `conf`. In this directory is a filed named `httpd.conf`.

1. Open `httpd.conf` to edit.

2. Ensure that the following lines of code are available and not commented:

   ```
   LoadModule rewrite_module modules/mod_rewrite.so
   LoadModule proxy_module modules/mod_proxy.so
   [9672_10_3.txt]
   ```

These modules will allow Apache to act as a proxy server and rewrite incoming URL requests to the internal representation of the APEX application.

In older versions of Apache, the next steps have to be done in the `httpd.conf` files. In newer versions, it has to be done in the `httpd-vhosts.conf` file. To see if we are working with a newer version, see if the following code is available in `httpd.conf`.

```
# Virtual hosts
Include conf/extra/httpd-vhosts.conf
[9672_10_4.txt]
```

If this line is present, open `httpd-vhosts.conf` in the `\conf\extra` directory. In the other case, keep editing the `httpd.conf` file which is already open.

We are going to make some assumptions, so the code below will be more clear:

▸ The URL of our website is the fictional website `http://www.apexbook.xyz`

▸ Our APEX application runs on a server with IP address `192.168.0.1` on port `7001`

▸ We have used the recipes in *Chapter 6, Creating Multilingual APEX Applications*, and made it a translatable application using the `LANG` request and `FSP_LANGUAGE_PREFERENCE`

▸ The Application ID is `200` and the ID of the login page is `101`

▸ We want the visitors to be able to use the URL `http://nl.apexbook.xyz` to directly access the Dutch version of the application

We now have enough information to create the configuration in the `.conf` file:

1. Open `httpd.conf` or `httpd-vhosts.conf` depending on your situation.

2. Enter the following code (replace the pieces where necessary for your situation):

   ```
   <VirtualHost *:80>
     ServerName nl.apexbook.xyz
   ```

```
    ServerAlias nl.apexbook.xyz

    RewriteEngine On
    RewriteRule ^/$ /apex/f?p=200:101::LANG:::FSP_LANGUAGE_
PREFERENCE:nl [R=301,L]

    ProxyPass /apex http://192.168.0.1:7001/apex
    ProxyPassReverse /apex http://192.168.0.1:7001/apex
    ProxyPass /i http://192.168.0.1:7001/i
    ProxyPassReverse /i http:// 192.168.0.1:7001/i
</VirtualHost>
```

What happens is that whenever `http://nl.apexbook.xyz` is called, the rewrite engine will paste `/apex/f?p=200:101::LANG:::FSP_LANGUAGE_PREFERENCE:nl` behind it. The Proxy is then learnt to redirect a call to `/apex` via `http://192.168.0.1:7001/apex` (and the other way around, hence the `ProxyPassReverse`). To also allow the `images` directory to be found, we do the same thing for any call to the `/i` directory.

With this code in place, any call to `http://nl.apexbook.xyz` will automatically redirect the user to `http://192.168.0.1:7001/apex/f?p=200:101::LANG:::FSP_LANGUAGE_PREFERENCE:nl`. Much friendlier isn't it?

# Setting up the APEX Listener on Tomcat

Together with the production release of APEX 4.0, the APEX Listener became available. The Listener is certified to run on three different web containers: Oracle WebLogic, OC4J (only APEX Listener 1.0), and Glassfish (in theory it can run on almost any web container, but these three are supported by Oracle).

In this recipe we will use Tomcat to be the container in which the listener will run. This choice is arbitrary and does not express an opinion of which web container is best.

## Getting ready

Make sure Tomcat is installed on your system; it can be downloaded from `http://tomcat.apache.org`.

Configure Tomcat to run on a free port. For this example, we will assume port `8080`, but when that is not available in your environment, replace `8080` with your port.

Also download the Application Express Listener from the Oracle website at `http://technet.oracle.com` and unzip the archive to reveal what's inside.

Lastly, have the `images` directory available that we want to use in this container.

## How to do it...

First we have to make sure `APEX_PUBLIC_USER` is available and unlocked:

1. Stop Tomcat.
2. Log in as SysAdmin on the database.
3. Execute the following commands to unlock the user and change its password:

   ```
   alter user APEX_PUBLIC_USER account unlock;
   alter user APEX_PUBLIC_USER identified by <password>;
   [9672_10_6.txt]
   ```

4. Open a DOSBox (or a terminal window in Linux) and set the APEX configuration directory by entering the following command:

   ```
   Java -jar <dir_where_listener_unpacked>\apex.war configdir "<base_
   dir>\tomcat\conf\Catalina\localhost"
   ```

5. The next step is to configure the APEX listener:

   ```
   Java -jar <dir_where_listener_unpacked>\apex.war
   ```

You will be asked to enter a number of parameters, such as the name of the database server, the port, the SID, the name of the database user for all PL/SQL gateway operations, and its password.

The next part is placing the APEX files in the right directory.

1. From the APEX Listener archive, copy the file called `apex.war` and place it into the webapps directory under `<base_dir>\tomcat\`.
2. Copy the content of the `images` directory (not the directory itself) from APEX and place it into `<base_dir>\tomcat\webapps\ROOT\i`.

All files are now where they should be. It's time to configure Tomcat to use the APEX Listener.

For this, two users with two roles have to be created that can use the administration pages of the listener. These roles have to be called `Admin` and `Manager`.

1. Edit the `tomcat_users.xml` file under `\tomcat\conf\`.
2. Add the following code to the file:

   ```
   <role rolename="Manager"/>
   <role rolename="Admin"/>
   <user username="manager" password="<password>" roles="Manager"/>
   <user username="admin" password="<password>" roles="Admin"/>
   [9672_10_7.txt]
   ```

3.  Start Tomcat.

4.  Now the Application Express environment can be reached by navigating to the URL `http://<YourApplicationServer>:8080/apex`.

## There's more...

As of APEX Listener 2.0, it has a command-line setup and not a graphical setup such as the one from the versions prior to 2.0. If you still want a graphical setup, you can use Oracle SQL Developer release 3.2 or later.

# Creating an error handling

Since APEX 4.1, it is possible to create a custom error handling. With the custom error handling, you can not only control error messages but also the location of the message. It is also possible to log the errors. In this recipe we will show you how to create an error handling function and how to use it in APEX. We will use a form based on the EMP table. When the user enters erroneous data and clicks on the **Submit** button, an error message will be displayed along the concerned text item and the error will be logged in to an error table. However, when the user enters a hire date in an invalid format, the error will be logged and an error message will be displayed in the **Notification** area (in the upper part of the screen).

## Getting ready

Make sure you have access to the EMP and APP_ERROR_LOG tables. Create a form based on the EMP table. Just follow the Create wizard and use the default settings.

## How to do it...

Perform the following steps:

1.  Create the following function. You can use an IDE like SQL developer or just SQL Plus or even the SQL Workshop in APEX:

```
create or replace
function handle_apex_error (p_error in apex_error.t_error)
return apex_error.t_error_result
is
  l_result apex_error.t_error_result;
begin
  l_result := apex_error.init_error_result (p_error => p_error);
  --
  insert into app_error_log
  (message
```

```
    ,display_location
    ,association_type
    ,page_item_name
    ,region_id
    ,row_num
    ,apex_error_code
    ,ora_sqlcode
    ,ora_sqlerrm
    ,error_date)
    values
    (p_error.message
    ,p_error.display_location
    ,p_error.association_type
    ,p_error.page_item_name
    ,p_error.region_id
    ,p_error.row_num
    ,p_error.apex_error_code
    ,p_error.ora_sqlcode
    ,p_error.ora_sqlerrm
    ,sysdate);
    --
    if l_result.page_item_name = 'PX_HIREDATE'
    then
       l_result.display_location := apex_error.c_inline_with_field_
and_notif;
    end if;
    --
    return l_result;
end;
[9672_10_1A.txt]
```

Where X in `PX_HIREDATE` is the page number.

2.  In the **Application Builder**, click on **Edit Application Properties**:

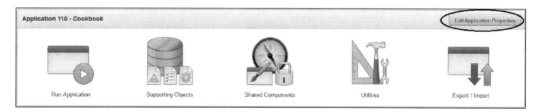

3. In the **Error Handling** section, enter `handle_apex_error` in the **Error Handling Function** text field.

4. In the **Default Error Display Location** select list, select **Inline with Field**.

5. Click on **Apply Changes**.

Run the page, try to enter some erroneous data, such as letters in the **Mgr** or **Sal** field. You will see that error messages will be displayed along the text fields, but when you enter a hire date in an invalid format, you will also see the error message on top of the page:

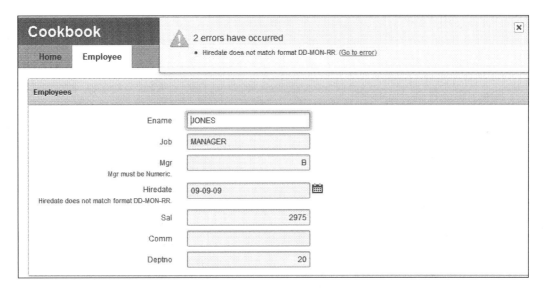

# How it works...

Whenever an error occurs, the error handling function is called. This function needs to meet some conditions:

▶ The input parameter is of type `APEX_ERROR.T_ERROR`

▶ The return value of the function is of type `APEX_ERROR.T_ERROR_RESULT`

The `APEX_ERROR.T_ERROR` type looks like the following:

| Column | Datatype | Description |
|---|---|---|
| message | varchar2(32767) | The error message |
| additional_info | varchar2(32767) | Additional error info which is only displayed on the error page |
| display_location | varchar2(40) | The location of the error message |

| Column | Datatype | Description |
|---|---|---|
| association_type | varchar2(40) | Type of the object where the error occurred |
| page_item_name | varchar2(255) | The concerned page item |
| region_id | number | The region ID when using a tabular form |
| column_alias | varchar2(255) | The column alias when using a tabular form |
| row_num | pls_integer | The tabular form row |
| is_internal_error | boolean | Internal error (when the error was raised by APEX) |
| apex_error_code | varchar2(255) | The APEX error code when the error was raised by APEX |
| ora_sqlcode | number | The ORA error code (that is ORA-000001) |
| ora_sqlerrm | varchar2(32767) | The ORA error message (SQLERRM) |
| error_backtrace | varchar2(32767) | The output of dbms_utility. format_error_backtrace or dbms_ utility.format_call_stack |
| component | wwv_flow.t_ component | The component where the error was raised |

The APEX_ERROR.T_ERROR_RESULT return type consists of the following:

| Column | Datatype | Description |
|---|---|---|
| message | varchar2(32767) | The error message |
| additional_info | varchar2(32767) | Additional error info which is only displayed on the error page |
| display_location | varchar2(40) | The location of the error message |
| page_item_name | varchar2(255) | The concerned page item |
| column_alias | varchar2(255) | The column alias when tabular form |

When you want to set the location of the error message, you have to use constants:

| Constant | Description |
| --- | --- |
| c_inline_with_field | Inline with field |
| c_inline_with_field_and_notif | Inline with field and notification |
| c_inline_in_notification | Inline with notification |
| c_on_error_page | On error page |

The content of T_ERROR can be used to insert the values into the error table or can be used to check, let's say, what the name of the item is where the error occurred. In this case, when the item where the error occurred is PX_HIREDATE, show the error message along the text item as well as in the **Notification** area.

# Using packaged applications

A long time ago, in earlier versions of Application Express, APEX was shipped with sample applications. These samples showed some of the techniques available in APEX.

As of Version 4.2, APEX is shipped with packaged applications. Packaged applications are prebuilt applications. There are two types of packaged applications: applications that offer productivity and sample applications that demonstrate the several features of APEX. The sample applications are very useful when you want to know how things work in APEX.

The productivity applications help you manage your APEX project. Productivity applications include bug tracking, application archive, and many more. Oracle offers support and updates on packaged applications, but only as long as the application is locked, which means that you cannot view or edit the application. Sample applications don't have to be unlocked. You can always view and edit them. In this recipe we will see how we can embed packaged applications into our own application landscape.

## Getting ready

To follow this recipe, APEX 4.2 (or higher) is required.

## How to do it...

First we will install a packaged application into our own list of applications:

1.  Navigate to the **Application Builder**.

2.  Click on **Create** and then select **Packaged Application** or go directly to the tab named **Packaged Applications**.

    We now see a list of available applications that can be installed. This list changes with every (sub) version of APEX, so it might look different in your environment. Our example application might not even be available or renamed. So replace it when necessary.

3.  Click on the application named **Incident Tracking**. On the next screen we can see an overview of the application and the requirements.

4.  Click on **Install Application**.

5.  Click on **Next**.

6.  And then click on **Install Application**.

After a short wait we can choose to run the new application and see what it looks like or we can go back to the **Application Builder**.

When we return to the application overview, we can see that the new application has been added to the list. Besides the icon, it is shown that the application is a **Packaged Application** and its status is **Locked**. This means that the application cannot be altered:

The application has been locked because Oracle offers support on these applications. Once the application is unlocked, we can change it the way we want.

To unlock this application, perform the following steps:

1. Navigate to the **Packaged Applications** page.
2. Click on the icon of the **Incident Tracking** application (notice that it now has a green indicator next to it saying it is installed).
3. Click on **Manage**.
4. Select **Unlock Application** and click on **Next**.
5. Click on **Unlock Application**.

When we return to the **Application Builder**, we can see the **Edit** button is available, just like any other application that we built ourselves.

 Unlocking this packaged application has now voided all warranty and we are no longer eligible for support or future updates for this specific application.

# 11
# APEX Administration

In this chapter, we will cover:

- ▸ Creating a workspace manually
- ▸ Creating a workspace by request
- ▸ Creating a user
- ▸ Adding a schema to your workspace
- ▸ Setting up a system message
- ▸ Setting up a workspace announcement
- ▸ Setting up news items on the home page
- ▸ Creating a site-specific task list
- ▸ Creating a public theme
- ▸ Locking a workspace
- ▸ Creating table APIs

## Introduction

In this chapter we will discuss the tasks that enable APEX developers to do their work. Before a developer can do anything in APEX, there needs to be a workspace where the developer can create his/her applications. This workspace uses one or more schemas in the database where tables, views, procedures, and so on reside. We will show you how to create a workspace, how to create users in the workspace, and how to manage workspaces.

# Creating a workspace manually

Before a developer can do something in APEX, he/she needs to have a workspace. The workspace is linked to a schema. In this recipe, you will be creating a workspace manually and assigning a schema to it.

## Getting ready

Before you can implement this recipe, you need to have access to the internal workspace. The internal workspace is a special workspace where the APEX administration applications reside. There is one user created already and that is the admin user.

There are two ways to start the APEX administration:

1. Go to `http://yourhost:port/apex/apex_admin` and log in using the admin login credentials. Use the link in the lower-left corner of the login page (**Administration**).

2. Go to `http://yourhost:port/apex` and log in as admin on the internal workspace.

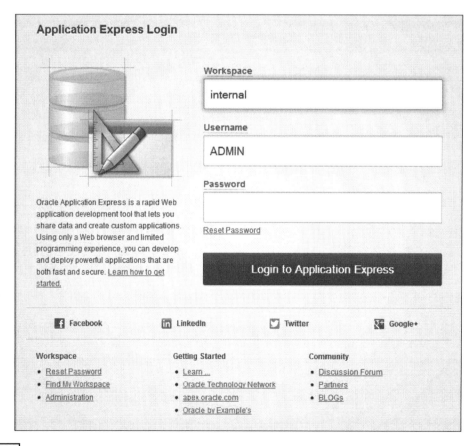

The password can be set using the `apxxepwd.sql` script. You can find this script in the APEX directory, that is, in Oracle home of the RDBMS installation or in the downloaded ZIP file of APEX. It is the same directory where the APEX install script is in. Run the script as the sys user with `password` as the first parameter:

```
@apxxepwd <password>
```

In the previous code, you should substitute `<password>` with your own chosen password. The next time you log in as admin user, you need to change the password; provide the current just created password, and the new password twice (to confirm), and after that, log out and log in using the new changed password and you're in.

## How to do it...

1.  Go to **Instance Administration | Manage Workspaces**.

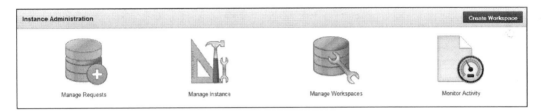

2.  In the **Workspace Actions** section, click on **Create Workspace**.

3.  In the next step, enter a workspace name, for example, `Test`.

4.  You can also enter a workspace ID and a description to explain what the workspace is used for.

5.  Click on **Next**.

6.  If you want to create a workspace on an existing schema, enter the schema name and select **Yes** in the **Re-Use Existing Schema** listbox. If you want to create a new schema, select **No** in the **Re-Use Existing Schema** listbox and enter a username, a password, and the size of the tablespace. Click on **Next**.

7.  Then, enter the administrator username and password. Usually, the administrator username is ADMIN (it is also displayed by default). Also enter the e-mail address of the administrator user. Click on **Next**.

8.  Click on the **Create Workspace** button.

9.  The workspace is ready now and it already has one user, the ADMIN user. You can now add users to the workspace. We'll cover that later in the chapter.

## How it works...

Every workspace initially has one user, the workspace administrator user. This user can create more users in the workspace, set workspace preferences, and make a request for more storage or a new schema. Every user can be made the workspace administrator. Log in as workspace administrator and go to **Administration | Manage Users and Groups**.

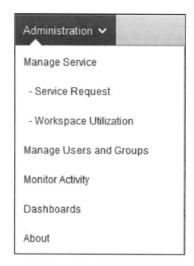

Select the user to be changed by clicking on the **Edit** pencil to the left of the user. In the **Account Privileges** section, select **Yes** from the options under the **User is a workspace administrator:** radio button.

# Creating a workspace by request

In the previous recipe, we showed you how to create a workspace manually. You can semiautomate this process by putting a link by request on the login page so any end user can request their own workspace. This request will be handled by the instance administrator. This recipe will show you how to create a workspace by request.

## Getting ready

First of all, you need to put the link on the login page:

1.  Log in as admin on the internal workspace.
2.  Click on **Manage Instance**.
3.  In the **Instance Settings** section, click on **Instance Settings**.
4.  In the **Self Service** section, click on the **Request- Link displayed on login page enabling users to request workspaces** radio button.
5.  Select **Yes** in the **Require Verification Code** select list.
6.  In the **Email** section, enter the name of the SMTP server that you use to send outgoing mails. If you don't know the name of your SMTP server, contact your system administrator.
7.  Click on the **Apply Changes** button.

The result is that you will see a link **Request a Workspace** in the **Workspace** section.

## How to do it...

1.  Go to the login page of APEX.

2. In the **Workspace** section in the lower-left corner, click on **Request a Workspace**.

3. A wizard is started with a welcome message. Click on **Get Started**.

4. Enter your name and your e-mail address and click on **Next**.

5. Enter a name for the workspace and click on **Next**.

6. In the next step, you can choose whether to use an existing schema or a new schema. We will request a new schema, so click on **Next**.

7. Enter the name of the new schema and click on **Next**.

8. In the next step, enter the reason why you want to request for the workspace and click on **Next**.

9. In the last step, confirm your request by entering the verification code (this is an extra check confirming that the request comes from you and not from any search robot) and clicking on **Submit Request**.

10. The request is made now and the administrator gets a signal that there is a request. Log in as administrator to the internal workspace and go to the home page. You will see something like the following screenshot:

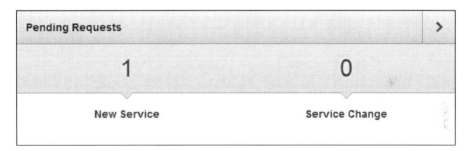

11. Click on the number **1** to see the request.

12. Then click on the **Provision** link.

13. In the next step you can approve or decline the request. If you decline the request, you will get a text area with a standard mail text where you can put some text yourself; for example, why you declined the request. In this recipe, we will approve the request for the workspace.

14. Click on the **Approve** button.

15. You will see a text area that shows a standard mail text to the requestor of the workspace. Here, you can put some additional text if you want to. After that, click on **Approve and Send Email** button.

16. A message appears that the workspace is accepted and that an e-mail is sent.

17. The requestor will receive the e-mail with the login details.

18. With these details, the user can log in to the new workspace.

## There's more...

If the requestor does not receive an e-mail, something must be wrong with the outgoing Internet connection. You can check a few things to make sure your Oracle database has Internet access.

First of all, check whether the mail is really sent. You can check that by going to **Manage Instance | Mail Queue** in the **Manage Meta Data** section.

All pending e-mails that have not been sent yet are in the list. If an error occurs, you can see the error message in the error column. If you think that this error has been fixed, you can resend the e-mail by clicking on the **Send All Mail** button. APEX will then try again.

Another possible reason for not sending e-mails is that you have not set up the e-mail facility yet. Go to **Manage Instance | Instance Settings** in the section **Instance Settings**. Go to the **Email** section and verify that the SMTP host address and administration e-mail address are entered.

If you request a workspace, you usually get a username that is the same as your e-mail address. This user is also the workspace administrator.

# Creating a user

If you want to work in APEX with more developers, you can create a user for each developer. There are three types of users in APEX: administrators, developers, and runtime users. Runtime users only have access to team development (to provide feedback on applications) and to use an application. Developers can have access to the application builder, SQL workshop, and team development. Administrators have access to all the components. This recipe shows how to create a `developer` user.

## Getting ready

Make sure you have an administrator user to be able to create a user.

## How to do it...

There are two ways to create a user:

1. Log in as administrator to the internal workspace and go to **Manage Workspaces | Manage Developers and Users**.

2. Log in as the workspace administrator and go to **Administration | Users**.

We choose the second option. The difference with the first option is that here you don't have to select the workspace.

1. Click on the **Create User** button.

2. Enter the username, e-mail address, and the desired password.

3. You can also enter the first and last names of the user, but this is optional.

4. In the **Account Privileges** section, select the appropriate option from the **Default Schema** dropdown.

5. In the **Accessible Schemas** text field, enter the schemas to which the user should have access to in the SQL workshop. The schemas should be separated by colons.

6. If you want this user to be a workspace administrator, select **Yes** from the options under the **User is a workspace administrator:** radio button, otherwise, select **No**.

7. If you want to create a developer user, select **Yes** from the options under the **User is a developer:** radio button. If you select **No**, this user will have no access to the application builder and the SQL workshop.

8. Furthermore, you can choose to have the user change his/her password upon first use and whether the account should be locked or unlocked.

9. If you want to create another user, click on **Create and Create Another**, otherwise, click on **Create User**.

# Adding a schema to your workspace

By default, a workspace has got one schema from where it uses the objects. You can add more schemas to a workspace. This recipe tells you how to do that.

There are several ways to add a schema to a workspace:

▶ Log in to the internal workspace as administrator and go to **Manage Workspaces | Manage Workspace to Schema Assignments**

▶ Log in as the workspace administrator and go to **Administration | Manage Service | Make a Service Request**

▶ Using the API, apex_instance_admin.add_schema('<workspace>','<schema>');

## Getting ready

Make sure you can log in to the internal workspace as administrator.

## How to do it...

1. Go to **Administration | Manage Service | Make a Service Request**.

2. Click on the **Request Schema** icon.

3. In the next step, select **Use an Existing Schema** and enter the name of the schema you want to add. Click on **Next**.

4. You will get the message you have requested stating that the existing schema be assigned to the workspace.

   We will now continue as the instance administrator, so log on to the internal workspace as administrator.

The internal administrator will now get a message when he or she logs on to the internal workspace.

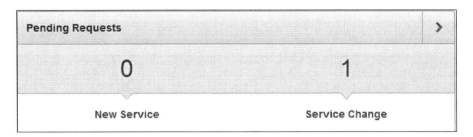

5. Click on **1** above **Service Change**.

6. You will get an overview of open requests. Click on the **View Request** link.

7. An overview of the request is shown now. Click on the **Assign Schema** button in the upper-right corner to approve the request.

8. The requestor of the schema will get an e-mail with the message that the request is approved.

## How it works...

You can add one or more schemas to a workspace. When you create an application, you can choose which schema you will use for the application. But you can of course add references to tables from another schema if your schema is granted with the necessary privileges; for example, the well-known scott/tiger. So, a workspace can access more schemas, but an application is limited to only one schema. You can see which parsing schema an application uses. Log on to the internal workspace and click on **Manage Workspaces** and then click on the **Parsing schemas** link in the **Manage Applications** section.

You can also control which schemas a user can access in the SQL workshop. Log on as the workspace administrator and go to **Administration | Manage Users and Groups**. Edit a user by clicking on the **Edit** pencil. You will see that in the **Account Privileges** section, there is an item called **Accessible Schemas** where you can enter the names of the schemas the user has access to in the SQL workshop. This item is not available when you edit a user via the internal workspace.

## Setting up a system message

To customize your APEX environment, it is possible to set a system message for all the users of APEX. This message will be visible at the top of the screen when the user is logged on. The system message can be of any type. Let's say you want to set a system message where you welcome the user to the new APEX 4.2 environment.

## Getting ready

You need to be logged in as the administrator user to the internal workspace, so make sure you have access to this environment.

## How to do it...

1. Click on **Manage Instance**.

2. In the **Messages** section, click on the **Define System Message** link.

3. Then, click on **Custom Message**.

4. In the message text area, enter the text Welcome to APEX 4.2, your totally new APEX environment. If you have any problems or questions, please contact your System Administrator.

5. Click on the **Apply Changes** button.

The system message is set and is now visible to all the users:

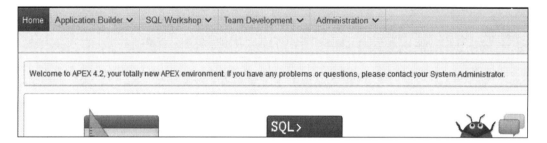

## There's more...

You can use HTML in your text, for example, to format the code or to put a hyperlink to a URL. If you enter <a href=http://apex.oracle.com>APEX</a>, the user will see the text **APEX** that is clickable and will redirect the user to http://apex.oracle.com.

# Setting up a workspace announcement

The success of the development of an application depends on good communication. That is why APEX supports various ways of communicating with the APEX user. One of them is the announcement. You can use announcement to notify the users with all kinds of messages, for example, for maintenance activities. In this recipe we will show you how to set an announcement telling the users that the APEX environment will be offline this weekend.

## Getting ready

You need to log in as a workspace administrator, so make sure you have a user with workspace administrator rights.

## How to do it...

1. Log on as the administrator.
2. Click on **Administration**.
3. Click on the **Manage Service** icon.
4. Click on the **Edit Announcement** icon.
5. In the text area, enter the desired text.

---

### Workspace Announcement

Message

```
Due maintenance activities, the entire APEX development environment
will be offline this weekend from saturday 08:00 CET till sunday
evening 23:00 CET. We apologize for the inconvenience.
```

---

6. Click on the **Apply Changes** button.
7. The announcement is ready. You can already see the announcement!

## There's more...

Like the system message, you can also use HTML in your text here.

# Setting up news items on the home page

Besides the system and workspace messages, you can also put news items on the APEX user's home page. The difference with the system and workspace messages is that you can add more news items that appear one by one like a carousel. Everyone can add news items, so this offers a good way of communication between the team members.

## Getting ready

No actions needed. Well, just make sure you have access to APEX.

## How to do it...

1. Log on to APEX. You will see the home page.

2. If no one in the workspace has added a news item yet, the **News** bar will show nothing (except **News**).
3. Click on the **Add** icon on the right-hand side of the **News** bar.
4. In the news entry text area, enter some text, for example, New project started.
5. Click on the **Add News** button. The news item is added.
6. If you click on the **Home** link, you will see the home page together with the news item.

7. Add another news item by again clicking on the **Add** icon on the right-hand side.
8. Enter some new text, for example, Finished functional design, and click on the **Add News** button.
9. Go back to the home page and you will see that the two news items will appear one by one.
10. Click on the right arrow icon on the right-hand side of the news bar.

11. You will see an overview of all the news items:

12. You can edit news items by clicking on the pencil icon to the left of the item.

13. You can also delete news items by first clicking on the pencil icon and then clicking on the **Delete** button.

## There's more...

Unlike the system message and the workspace message, it is not possible to use HTML in the news items.

# Creating a site-specific task list

You can customize the workspace home page for developers when they have logged in. You can add a site-specific task list. This is a section on the page with links to websites or APEX applications. For example, you can put a link to an APEX application that needs to be tested or a link to a relevant website. You can choose to add the site-specific task list to the login page or to the workspace home page.

## Getting ready

You need to have access to the internal workspace.

## How to do it...

1. Log on to the internal workspace.

2. Click on the **Manage Instance** icon.

3. In the **Messages** section, click on **Manage Site-Specific Tasks**.

4. Click on the **Create** button. The following screen appears:

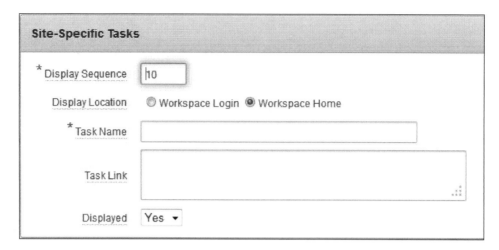

5. Enter a number in the **Display Sequence** text field. This determines the order of the tasks.

6. In the **Display Location** radio group, select where you want to see the task list. If you select **Workspace Login**, the task list will be displayed on the login page. If you select **Workspace Home**, the task list will be displayed on the right-hand side of the workspace home page. Select **Workspace Home**.

7. In the **Task Name** text field, enter a name for the task, for example, Testpage.

8. In the **Task Link**, enter the URL of the test application. You can enter the complete URL, for example, http://www.website.com, or you can use a relative URL such as f?p. So let's say you have an APEX application with the ID 108 and a starting page with the ID 1, enter f?p=108:1.

9. Make sure the Displayed select list is set to **Yes**. Click on the **Create** button.

10. A task is added to the task list. When a user logs into the concerned workspace, he/she will see the following:

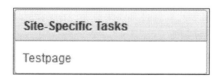

## How it works...

If a task is created, the site-specific task list will not be shown. If there is at least one task defined, a section will be displayed showing the task as a hyperlink.

To delete a task, go to **Manage Instance** | **Manage Site-Specific Tasks**, click on the task, and click on the **Delete** button.

# Creating a public theme

When you have a theme that you want to use in more applications, you can create a public theme. Creating a public theme is actually copying a theme to the theme repository so that all the applications can make use of it.

We will demonstrate how to create a public theme.

## Getting ready

Make sure you have access to the internal APEX workspace.

## How to do it...

1. Log on to the APEX internal workspace.
2. Click on **Manage Instance**.

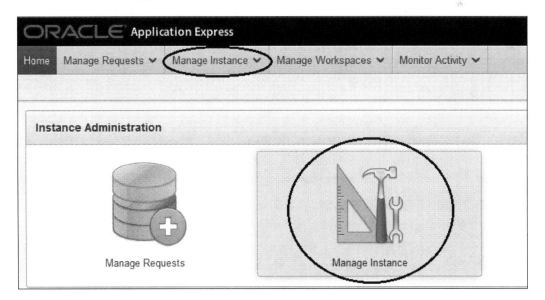

3. In **Manage Shared Components**, click on the **Public Themes** link.

4. Click on the **Create Public Theme** button.

5. In the **Workspace** text field, enter the name of the workspace that owns the theme. You can use the button next to the text field to select a workspace from the list of available workspaces. Click on **Next**.

6. In the **Application** select list, select the application through which the theme was created. Click on **Next**.

7. In the **Theme to Copy** select list, select the theme that you want to make public. Click on **Next**.

8. In the **Theme Number** field, enter a number for the theme.

9. In the **Theme Name** field, enter a name for the theme.

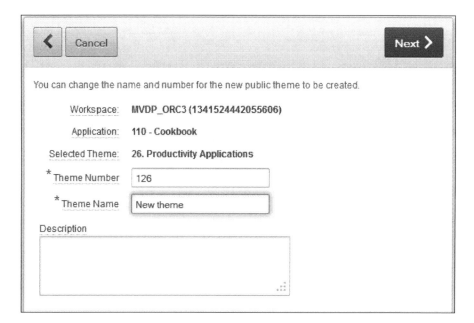

10. You can also enter a description in the **Description** text area, but this is optional. Click on **Next**.

11. If everything is okay (no template class is missing), click on the **Create Public Theme** button.

The theme is now added to the theme repository, and every application can now make use of it. To test this, log on to a workspace, go to **Shared Components | Themes**, click on the **Create** button, select **From the Repository**, click on **Next**, select **Desktop** as the user interface, click on **Next**, and select **Custom Themes** from the **Theme Type** select list. You will see something like the following:

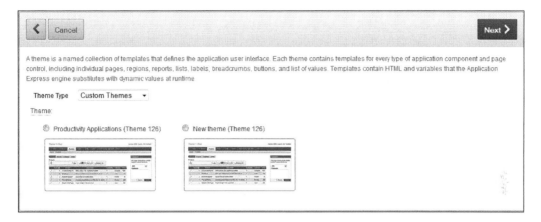

## How it works...

Themes that are created within an application are only available to that application. You can create an export of the theme and import it into another application. But it is much easier to make the theme public so that it is available to all the applications and workspaces.

## There's more...

Once you make a theme public, you cannot directly edit the theme. If you want to edit a public theme, create an application or go to an existing application, switch to the theme, edit the theme within the application, and then create a new public theme from this edited theme.

# Locking a workspace

There may be situations when you want to immediately lock an application for all the users; for example, when there are security issues. In that case, you can (temporarily) lock the workspace. Locking a workspace means locking all the user accounts in the workspace. Besides that, the status of all the applications in the workspace will be "unavailable". When the workspace is locked, all the users will not be able to log on to the workspace. Starting an APEX application of a workspace that is locked will result in a message that the application is unavailable.

## Getting ready

You need to have access to the APEX internal workspace.

## How to do it...

1. Log on to the internal workspace.
2. Click on **Manage Workspaces**.
3. In the **Workspace Actions** section, click on the **Lock Workspace** link.

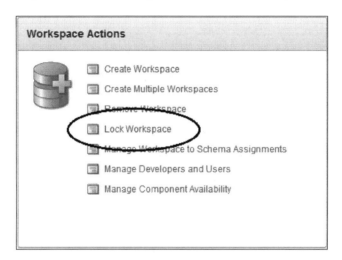

4. In the **Workspace** text field, enter the name of the workspace you want to lock. You can also click on the **List of Values** button next to the text field to choose from a list of workspaces. After you have selected or entered a workspace, click on **Next**.
5. In the next page, you see an overview of the workspace applications and their status. You also see an overview of all the users in the workspace and their availability. If everything is okay, click on the **Lock Workspace** button.

The workspace is now locked.

## How it works...

As stated before, locking a workspace means actually locking all the user accounts in the workspace and setting the status of all the applications in the workspace to unavailable. This means that users can no longer log on to the workspace and that it is not possible anymore to run an application from that workspace.

## There's more...

According to the APEX administration guide, locking a workspace makes it permanently inaccessible. However, you can make the users and the applications accessible again:

First, unlock the administrator user of the workspace:

1. Log on to the internal workspace.
2. Click on **Manage Workspaces**.
3. In the **Workspace Actions** section, click on the **Manage Developers and Users** link.

4. In the list that appears, look for a user from the workspace and click on the **Edit** icon (the pencil).
5. In the **Account Privileges** section, set the **Account Availability** select list to **Unlocked**.
6. Click on the **Apply Changes** button.

Second, unlock the application:

1. Log on to the workspace using the unlocked user.
2. Go to the application that you want to unlock.
3. Click on **Shared Components**.
4. Click on the **Edit Definition** link on the right-hand side.
5. In the **Availability** section, select **Available with edit links** in the **Status** select list.
6. Click on the **Apply Changes** button.

The application is available now, and you can run it again.

# Creating table APIs

APEX can create a table **Application Programmatic Interface** (**API**) for you. A table API is a package that takes care of the DML, rather than having to implement DML yourself. So you will get a package that you can use to insert, update, delete, or retrieve data from the concerning table. The APIs can be referenced from within APEX, so you can call the API from a PL/SQL region. In this way you can keep the database and the client interface separated.

## Getting ready

Make sure you have access to the table APP_DEALERS and that this table has a primary key.

## How to do it...

1. Click on **SQL Workshop**.
2. Then, click on **Utilities**.

3. Click on **Methods on Tables**.

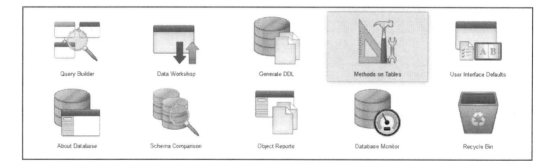

4. Enter a name for the package, for example, DLR_PACKAGE.
5. Click on **Next**.
6. In the **Table 1** text field, enter the table name, APP_DEALERS, or select it from the list of values that pops up when you click on the icon next to the text field. You can select more tables in the following text fields. Click on **Next**.

7.  In the last step, you will see an overview of the created package. You can see which subprograms APEX created, and you can show or download the contents of the package. If everything is okay, click on **Create Package**.

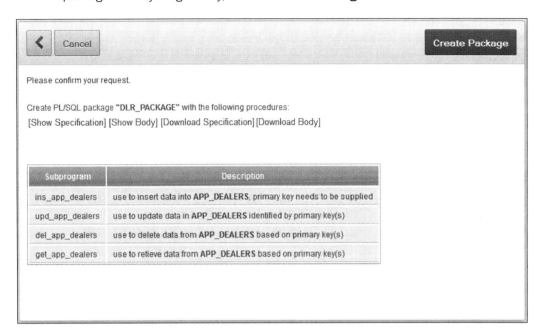

8.  After clicking on the **Create Package** button, the object browser will be displayed, and it will show the newly created package.

## How it works...

APEX created a package with five subprograms:

- ▸ INS_APP_DEALERS
- ▸ UPD_APP_DEALERS
- ▸ DEL_APP_DEALERS
- ▸ GET_APP_DEALERS
- ▸ GET_APP_DEALERS with MD5
- ▸ BUILD_APP_DEALERS_MD5

The insert and the update procedures have all the columns of the table as parameters. Mind that the primary key, DLR_ID, is also an input parameter, and it will not use a sequence. You have to supply the ID yourself, if possible, using a sequence.

The delete procedure only uses the primary key as the input parameter.

With the `GET_APP_DEALERS` procedure, you can retrieve data from the `APP_DEALERS` table. The procedure has an `out` parameter for each column. You can retrieve data in the following way:

```
declare
  p_dlr_id          number(3);
  p_dlr_name        varchar2(100);
  p_dlr_address1    varchar2(100);
  p_dlr_city        varchar2(100);
  p_dlr_state       varchar2(100);
  p_dlr_country_cd  varchar2(100);
  p_md5             varchar2(100);
begin
  p_dlr_id := 14;
  dlr_package.get_app_dealers(p_dlr_id,p_dlr_name, p_dlr_address1,
    p_dlr_city, p_dlr_state, p_dlr_country_cd);
  dbms_output.put_line('Result:
    '||p_dlr_name||'..'||p_dlr_address1);
end;
/
[9672_11_1.txt]
```

## There's more...

The `BUILD_APP_DEALERS_MD5` procedure calculates an MD5 checksum. This can be useful when you want to ensure that the data in the database has not changed when you try to update the table. You can use it in the following way:

```
declare
  p_dlr_id          number(3);
  p_dlr_name        varchar2(100);
  p_dlr_address1    varchar2(100);
  p_dlr_city        varchar2(100);
  p_dlr_state       varchar2(100);
  p_dlr_country_cd  varchar2(100);
  p_md5             varchar2(100);
  p_ctr             number(9)  := 1;
begin
  p_dlr_id := 14;
  dlr_package.get_app_dealers(p_dlr_id,p_dlr_name, p_dlr_address1,
    p_dlr_city, p_dlr_state, p_dlr_country_cd,p_md5);
  dbms_output.put_line('Result: '||p_md5);
  while p_ctr <= 100000000
  loop
    p_ctr := p_ctr + 1;
```

```
    end loop;
    dlr_package.upd_app_dealers(p_dlr_id,'Media Markt
      Ehv','Boschdijktunnel 1','Eindhoven','Noord-
      Brabant','NL',p_md5);
  end;
  /
  [9672_11_2.txt]
```

This script calls the GET_APP_DEALERS procedure in the package DLR_PACKAGE and gets an MD5 checksum. After that, it loops (count till 100000000) so that you have time to update and commit in another session. In that other session, update the same row in the APP_DEALERS table and commit. When the loop is done, the script calls the UPD_APP_DEALERS procedure with some changed data and the MD5 checksum. In the UPD_APP_DEALERS procedure, an MD5 checksum is recalculated from the retrieved data, based on the primary key. The passed MD5 checksum is compared with the calculated MD5 checksum, and when the two numbers differ, an error message will be displayed.

```
Administrator: Command Prompt - sqlplus                            _  □  X
 10    begin
 11       p_dlr_id := 14;
 12       dlr_package.get_app_dealers(p_dlr_id,p_dlr_name, p_dlr_address1, p_dlr_ci
ty, p_dlr_state, p_dlr_country_cd,p_md5);
 13       dbms_output.put_line('Result: '||p_md5);
 14       while p_ctr <= 100000000
 15       loop
 16          p_ctr := p_ctr + 1;
 17       end loop;
 18       dlr_package.upd_app_dealers(p_dlr_id,'Media Markt Ehv','Boschdijktunnel 1
','Eindhoven','Noord-Brabant','NL',p_md5);
 19    end;
 20    /
declare
*
FOUT in regel 1:
.ORA-20001: Current version of data in database has changed since user initiated
update process. current checksum = "CB40959BCF29764834A89CC01AF45BF0", item
checksum = "5A5A61D4DA9D0CBD8CF3D18E856F993D".
ORA-06512: in "MUDP.DLR_PACKAGE", regel 77
ORA-06512: in regel 18

SQL>
```

# 12
# Team Development

In this chapter, we will cover:

- ▶ Creating a list of features
- ▶ Creating and assigning To-dos
- ▶ Keeping track of bugs in the Bugtracker
- ▶ Creating Milestones
- ▶ Using Feedback
- ▶ Using follow-ups

## Introduction

Team Development is a suite of built-in applications to help developers organize their projects. It is a part of the workspace, so it can be used for multiple applications at the same time.

The suite consists of five main applications: a list of features, a milestones planner, a to-do list, a Bugtracker, and a feedback application. These five applications integrate into one dashboard overview, to offer an insight into the status of a project at a single glance.

In this chapter, we will see how we can take advantage of the features in Team Development in our project. Each recipe will show how a part of Team Development can be put to use in a specific part of the project cycle.

Team Development can be found on the Workspace Home, as shown in the following screenshot:

Click on Team Development to enter its environment, as shown in the following screenshot:

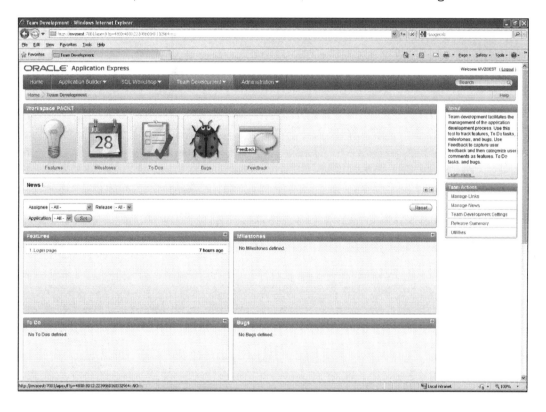

Since Team Development is not a part of a single application, it can be used in smaller and bigger projects spanning multiple applications.

Because of its possibilities, Team Development is an excellent tool to support a project using Agile principles.

# Creating a list of features

Each project will eventually get to the point where there is a list of features populated. In a Scrum project for instance, the team will eventually start off with a backlog of User Stories. Each User Story can be seen as a feature.

A feature is not necessarily a piece of software, but rather a collection of software developed to perform a requested task. For instance, if the client asks for a Login, this can consist of a login page, a table of users, a function to encrypt passwords, and so on.

In this example, the Login will become a feature to be assigned to a number of developers. The creation of the login page, the table of users, and the other smaller tasks will be To-do's, as we will see in a later recipe in this chapter.

In this recipe, we will see how we can create a list of features and assign them to certain project members.

## Getting ready

For this recipe, we don't need any physical pages or code. All we need is an application.

Create a new application named `Enterprise Application` and add a blank page named `Home` inside it.

## How to do it...

For this recipe, we have to assume a lot of things. Because we will not actually be creating the Enterprise Application, we just need to theorize what kind of features such an application should contain.

Let's assume that the following features at least need to be built:

- Users need to be authenticated in a secure way
- Users need to be able to see a list of employees
- Users need to be able to see a list of departments
- Administrators need to be able to edit the list of departments

Now we can start to build our List of Features in Team Development.

1. Navigate to **Team Development** from the Workspace Home Page.
2. Click on **Features**.

We can now see a large **Dashboard** screen that is completely empty as seen in the following screenshot. This **Dashboard** will be filled with data once we add items in **Team Development**.

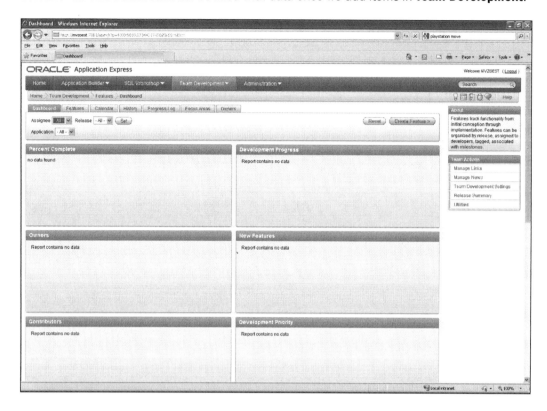

There are also some tabs near the top of the screen. We will leave them alone for now. Once we have added something, it is more prudent to explain this screen.

1. Click on the button labeled **Create Feature**.

2. In the first text field, enter Users need to be authenticated in a secure way.

3. Enter Security Manager in **New Owner** text field.

4. Enter HR Manager in **New Contributor** text field.

5. In **New Release** enter 0.1.

6. For **Status** select **Not Started - 0%**.

7. For **Desirability** select **1. Marquee feature**.

8. For **Priority** select **1. As soon as possible**.

9. **Start Date** will be January, 3rd 2011.

10. **Due Date** will be February, 4th 2011.

11. The **Public Feature Summary** is a piece of text to describe the Feature. Since we don't need to be very elaborate, just enter the text `Users need to be authenticated in a secure way`.

12. Set **Publish this feature** to **Yes**.

13. The **Description** can be more elaborate, and the text can even be formatted. Again, we don't need to be elaborate. Use the text `Users need to be authenticated in a secure way`

14. Use the List of Values to select the "Enterprise Application" in the corresponding field.

15. The **Estimated Effort** will be `120` hours.

16. Click on the **Create Feature** button to save.

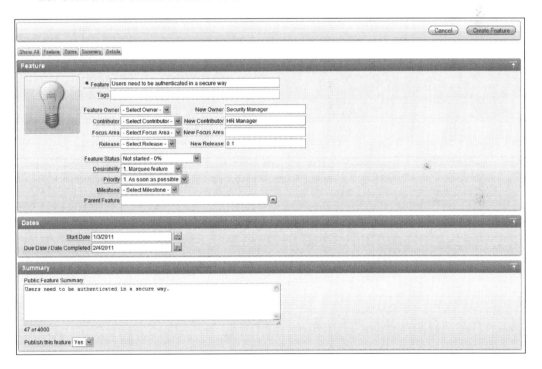

17. The first feature is now done. In the same manner, we will now create the other three features. The required data to be entered can be found in the following table:

| Item name | Feature 2 | Feature 3 | Feature 4 |
|---|---|---|---|
| **Feature** | Users need to be able to see a list of employees | Users need to be able to see a list of departments | Administrators need to be able to edit the list of departments |
| **Owner** | HR Manager | HR Manager | HR Manager |
| **Contributor** | N/A | N/A | Security Manager |
| **Release** | 0.1 | 0.2 | 0.2 |
| **Feature Status** | Under consideration – 10% | Not started – 0% | Not started – 0% |
| **Desirability** | 1. Marquee feature | 2. Highly desirable | 2. Highly desirable |
| **Priority** | 1. As soon as possible | 2. Prioritized | 3. Normal priority |
| **Parent Feature** | N/A | N/A | Users need to be able to see a list of departments – 0.2 |
| **Start Date** | February 7th 2011 | February 21st 2011 | March 7th 2011 |
| **Due Date** | February 25th 2011 | March 11th 2011 | March 25th 2011 |
| **Public Feature Summary** | Users need to be able to see a list of employees | Users need to be able to see a list of departments | Administrators need to be able to edit the list of departments |
| **Publish this feature** | Yes | Yes | Yes |
| **Description** | Users need to be able to see a list of employees | Users need to be able to see a list of departments | Administrators need to be able to edit the list of departments |
| **Application** | Enterprise Application | Enterprise Application | Enterprise Application |
| **Estimated Effort** | 80 | 40 | 80 |

After entering all this data, we have a nice start for a small project.

When we now take a look at the different tabs of the **Features** page, we can see that they start to make more sense.

1. Open the tab **Calendar**.

2. Navigate to the month of **February 2011**.

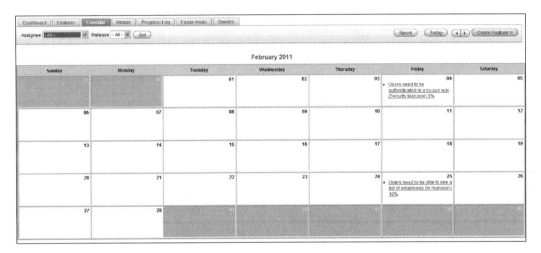

In this overview, all due dates for **Features** can be found. This overview is very helpful for all participants in the project to keep a grip on the planning.

Browse the other tabs to see what kind of information is offered.

## There's more...

A development team consists of people with many different skills and levels of authority. Not all of these team members should have access to the development environment. To assure that these people can use Team Development, but not look into the actual development environment, we can create an End User with just a few privileges through the following steps:

1. Go to the **Administration** section and click on **Manage Users and Groups**.

2. Click on the **Create User** button.

3. Enter the username as EndUser.

4. Enter an e-mail address such as enduser@company.com.

5. In the **Account Privileges** section set all privileges to **No**, except for **Team Development Access**. That should be **Yes**.

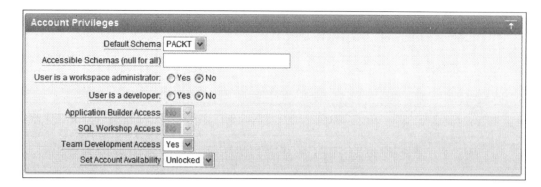

Now enter a password and click on the **Create User** button.

When we log into the Workspace with this user, we can see that only the **Team Development** button and the **Administration** button are available, with the latter being restricted to just the possibility to change our own password.

This user can now be used to do tasks in Team Development that do not require access to the Application Builder or SQL Workshop, like reporting bugs or performing administrative tasks.

# Creating and assigning To-dos

In the previous recipe, we have seen how we can use Features. In that recipe, we defined Features as an equal to Scrum's User stories, but a word like deliverable can also be used. If we keep that analogy, then To-do's are tasks within a user story. If you are building the Feature "barn" then To-do's could be: "erect walls", "place roof", and "put in door".

In this recipe, we will see how we can create To-do's and add them to Features.

## Getting ready

For this recipe, we will need the Features created in the previous recipe.

## How to do it...

Let's start with creating a few To-do's. First, we need some To-do's that can be connected to the Feature for **Users need to be authenticated in a secure way**. These To-do's will be: Create a user table, Create an authentication scheme, and Build a login page.

1. Open **Team Development** and click on the **To Dos** icon.

2. Click on the button **Create To Do**.

3. The **To Do Action** will be called `Create a user table`.

4. **Assigned To** is **Michel van Zoest**.

5. **Status** is **Complete – 100%**.

6. **Start Date** is January 3rd 2011.

7. **Due Date** is January 7th 2011.

8. **Date Completed** is January 6th 2011.

9. Select **0.1** from the **Release** listbox.

10. The **Description** is `Create a user table that contains username and encrypted password`.

11. Select the Feature **1 - Users need to be authenticated in a secure way** using the LOV button.

12. Select **Enterprise Application** using the **Application** LOV button.

13. Because we will be building a page 101 as the login page, enter `101` in the **Page** field even though it doesn't exist yet.

14. **Estimated Effort (in hours)** is **24**.

15. Click on the **Create To Do** button.

When we now take a look at the **To Do** dashboard, we can see that there is already something interesting happening. The charts showing the number of To-do's per assignee and the number of To-do's completed are giving a glimpse of things to come as shown in the following screenshot:

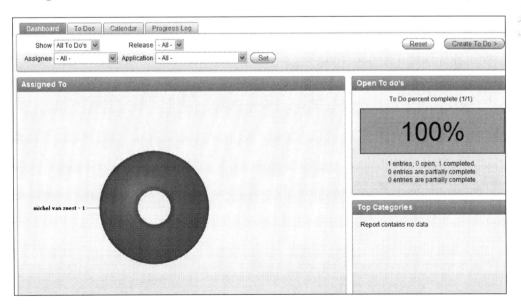

We can now enter the other To-do's.

The second To-do can be created as follows:

1. The **To Do Action** will be called `Create an authentication scheme`.
2. **Assigned To** is **Michel van Zoest**.
3. **Parent To Do** is **Create a user table**.
4. Status is **Complete – 50%**.
5. **Start Date** is January 10th 2011.
6. **Due Date** is January 15th 2011.
7. Select **0.1** from the **Release** listbox.
8. The description is `Create an authentication scheme`.
9. Select the Feature **1 - Users need to be authenticated in a secure way** using the LOV button.
10. Select **Enterprise Application** using the **Application** LOV button.
11. Enter `101` in the **Page** field.
12. **Estimated Effort (in hours)** is `24`.
13. Click on the **Create To Do** button.

The third To-do can be created as follows:

1. The **To Do Action** will be called `Build a login page`.
2. **Assigned To** is **Marcel van der Plas**.
3. **Contributor** is **Michel van Zoest**.
4. **Parent To Do** is **Create an authentication scheme.**
5. **Status** is **Not started – 0%**.
6. **Start Date** is January 12th 2011.
7. **Due Date** is February 4th 2011.
8. Select **0.1** from the **Release** listbox.
9. The **Description** is `Build a login page based on the authentication scheme`.
10. Select the Feature **1 - Users need to be authenticated in a secure way** using the LOV button.
11. Select **Enterprise Application** using the **Application** LOV button.
12. Enter `101` in the **Page** field.
13. **Estimated Effort (in hours)** is `72`.
14. Click on the **Create To Do** button.

When we return back to the dashboard, we can see that the graphs now contain more information that we can use to monitor the progress of the project. For instance, the total progress of all To-do's as shown in the following screenshot:

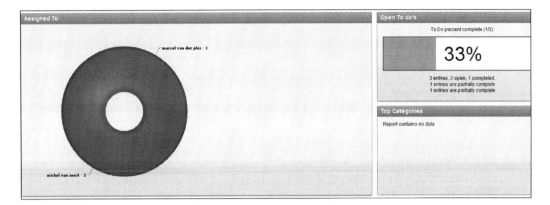

Or, the progress for each individual assignee which is shown in the following screenshot:

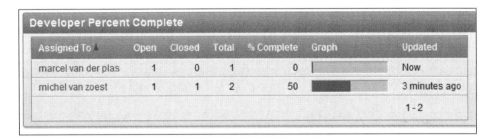

# Keeping track of bugs in the Bugtracker

At some point during every project, bugs will start to appear. They might be mistakes made by the developer, they might originate from a different perspective on the specifications, or they might be caused by a million other reasons.

The fact is, every project needs a good system to store bug reports and keep track of their resolution. Sometimes, companies use a standard piece of software, or they use a spreadsheet.

Application Express offers a built-in Bugtracker in Team Development. In this recipe, we will see how we can create an administration for bugs and track their progress.

## Getting ready

Complete the first two recipes of this chapter, so we have a base to start from.

## How to do it...

1. Click on the **Bugs** button in **Team Development**.

2. Click on the button labeled **Create Bug**.

3. The Bug's title is `Passwords are not encrypted.`

4. **Status** is **10. Entered**.

5. **Severity** is **2. No Workaround Available**.

6. **Priority** is **1. As soon as possible**.

7. **Fix by Release** is **0.2**.

8. **Bug Description** is `When creating a new user, I noticed that the password for this user is not encrypted on the database.`

9. The **Application** is **Enterprise Application**.

10. Select Feature **1 - Users need to be authenticated in a secure way** using the LOV button.

11. Select the To Do **1 – Create a user table** using the LOV button.

12. **Impact** is `The application is not secure enough.`

13. Click on the **Create Bug** button.

This Bug is now available for the Team to investigate. The first steps are to confirm the problem and assign it to a team member that will identify the cause and solution.

1. Go to the **Bugs** tab and click on the Edit icon in front of the Bug we just created.

2. Select the **Status** as **30. Assigned**.

3. **Assigned To** is **Michel van Zoest**.

4. Select an **Estimated Fixed Date** of February 16th 2011.

5. Click on **Apply Changes**.

In the same manner, we can change the status and other properties of bugs as we go along. The Dashboard can be used to get an overview of all bugs and their current status.

## There's more...

When a bug is fixed, we can change its status and communicate this to the team. Two things need to be set. Go back to the Bug we created earlier in this recipe

If we take a deeper look at the **Status** field, we can see a lot of possible statuses our bug can have. When development starts working on it, status should be **40. In progress**. The next step is **80. Fixed in development** if the developers feel they have corrected the problem. After the bug has been tested by the reporter, the status would become **90. Confirmed by QA** and after that **100. Complete.**

The second field that needs to be set is the **Actual Fix Date**.

So to close this bug, take the following steps:

1. Use the listbox to change **Status** to **100. Complete**.
2. Use the datepicker to set **Actual Fix Date** to February 18th 2011.
3. Click on **Apply Changes**.

Anyone looking at the dashboard can now see that the bug has been resolved.

# Creating Milestones

In the previous three recipes of this chapter, we have created Features, To-do's, and Bugs. When creating those, we also noticed the possibility of linking these to Milestones.

Milestones are moments of significance in a project. This is different for every project of course, but examples of a Milestone can be a release, a demo, or (when in a Scrum project) the end of a sprint.

In this recipe, we are going to see how we can create a Milestone, link it to existing objects in Team Development, and how the calendar can help in keeping track of progress.

## Getting ready

Make sure that the Features, To-do's, and Bugs from the previous recipes are present.

## How to do it...

Open the **Milestones** tab in **Team Development**. This section also has a **Dashboard** overview. One of the pieces of this Dashboard is especially interesting. Have a look at the **Component Counts** section, as shown in the following screenshot:

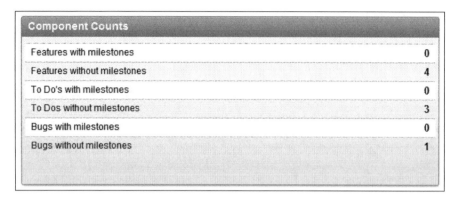

| Component Counts | |
| --- | --- |
| Features with milestones | 0 |
| Features without milestones | 4 |
| To Do's with milestones | 0 |
| To Dos without milestones | 3 |
| Bugs with milestones | 0 |
| Bugs without milestones | 1 |

This overview shows exactly how many Features, To-do's, and Bugs there are and if they are linked to a Milestone. Using this, we can see if all pieces of the project are assigned.

For this example, we are going to create the Milestone First Demo.

1. Click on the **Create Milestone** button.

2. The Milestone is called `First Demo`.

3. Select the **Date** as March 29th 2011.

4. Enter a **New Type** called `Demo`.

5. Enter a **New Owner** called `Project Manager`.

6. Select **0.2** as **Release**.

7. Leave **Selectable for Features** as **Yes**.

8. Enter the description: **This is the first demo for the management team**.

9. Click on the **Create Milestone** button.

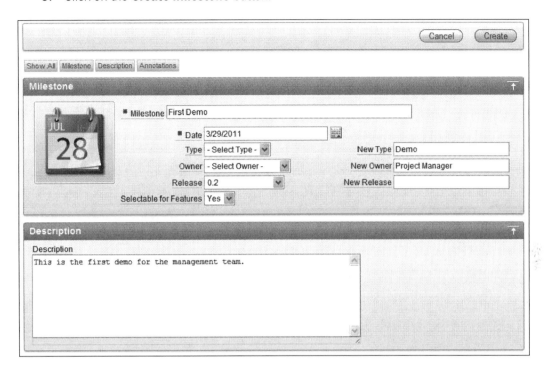

We are automatically returned to the Milestone **Dashboard**. Prominent in the screen is now a large number that counts down the number of days until the final Milestone is reached as shown in the following screenshot:

To assign the Features, To-do's, and Bugs to this Milestone, we have a bit of a cumbersome task ahead of us. Because we can't assign them from within a Milestone, we are going to have to open each Feature, To-do, and Bug and assign them to a Milestone from there.

1. Return to the **Team Development** overview.

2. Click on **Features**.

3. Click on the **Features** tab.

4. Click on the Edit icon in front of the first Feature.

5. Select **First Demo** from the **Milestone** listbox.

6. Click on the **Apply Changes** button.

7. Repeat this for the other Features.

8. Repeat the procedure for To-do's and Bugs.

This showed that it can be a big job to assign Features, To-do's, and Bugs to a Milestone afterwards. It is better to have a decent planning of Milestones ready before starting a project. Then we can directly assign all project deliverables to a Milestone when the deliverable is created.

Now that we have assigned all Features, To-do's, and Bugs to the Milestone, we can take a look at the Milestone Dashboard again. The content of this is a lot more interesting now as seen in the following screenshot:

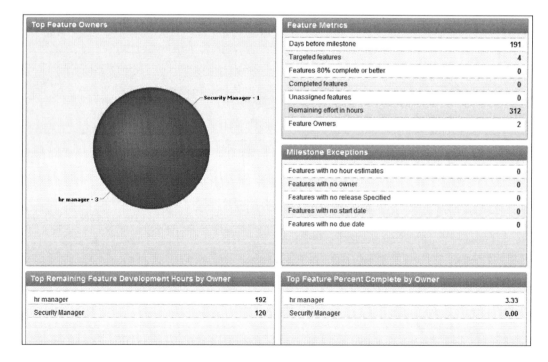

On top of the screen is an Edit button. This is the same as the Edit icon on the **Milestones** tab. Click on it to open the **Milestone Edit** window.

In this window, there are now two new sections to give an overview of the associated To-do's and Features.

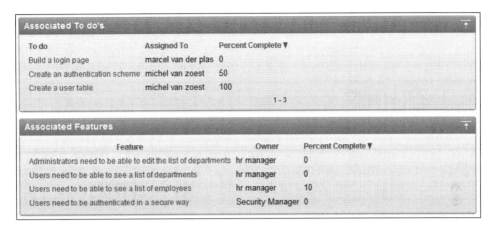

This is also a nice way to keep track of the progress of the project.

The **Milestone Edit** window can also be reached by going to the **Calendar** tab and clicking on the link of the corresponding Milestone. When more Milestones are created, the Project Managers can quickly see the status of their project and take action if necessary.

| | | | March 2011 | | | |
|---|---|---|---|---|---|---|
| Sunday | Monday | Tuesday | Wednesday | Thursday | Friday | Saturday |
| 27 | 28 | 01 | 02 | 03 | 04 | 05 |
| 06 | 07 | 08 | 09 | 10 | 11 | 12 |
| 13 | 14 | 15 | 16 | 17 | 18 | 19 |
| 20 | 21 | 22 | 23 | 24 | 25 | 26 |
| 27 | 28 | 29 • First Demo (project manager) | 30 | 31 | 01 | 02 |

# Using Feedback

When Oracle launched the first Early Adopters Release of Application Express 4.0 on the Amazon EC2 Cloud at `http://www.tryapexnow.com` we could see a feedback link on the application, so people testing APEX 4.0 could quickly send findings to the development team.

This functionality is also available for our own applications. This recipe will show us how we can set up Feedback on an application and handle responses in Team Development.

## Getting ready

In a previous recipe there is an explanation on how we can add a Feedback link on an application. Use this part of the recipe to add a Feedback link to the Navigation Bar of the Enterprise Application we used in the other recipes of this chapter.

Also allow Feedback on the application by editing the Application Properties.

## How to do it...

To have something to work with, we will first create a Feedback entry.

1.  Run the Enterprise Application.

2.  Click on the **Feedback** link in the Navigation Bar.

3.  In the pop-up screen, add the following in the **Feedback** textarea: `The information on the Home page is not complete.`

4.  **Feedback Type** is **General Comment**.

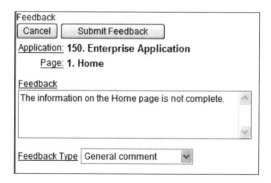

5.  Click on the **Submit Feedback** button.

We can now go back to the **Team Development** environment to process this Feedback. When we open up the Team Development Dashboard, we can see an entry for the Feedback that we have just created among the other pieces of information as seen in the following screenshot:

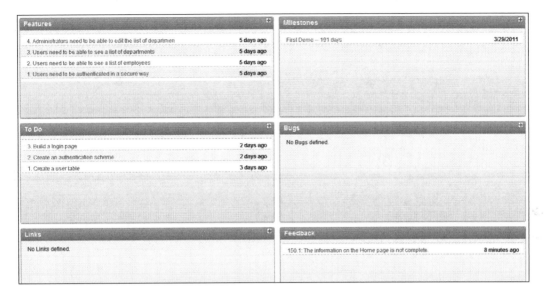

1. Click on the new Feedback entry.

2. This will take us directly into the **Edit Feedback** screen. We can now change the properties of the Feedback and log in.

3. Set **Status** to **1. Acknowledged**.

4. Developer comment is **Still waiting for input from management**.

5. Public Response is **Will be fixed as soon as possible**.

6. Click on **Apply Changes**.

After applying the changes, we are taken to the Feedback overview screen. This overview offers a lot of information about the Feedback, its status, and the environment of the person that gave us the Feedback in the first place.

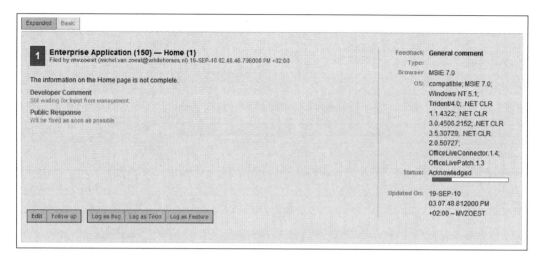

The information about the user environment can be especially important when a bug is reported that is not reported on all web browsers.

We will now log this Feedback as a To Do.

1. Click on the button labeled **Log as Todo**.

2. Enter information for the To-do using the data given in the next steps.

3. **Name** and **Description** are taken from the Feedback, so they can stay the same.

4. **Release** is **0.2**.

5. **Assigned To** is **Project Manager.**

6. **To do status** is **Work Progressing – 50%.**

7. Click on the **Create To Do** button.

It can now be found among the other entries in the Todo section. All information is already available, except for the Milestone. Follow the steps in the previous recipe to assign the Milestone as well.

## There's more...

Now that we have filled our Team Development environment with Milestones, Features,
To-Do's, Bugs, and Feedback, we can take a look at an overview.

1. Go to the **Team Development** main overview.

2. In the **Team Actions** list on the right-hand side of the screen click on
   **Release Summary**.

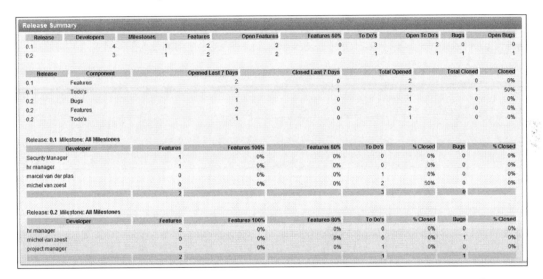

The overview that is now presented shows all kinds of information about the available
releases in the workspace as shown in the preceding screenshot. This overview can
also be used to follow the progress of development.

# Using follow-ups

We have facilitated the users of our application to send Feedback to the development team.
However, we have not implemented an option for the team to receive follow-up information
about their Feedback yet.

There are several possibilities to return follow-up information to the user. The least
appealing would be to create a new APEX account for the user so he can look into
Team Development himself.

Another option would be to return an e-mail whenever a follow-up is produced.

A third option that we will explain further in this recipe is to build a page using built-in APEX views.

## Getting ready

Make sure that the environment created in the previous recipe on *Using Feedback* is available.

## How to do it...

In the first place, we have to create some follow-up.

1. Go to **Team Development**.
2. Navigate to the **Feedback** section and select the **Feedback** tab on the overview.
3. Go to the expanded view.
4. Press the **Follow up** button on the Feedback entry.
5. In the **Enter follow up** text area, enter We have added more information.
6. Click on **Create Follow Up**.

Now, we have to communicate this new information to the user.

First, we'll build a simple Interactive Report to show all feedback given by the current user.

1. Go to **Enterprise Application** in the **Application Builder**.
2. Click on **Create Page**.
3. Select **Report** and click on **Next**.
4. Select **Interactive Report** and press **Next**.
5. Name the Page and Region Feedback Overview and click on **Next**.
6. Select **Use an existing tab set and create a new tab within the existing tab set** from the radio group and enter the **New Tab Label** text as Feedback.
7. Click on **Next**.
8. Use the following query in the SQL Statement area:

```
select feedback_id
     , feedback_number
     , feedback
     , public_response
  from apex_team_feedback
 where logging_apex_user = :APP_USER
[9672_12_01.sql]
```

9. Change **Link to Single Row View** to **No** and click on **Next**.

10. Click on **Finish**.

We now have a page that will show some information about the logged Feedback that the application user has added.

Now, we'll create a page to show the follow-ups for this Feedback.

1. Go to the **Enterprise Application** in the **Application Builder**.

2. Click on **Create Page**.

3. Select **Report** and click on **Next**.

4. Select **Interactive Report** and click on **Next**.

5. Name the Page and Region Feedback follow-up and click on **Next**.

6. Select **Use an existing tab set and reuse an existing tab within that tab set** from the radio group and click on **Next**.

7. Select the Feedback tab from the pulldown list and click on **Next**.

8. Use the following query in the **SQL Statement** area (change P7 if your page has another ID).

```
select follow_up
  from apex_team_feedback_followup
 where feedback_id = :P7_FEEDBACK_ID
[9672_12_02.sql]
```

9. Change **Link to Single Row View** to **No** and click on **Next.**

10. Click on **Finish**.

11. Click on **Edit Page**.

12. Right-click on the Feedback follow-up region and select **Create Page Item**.

13. Select **Hidden** and click on **Next**.

14. Name it P7_FEEDBACK_ID (or change the page number according to what your situation might be) and click on **Next.**

15. Set **Value Protected** to **No** and click on **Next.**

16. Click on **Create Item**.

Now, we just have to link the two pages together.

1. Go to the **Feedback Overview Page** in the **Application Builder**.

2. Right-click on the **Feedback Overview** region and select **Edit Report Attributes**.

3. Press on the pencil icon next to **FEEDBACK_ID**.

4. Scroll down to the **Column Link** section.

5. Enter #FEEDBACK_ID# into the **Link Text** (or use the shortcut under the text item).

6. Make sure target is set to **Page in this Application** and enter 7 (or the number of your page) into the **Page** field.

7. In the **Item List** set **Name** to **P7_FEEDBACK_ID** and Value to **#FEEDBACK_ID#** for item 1.

8. Click on **Apply Changes** twice.

9. Run the **Feedback Overview Page** logging in as the user that entered the Feedback earlier in the recipe.

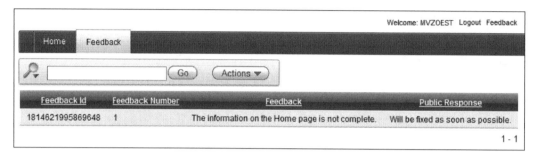

As we can see, the Feedback we entered in the recipe *Using Feedback* in this chapter is shown in the preceding screenshot.

Click on the link on the FeedbackId column to see the next page as shown in the following screenshot:

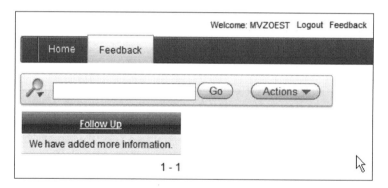

And there we have it. This is a very simple page, but it can be expanded much further.

## How it works...

Application Express in general and Team Development in particular offer some built-in views to select information directly from the database. Two of those views have been shown here: `apex_team_feedback` and `apex_team_feedback_followup`.

Besides the columns that we have used in the example, much more information can be gathered to use to our advantage.

# 13
# HTML5 and CSS3

In this chapter, we will cover:

- ▸ Using a responsive HTML5 and CSS3 template
- ▸ Creating a form with HTML5 item types
- ▸ Creating a UI with drag-and-drop
- ▸ Creating storage events
- ▸ Geolocation – creating a tracker
- ▸ Creating a video plug-in
- ▸ Creating HTML5 charts

## Introduction

HTML5 is the new industry standard for formatting web pages. Its predecessor HTML 4.0 has been around since December 1997, so a new version has been long overdue.

**HTML** (**Hypertext Markup Language**) is the language in which all of the World Wide Web speaks to browsers like Google Chrome, Internet Explorer, Firefox, Safari, and so on. Because HTML is a standard enforced by the **W3C** (**World Wide Web Consortium**), all browsers have agreed to handle HTML code in roughly the same manner.

Because Application Express also generates HTML, this development also brings new opportunities to use in APEX applications.

Despite HTML5 still being in draft at the time of writing this, most of the browsers and many websites already support and use the new features that HTML5 brings. These features include things like new tags and item types and many others.

Also available in APEX is support for the third version of Cascading Style Sheets, better known as CSS3. CSS supports the separation of content and style. Things like font size, background color and many more style elements are defined separately from the content of a website. Thus, it's possible to quickly change the look of a complete web application by just changing a single property.

In CSS3, many more functions and features are introduced. But just like HTML5, the standard is not yet fully ratified. Not all browsers offer full support, but that's likely to change in the near future as well.

APEX already offers the possibility to use the new CSS3 features, so it will be ready for the ratification of the new standard.

This chapter will show several recipes for using HTML5 and CSS3 in an APEX application.

# Using a responsive HTML5 and CSS3 template

The new standards for HTML5 and CSS3 can already be used in APEX applications. To create such an application we can use one of the special HTML5 and CSS3 templates.

Some of these templates can also be used as a responsive theme. Responsiveness not only allows the application to be highly scalable on any screen size (items will move automatically according to the screen size it is shown on), but it also supports gestures that are common on those types of devices, such as pinching, swiping, and flicking.

This recipe will show how to create an APEX application using a responsive HTML5 and CSS3 theme.

## Getting ready

The only thing necessary to start this recipe is an Application Express 4.2 (or higher) installation on your device.

## How to do it...

The next steps will show how to create an application that uses an HTML5 template:

1. Click on **Application Builder** and click on **Create**.

2. Select **Database** and click on **Next**.

3. Enter an application ID and name. Leave the **Create Options** as **Include Home Page** and **User Interface** as **Desktop**, and click on **Next**.

4. Click on **Next** again until we reach the page to select the **User Interface Theme**.

   On this page, we can see several selectable themes. Some of them show the HTML5 logo on its thumbnail preview (themes 23, 24, 25 and 26). These themes allow usage of HTML5.

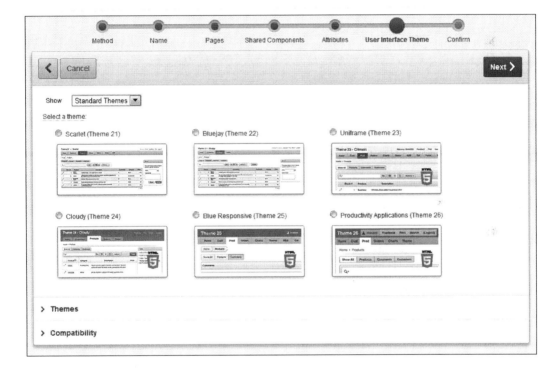

5. Select **Blue Responsive (Theme 25)** and click on **Next**.

6. Click on **Create Application**.

## How it works...

Blue Responsive (Theme 25) is (as its name indicates) a responsive theme. For instance, when we open this new application in a browser on a tablet, it will automatically resize to fit the size of the screen. But that's not all it does. When the screen is turned from landscape to portrait or vice versa, the application will change along with it.

## There's more...

This theme also supports the use of CSS3 elements. We'll now see how to implement some of these features in the form of a styled button:

1.  Open **Page 1** of **Application Builder**.

2.  Create a new HTML region on this page.

3.  Add an item-type button to this region.

4.  Switch the **Application Builder** view to **Component View**.

5.  On the page section click on **Edit**.

6.  In the section **CSS** add the following code to the **Inline** item:

```css
/* button */
.button {
    display: inline-block;
    zoom: 1;
    *display: inline;
    vertical-align: baseline;
    margin: 0 2px;
    outline: none;
    cursor: pointer;
    text-align: center;
    text-decoration: none;
    font: 14px/100% Arial, Helvetica, sans-serif;
    padding: .5em 2em .55em;
    text-shadow: 0 1px 1px rgba(0,0,0,.3);
    -webkit-border-radius: .5em;
    -moz-border-radius: .5em;
    border-radius: .5em;
    -webkit-box-shadow: 0 1px 2px rgba(0,0,0,.2);
    -moz-box-shadow: 0 1px 2px rgba(0,0,0,.2);
    box-shadow: 0 1px 2px rgba(0,0,0,.2);
}
.button:hover {
    text-decoration: none;
}
```

```css
.button:active {
  position: relative;
  top: 1px;
}

/* blue */
.blue {
  color: #d9eef7;
  border: solid 1px #0076a3;
  background: #0095cd;
  background: -webkit-gradient(linear, left top, left
    bottom, from(#00adee), to(#0078a5));
  background: -moz-linear-gradient(top,  #00adee,
    #0078a5);
  filter:
    progid:DXImageTransform.Microsoft.gradient(startColorstr='#
    00adee', endColorstr='#0078a5');
}
.blue:hover {
  background: #007ead;
  background: -webkit-gradient(linear, left top, left
    bottom, from(#0095cc), to(#00678e));
  background: -moz-linear-gradient(top,  #0095cc,
    #00678e);
  filter:
    progid:DXImageTransform.Microsoft.gradient(startColorstr='#
    0095cc', endColorstr='#00678e');
}
.blue:active {
  color: #80bed6;
  background: -webkit-gradient(linear, left top, left
    bottom, from(#0078a5), to(#00adee));
  background: -moz-linear-gradient(top,  #0078a5,
    #00adee);
  filter:
    progid:DXImageTransform.Microsoft.gradient(startColorstr='#
    0078a5', endColorstr='#00adee');
}
```

This code will alter the appearance of buttons when the right class is chosen. There are several CSS3 specific pieces of code, such as `gradient` and `shadow`. More information about these and other options can be found on websites such as `http://www.w3.org/Style/CSS/` and `http://www.w3schools.com/css3/`.

7. Click on **Apply Changes**.

8. Click on the button name we created in step 3 to edit it.

9. Go to the **Attributes** section.

10. For the property **Style**, select **HTML Button**.

11. In the property **CSS Classes**, enter `button blue` according to the two main CSS classes in the code we entered.

12. Click on **Apply Changes**.

13. Run the page in a CSS3 compliant browser such as Google Chrome or Safari to see the effects.

14. When the browser supports CSS3, the button will be shown as a blue button with rounded corners. If we hover with the mouse pointer over the button, its color will change to a darker gradient. When the button is pressed, the color will change again as well as the color of the text.

## See also

▸ The recipe, *Creating a form with HTML5 item types*, will explain how to use HTML5 features.

# Creating a form with HTML5 item types

With the introduction of Application Express 4.2, Oracle decided to add native support for several HTML5 item types. By adding this support, it is now possible to use these item types like you would use any other item type.

This recipe will show how to use these item types in an APEX application.

## Getting ready

First, we have to make sure that we have an application available that uses a template that supports HTML5. To do so, follow the steps in the previous recipe.

Also we have to make sure that the database schema we are using for this application has access to the EMP table.

## How to do it...

First of all, we need to add a form to **Page 1**, so we can add some items.

1. In the new application that uses Theme 25, find the blank **Page 1** in **Application Builder** and open it.

2. Right-click on **Regions** and click on **Create** to start making a new region.

3. Select **Form** and click on **Next**.

4. Select **Form on a Table or View** and click on **Next**.

5. Under **Table / View Name**, select the option **EMP (table)**, and click on **Next**.

6. Change the name and title to **Employees** and click on **Next**.

7. Select **Managed by Database (ROWID)** and click on **Next**.

   This option eliminates the need for a primary key sequence in this case. This is not recommended in production environments, but will suffice for this demonstration.

8. Make sure all columns are selected to the right of the shuttle-item and click on **Next**.

9. Leave all options as they are and click on **Next**.

10. Enter 1 for both **After Page Submit and Processing Branch to Page** and **When Cancel Button Pressed Branch to Page** and click on **Next**.

11. Finally click on **Create** to create the Form region.

Now when we run the page, we can see the form is made up of several standard items. With the exception of the **Hiredate** (a date column in a table is automatically shown as a calendar item in APEX), all items are simple text items.

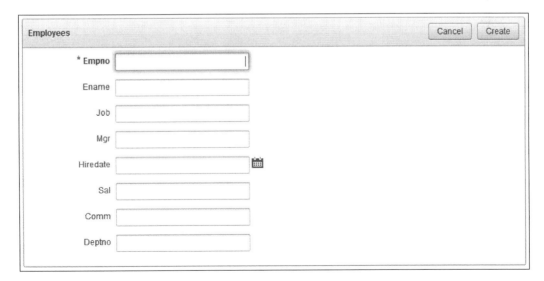

To enhance this form, make it more appealing to end users, and easier to use, we are going to change some of the items into native HTML5 item types.

1.  Edit **Page 1** and expand the items node under the **Employees** region.

2.  Double-click the **P1_HIREDATE** item.

3.  Find the attribute labeled **Display As** and expand the listbox next to it.

4.  Click on the last item **Show Unsupported**.

5.  Re-expand the listbox and now select the option **Date Picker (HTML5) [Unsupported]**.

    This item is shown as 'Unsupported', not because it's impossible to use in your application, but because it is enhanced for usage in another type of User Interface.

6.  Click on **Apply Changes**.

7.  Run the page to see the results.

The first thing that can be noticed, is that the item shows the format mask when no data is yet selected.

Remember that we saw the HTML5 Calendar item type was unsupported? When we open this page in a browser on a mobile device such as a tablet or smartphone, we can see that the item is now actually looking pretty good.

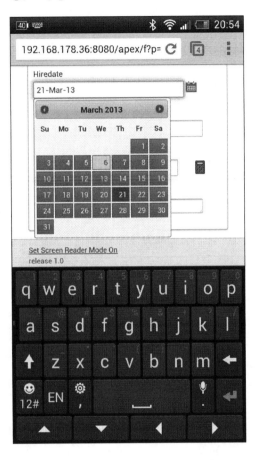

In this manner, other item types can be used as well. For instance, when a field requires a choice of two values, the **Yes/No** item can be used.

Another change that is now available, is an enhancement to the regular text field in the following manner:

1. Return to the **Employees** region and double-click on the **P1_ENAME** item.

2. Scroll down to the **Settings** section.

3. In the attribute **Subtype**, select the option **E-mail**.

4. Click on **Apply Changes**.

Other types that are available are **URL** and **Phone Number**. These subtypes tell the browser to do a pre-check on the contents of the item. An e-mail address should always hold a username, an @ sign and a domain. Also the browser on a mobile device will change the on-screen keyboard to ease the entry of e-mail addresses. The lay-out will change slightly with the @ sign available for input directly and a shortcut to . com.

When viewed on another device, for example, an Apple iPad, it will look a bit different. This shows that there is no coding necessary to make an application look good on several different devices.

If an item is created with type **Phone Number**, the layout of the keyboard will be changed to be able to quickly type numbers and other signs that are used in a phone number.

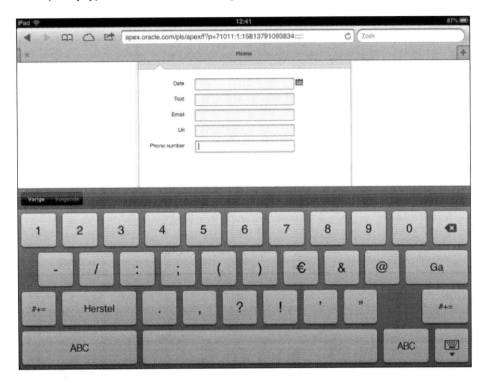

## How it works...

In the new W3C standard for HTML5, several new features are described and standardized. Unfortunately not all of these features are available in all browsers as the standard is not yet fully ratified at the time of writing this recipe.

This can be seen when the page is run and the text item that is using the E-mail subtype is filled with data. The validation is not performed when the form is submitted.

When inspecting the element with a tool like Firebug for the Firefox browser, the structure of the form can be seen:

```
<form id="wwvFlowForm" novalidate="" name="wwv_flow" method="post"
    action="wwv_flow.accept">
```

The option `novalidate` is added to the form declaration. This ensures that validations like the ones for E-mail, URL, and Phone Number are not executed.

In conclusion, we can say that APEX supports the creation of many HTML5 item types, but not all of them are usable yet, or not yet on all browsers and devices. Support for those item types will be available for future use when the HTML5 standard is finalized and browsers fully support it.

Developers should be aware of these issues when building applications.

## There's more...

Most of the HTML5 item types are created to facilitate easier data entry on several devices. Tablets and smartphones normally don't have a physical keyboard and they hold smaller (touch) screens. To support these differences from a laptop or desktop computer, HTML5 item types often require less usage of a keyboard or use large buttons.

Let's use some more HTML5 item types on our page. These are examples of a slider and a calculator item.

1. Double-click the **P1_COMM** item.
2. Go to the **Display As** listbox and choose **Slider [Unsupported]**.
3. Scroll down to the **Settings** section.
4. In the attribute **Minimum Value** enter 0.
5. In the attribute **Maximum Value** enter 1000.
6. In **Step Increment** enter 100.

   This will create a Slider item in which users can change values from 0 to 1000 in steps of 100 by simply sliding their finger over the item.

   Another item type that enhances a normal text field, is the Calculator Popup.

7. Return to the **Employees** region and double-click on the **P1_SAL** item.
8. Go to the **Display As** listbox and choose **Text Field with Calculator Popup**.
9. Click on **Apply Changes**.

When running the page with this item, we can see an icon that looks like a calculator next to the field. When clicking this icon, a pop up will show where a calculation can be made before the value is sent back to the item.

## See also

▶ *Chapter 14, Mobile,* will also show some item types new to APEX 4.2 specifically for smartphone devices.

# Creating a UI with drag-and-drop

Drag-and-drop is another new feature of HTML5. It was already possible to create drag-and-drop objects in web pages, but you needed to include a JavaScript library like jQuery or Prototype. As of HTML5, drag-and-drop is native supported by the use of a drag-and-drop API.

Drag-and-drop can offer a user-friendly user interface, where the user can easily move objects. We will create a web page where the user can drag-and-drop employees to other departments. On dropping the employee, the table EMP is updated with the new DEPTNO.

## Getting ready

Make sure, you have access to the EMP and DEPT tables. We will use these tables to demonstrate how easy it is to move an employee from one department to another department, using the drag-and-drop functionality.

## How to do it...

First, we will create the page:

1. In **Application Builder**, click on **Create Page**.
2. Click on **Blank Page**.
3. Enter the desired page number or leave the default value. Click on **Next**.
4. Enter a name for the page, for example, Reorganise Teams. Click on **Next**.
5. Select whether you like to use tabs or not. Click on **Next**.
6. Click on **Finish**.

    The page is created. Now we will add some CSS code.

7. Click the **Edit Page** button
8. In the **Page** section, click on the **Edit** icon

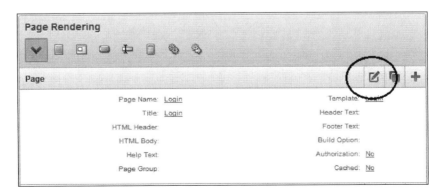

9. Click on the **CSS** tab.

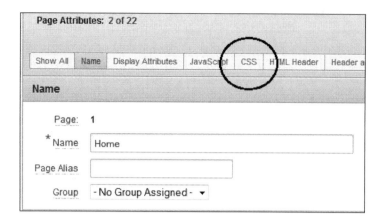

10. In the **Inline** text area, enter the following CSS code:

```
/* CSS code for the div where the employee can be dropped */
.dropdiv {
    border: 2px solid #838383;
    box-shadow: 3px 3px 3px #BDBEBD;
    border-radius: 5px 5px 5px 5px;
    display: block;
    min-height: 300px;
    width: 200px;
    padding: 16px;
    text-decoration: none;
    margin-right: 10px;
}
/* CSS code for the H1 tag */
h1 {
    font: bold 21px/21px Helvetica, Arial, Sans-serif;
    text-shadow: 0px -1px 2px rgba(0, 0, 0, 0.5);
    margin: 0px;
    -moz-box-flex: 1;
    text-align: center;
}
/* CSS code for the div to be dragged */
.dnddiv {
    background-image: linear-gradient(#A4A4A4, #848484);
    background-image: -o-linear-gradient(#A4A4A4, #848484);
    background-image: -moz-linear-gradient(#A4A4A4, #848484);
    background-image: -webkit-linear-gradient(#A4A4A4, #848484);
    background-image: -ms-linear-gradient(#A4A4A4, #848484);
```

```
        border: 1px solid #848484;
        cursor: pointer;
        display: block;
        min-height: 10px;
        width: 50px;
        padding: 4px;
        text-decoration: none;
        margin-bottom: 8px;
    }
    /* CSS code for the div to be dragged, when hovered with the mouse
    */
    .dnddiv:hover {
        box-shadow: 0px 1px 8px #BDBEBD;
        background-image: linear-gradient(#F4F4F4, #A4A4A4);
        background-image: -o-linear-gradient(#F4F4F4, #A4A4A4);
        background-image: -moz-linear-gradient(#F4F4F4, #A4A4A4);
        background-image: -webkit-linear-gradient(#F4F4F4, #A4A4A4);
        background-image: -ms-linear-gradient(#F4F4F4, #A4A4A4);
        border: 1px solid #151515;
        cursor: pointer;
        display: block;
        min-height: 10px;
        width: 50px;
        padding: 4px;
        text-decoration: none;
        margin-bottom: 8px;
    }
    [9672_13_01.txt]
```

11. Click the **Apply Changes** button.

12. Now, we will add the JavaScript code:

13. In the **Page** section, click the **edit** icon.

14. Click the **Javascript** tab.

15. In the **Function and Global Variable Declaration** text area, enter the following code:

```
function handle_drop_over(evt) {
  evt.preventDefault();
}

function handle_drag(evt) {
  evt.dataTransfer.setData("Text",evt.target.id);
}

function handle_drop(obj,evt) {
```

```
    evt.preventDefault();
    var data=evt.dataTransfer.getData("Text");
    evt.target.appendChild(document.getElementById(data));
    var ajaxRequest = new htmldb_Get(null,&APP_ID.,'APPLICATION_
PROCESS=save_emp_dept',0);
    ajaxRequest.add('PXX_EMPNO',data);
    ajaxRequest.add('PXX_DEPTNO',obj.id);
    ajaxResult = ajaxRequest.get();
}
[9672_13_02.txt]
```

In the above code, XX is the number of the page.

The three functions handle different events. The `handle_drop_over` function is called by the `ondragover` event and prevents the default handling of the element. Otherwise, you cannot use the element as a drop item. The `handle_drag` function copies the data from the dragged element, so that it can be used in the update. The `handle_drop` function calls an application process (`save_emp_dept`). The application process does the actual update.

16. Click on **Apply Changes**.

17. Now, we will create a PL/SQL region.

18. In the **Regions** section, click the Add icon.

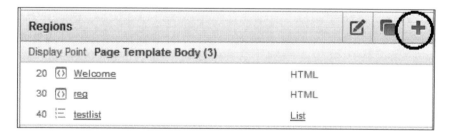

19. Click on **PL/SQL Dynamic Content**.

20. Enter a title. Click on **Next**.

21. In the **PL/SQL** source, enter the following code:

```
Declare
--Cursor to select the deptno and dname from
--the dept table.
--Put the output in a div to enable the
```

```
--Drop functions on the department
  cursor c_dept is
    select '<div class="dropdiv" id="'||deptno||'"
ondrop="handle_drop(this,event)" ondragover="handle_drop_
over(event)"><h1>'||dname||'</h1><br>' dropdept
    , deptno
    from dept;
  --
  -- cursor to select the empno and ename from
  -- the emp table. Put the output in a div
  -- to enable drag functions on the employee
  cursor c_emp (b_deptno in number) is
    select '<div id="'||empno||'" class="dnddiv" draggable="true"
ondragstart="handle_drag(event)">'||ename||'</div>' dragline
    from emp
    where deptno = b_deptno;
begin
  --Use a HTML table to format the output
  sys.htp.print('<table>');
  sys.htp.print('<tr>');
  for r_dept in c_dept
  loop
    sys.htp.print('<td>');
    sys.htp.print(r_dept.dropdept);
    for r_emp in c_emp(r_dept.deptno)
    loop
      sys.htp.print(r_emp.dragline);
    end loop;
    sys.htp.print('</div>');
    sys.htp.print('</td>');
  end loop;
  sys.htp.print('</tr>');
  sys.htp.print('</table>');
end;
[9672_13_03.txt]
```

22. Click on **Next**.

23. Click on **Create Region**.

Two hidden items need to be created:

1. In the **Items** section, click on the Add icon.

2. Click on **Hidden**.
3. In the **Name** text field, enter PXX_EMPNO. Click on **Next**.
4. Click on **Next**.
5. Click on **Create Item**.
6. In the **Items** section, click on the Add icon.
7. Click on **Hidden**.
8. In the **Name** text field, enter PXX_DEPTNO. Click on **Next**.
9. Click on **Next**.
10. Click on **Create Item**.
11. To create an AJAX process, go to **Shared Components | Application Processes**.

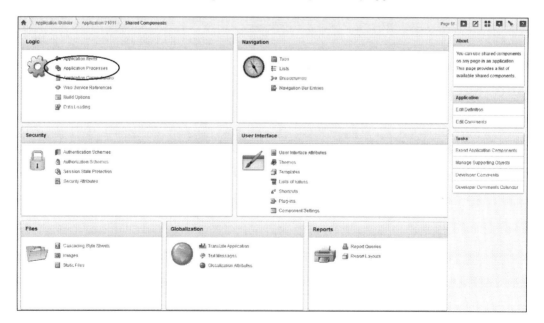

12. Click on the **Create** button.

13. In the **Name** text field, enter `save_emp_dept`.

14. In the **Point** listbox, select **On Demand: Run this application process when requested by a page process**. Click on **Next**.

15. In the **Process Text** text area, enter the following code:

```
begin
   update emp
   set     deptno = :PXX_DEPTNO
   where   empno  = :PXX_EMPNO;
   --
end;
[9672_13_04.txt]
```

16. Click on **Next**.

17. Click on **Create Process**.

The page is ready. Run it and try to move employees to other departments.

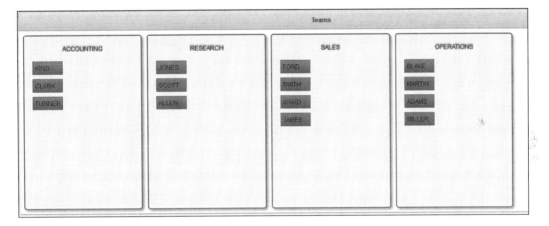

## How it works...

For the drag-and-drop feature we make use of a div. The advantage of a div is that you can give them an ID so that they can be found (DOM object) and divs can be made draggable using the attributes `draggable` and `ondragstart`, or droppable using `ondrop`. By including the class we can give the div the style which we defined in the CSS part.

The CSS is used to give the object some styling so that they look good. With CSS3, a number of new styles have been added; amongst others, the rounded corners and the shadow effects. There is a style for div where the employees are dropped. This div displays the departments. They have rounded corners, a background color, a margin right to see some spacing between the divs, and they have shadow effects.

The dnddiv style is for the employees. There are two styles for dnddiv: one for the normal display and one that is used when the user hovers over the employee. It will light up and show some shadow effect. The dnddiv style makes use of linear-gradient, which will show two colors changing from one color to another starting at the top and moving to the bottom. To support all browsers, the linear gradient is prefixed by different renderers like webkit (used in Apple Safari and Google Chrome), Mozilla (Firefox), Opera and Microsoft Internet Explorer.

In the JavaScript code, there are functions to support the drag-and-drop. The drop function calls an on-demand page process with the parameters PXX_EMPNO and PXX_DEPTNO. These parameters are used in the page process to update the emp table with the new department. empno can be found using the getData function. The deptno can be found using the ID of the DOM object. In this case, the DOM object is the div holding the employee name. The ID of the div is the empno.

# Creating storage events

With storage events you can store data on your local machine. This is similar to cookies but with storage events you can store more data than cookies. There are two types of storage events:

- ▸ Local storage
- ▸ Session storage

Local storage exists forever, or at least as long as the browser is installed and working. Session storage only holds the value for the lifetime of the session. A session holds the values of the items in an application for the time that a user is logged in in the application.

One important remark is that web storage can have different values for different browsers. Keep that in mind when working with web storage and multiple browsers.

Local storage can be used in APEX applications for user or machine specific settings. We will demonstrate this by putting a line on the login page telling when the last visit was.

## Getting ready

You need to have a global page. This used to be page 0 in previous releases but now it doesn't have to be page 0. It could also be page 8 for example. On a global page you can put items, regions, and page processes that will be displayed or executed on every page in the application. The benefit of this is that you don't have to create items, regions, or page processes on every page but you can reuse them. Since an application can have multiple user interfaces, it can also have multiple global pages. For this recipe we will use the desktop's global page. You can check what the desktop's global page is by going to **Shared Components | User Interface Attributes**. Scroll down to the bottom of the page and check what the global page is for the desktop user interface. If there is no global page you can create one:

1. In **Application Builder**, click on the **Create Page** button.

2. In the **User Interface** radio group, select **Desktop**.

3. Click on the **Global Page** icon.

4. In the next step, check the default page number. You can also enter your own page number if you want to. Click on **Finish**.

5. You now have a global page for the desktop user interface.

## How to do it...

Follow the given steps:

1. In **Application Builder**, Click on the **Global Page** icon.

2. In the **Dynamic Actions** section, click on the Add icon.

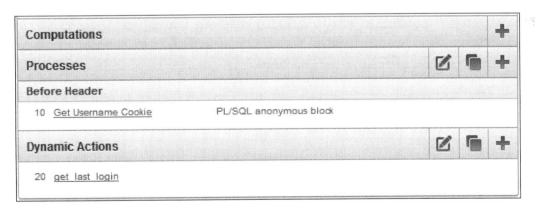

3. In the **Name** text field, enter `set_last_login_time`.

4. Click on **Next**.

5. In the **Event** select list, select **Page Load**.

6. Click on **Next**.

7. In the **Action** select list, select **Execute JavaScript Code**.

8. In the **Code** text area, enter the following JavaScript code:

```
localStorage.last_login_time=new Date();
[9672_13_05.txt]
```

9. Click on **Next**.

10. Click on **Create Dynamic Action**.

11. Click on the **set_last_login_time** dynamic action.

12. In the **Condition** section, select **User is Authenticated (not public)** in the **Condition Type** select list.

13. Click on **Apply Changes** button.

14. Now we need to modify the login page. For the desktop user interface, usually this is page 101. If you want to be sure, you can check it in the application builder. Click on the application so that you get an overview of all pages in the application. Search for the login page for desktop.

15. Click on the **Login Page** link.

16. Click on the **Login** region.

17. In the **Region Source** text area, enter the following code:

```
<div id="last_visit">
</div>
[9672_13_06.txt]
```

18. Click on **Apply Changes**.

19. In the **Dynamic Actions** section, click on the Add icon.

20. In the **Name** text field, enter get_last_login_time. Click on **Next**.

21. In the **Event** select list, select **Page Load**.

22. Click on **Next**.

23. In the **Action** select list, select **Execute Javascript Code**.

24. In the **Code** text area, enter the following code:

```
document.getElementById("last_visit").innerHTML="Last
  successful login on this machine: " +
  localStorage.last_login_time;
[9672_13_07.txt]
```

25. Click on **Next**.

26. Click on **Create Dynamic Action**.

The page is ready. Run the application. Log in, log out, and close the browser. Open the browser again and start the application again. Check that the last successful login is displayed.

## Login

| Username | | |
|----------|----------|-------|
| Password | | Login |

Last successful login on this machine:Sat Mar 09 2013 22:30:17 GMT+0100

## How it works...

We created two dynamic actions: one on the login page and one on the global page (previously page 0). The dynamic action on the login page reads the local storage variable and uses the inner HTML JavaScript function to display the contents. The dynamic action on the global page sets the local storage variable.

# Geolocation – creating a tracker

One of the features of HTML5 is the Geolocation API. The Geolocation API is a set of methods that help you share your location. It has a number of ways to determine your location:

- Using your IP address
- Using your wireless network connection
- Using your cell phone connection
- Using built-in GPS receiver

The most important parameters to show the location are the latitude and the longitude. But there is also the altitude and the accuracy. The Geolocation API can also show the direction you are moving to and the speed.

Sharing your location can be useful in a number of applications on your mobile device. One example is a tracking system where the mobile device stores the coordinates in a table at frequent times. In this way a transport company can see where the vehicles have been. We will create such a tracking system in this recipe. As mobile tracking is typically for mobile devices, we will create a page for mobile devices. Therefore, we will use the jQuery Mobile Smartphone theme.

## Getting ready

You need access to the table GM_COORDINATES. Make sure you have enabled the jQuery Mobile Smartphone theme for this application. If you haven't, please follow the given steps:

1. In **Application Builder**, click on **Shared Components**.

2. In the **User Interface** section, click on **User Interface Attributes**.

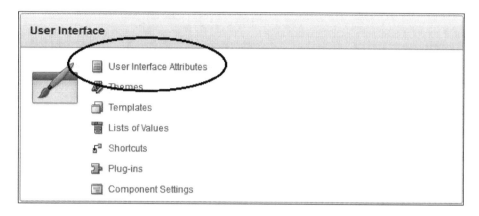

3. Scroll down to the bottom of the page and click on **Add New User Interface**.

4. In the **Type** select list, select **jQuery Mobile Smartphone**.

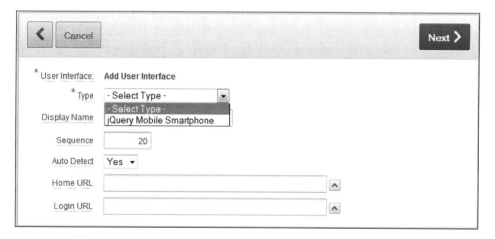

5. Click on **Next**.

6. Click on the **jQuery Mobile Smartphone theme (theme 50)**.

7. Click the **Create** button.

## How to do it...

First we will create the mobile tracking page:

1. Go to **Application Builder** and click on **Create Page**.
2. In the **User Interface** radio group, select **jQuery Mobile Smartphone**.
3. Click on the **Blank Page** icon.
4. Click on **Next**.
5. In the **Name** text field, enter a name for the page, for example `Tracking`.
6. In the **HTML Region 1** text field, enter a name for the region, for example, `Tracking`.
7. Click on **Next**.
8. Click on **Finish**.
9. Click on **Edit Page**.
10. In the **Page** section, click the **Edit Page** icon.
11. Click on the **JavaScript** tab.
12. In the **Function and Global Variable Declaration** text area, enter the following code:

```
--Function to get the location
function get_location_int() {
    if (document.getElementById('PX_SWITCH').value=='Y') {
    navigator.geolocation.getCurrentPosition(loop_coord);
    }
  }

--Function to write the coordinates into a table
  function loop_coord(position) {
    var latitude = position.coords.latitude;
    var longitude = position.coords.longitude;
    var ajaxRequest = new htmldb_Get(null,&APP_ID.,'APPLICATION_
PROCESS=write_coordinate',0);
    ajaxRequest.add('PX_LATITUDE',latitude);
    ajaxRequest.add('PX_LONGITUDE',longitude);
    ajaxResult = ajaxRequest.get();
    document.getElementById('PX_LATITUDE').value = latitude;
    document.getElementById('PX_LONGITUDE').value = longitude;
  }
[9672_13_08.txt]
```

In the above code, x is the number of the page.

13. In the **Execute when Page Loads** text area, enter the following code:

```
setInterval("get_location_int()",document.getElementById('P
   X_INTER  VAL').value);
[9672_13_13.txt]
```

14. Click on the **Apply Changes** button.

15. In the **Items** section, click on the Add icon.

16. Click on **Text Field**.

17. In the **Item Name** text field, enter PX_LATITUDE where X is the number of the page. Click on **Next**.

18. In the **Label** text item, enter Latitude. Click on **Next**.

19. Click on **Next**.

20. Click on **Create Item**.

21. Repeat steps 15 to 19 and name the item PX_LONGITUDE.

22. In the **Items** section, click on the Add icon.

23. Click on **Slider**.

24. In the **Item Name** text field, enter PX_INTERVAL where X is the number of the page. Click on **Next**.

25. In the **Label** text item, enter Interval. Click on **Next**.

26. In the **Minimum Value** text field, enter 1000.

27. In the **Maximum Value** text field, enter 10000.

28. In the **Step Increment** text field, enter 1000.

29. Click on **Next**.

30. Click on **Create Item**.

31. In the **Items** section, click the Add icon.

32. Click on **Yes/No**.

33. In the **Item Name** text field, enter PX_SWITCH where X is the number of the page. Click on **Next**.

34. In the **Label** text item, enter Switch. Click on **Next**.

35. Click on **Next**.

36. Click on **Create Item**.

1. In **Application Builder**, click on **Shared Components**.

2. In the **Logic** section (upper-left corner), click on **Application Processes**.

3. Click on the **Create** button.

4. In the **Name** text field, enter a name for the application process, for example, `write_coordinate`.

5. In the **Point** select list, select **On Demand: run this application process when requested by a page process**. Click on **Next**.

6. In the **Process text** text area, enter the following code:

```
declare
    l_ip_address gm_coordinates.ip_address%type;
begin
    --
    select sys_context('userenv','ip_address')
    into    l_ip_address
    from dual;
    --
    insert into gm_coordinates
    (date_time
    ,ip_address
    ,latitude
    ,longitude)
    values
    (sys_extract_utc(systimestamp)
    ,l_ip_address
    ,:PX_LATITUDE
    ,:PX_LONGITUDE);
    --
end;
[9672_13_09.txt]
```

Where X is the page number of the page that is being created.

7. Click on **Next**.

8. Click on **Create Process**.

The page and the page process are ready now. Run the page, preferably on a mobile device, set the interval and set the switch on. The page will show the latitude and longitude and refreshes every *x* seconds, dependent on the interval set.

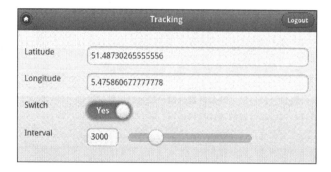

When you start this page in a browser for the first time, you might get the question to enable location services. Enable this to be able to get the coordinates.

Most mobile phones will dim the screen after a number of seconds. When the screen is dimmed, the page will most probably not work. Set the timeout to a number of minutes to keep the device on and working.

## How it works...

The new thing in APEX 4.2 is that you can enter the JavaScript code at header level without having to use the `<script>` tags. Just put the JavaScript code there and it will work. The same goes for `$function` which was used previously to execute JavaScript code as a first action when the web page was opened and all libraries and so on were loaded. The code that needs to be executed when opening a web page can be put in the **Execute when page loads** text area.

When opening the page, an interval is set. The timeout of the interval is determined by the slider. The interval calls a JavaScript function and in that function, the switch is checked. When set to `Yes`, it will call the Geolocation API.

The Geolocation API can be used via a so-called callback function. A call to the API is made and the result is passed in another called function.

The coordinates can be fetched using the following code:

```
navigator.geolocation.getCurrentPosition(callback function);
```

In the `callback function` as a parameter of `getCurrentPosition`, the latitude and longitude can be fetched. An on-demand page process is called where the coordinates are stored in the table `GM_COORDINATES`.

# Creating a video plug-in

With HTML5, two new tags are introduced: audio and video. This tag should make an end to all the struggles with browsers or operating systems that do not support Flash. Simply include the video or audio tag and add the source. We will create a page with a video player in it using the video tag. Since APEX does not have a native support for video or audio, we will have to create it ourselves. We can do that with an item type plug-in.

## Getting ready

For this recipe you need at least one video file of the type Ogg, MP4, or WebM. If you only have a video file in just one format available, and you want to have this file also in another format, you can convert it. An easy way to convert files is by using VLC media player. You can convert to Ogg, as well as to MP4 or WebM.

Mind that Ogg video files have an extension .ogv. MP4 video files can also have an extension .mov.

## How to do it...

Follow the given steps:

1. In **Application Builder**, click on **Shared Components**.
2. In the **User Interface** section, click on **Plug-ins**.
3. Click on **Create**.
4. In the **Name** section, enter Video in the **Name** text field.
5. In the **Internal Name** text field, enter the reversed domain name, for example, com.packtpub.video.
6. Make sure the type select list shows **Item**.
7. In the **Source** section, enter the following code in the **PL/SQL code** text area:

```
function render_video (
    p_item                  in apex_plugin.t_page_item,
    p_plugin                in apex_plugin.t_plugin,
    p_value                 in varchar2,
    p_is_readonly           in boolean,
    p_is_printer_friendly in boolean )
    return apex_plugin.t_page_item_render_result
is
  -- for every attribute a variable
```

```
    l_video_src_webm  apex_application_page_items.attribute_01%type
 := p_item.attribute_01;
    l_video_src_ogg   apex_application_page_items.attribute_02%type
 := p_item.attribute_02;
    l_video_src_mp4   apex_application_page_items.attribute_03%type
 := p_item.attribute_03;
    l_video_cap       apex _application_page_items.attribute_04%type
 := p_item.attribute_04;
    l_result          apex_plugin.t_page_item_render_result;
 begin
   -- print the video tag
   -- when available, print the source tag for the
   -- different types
   sys.htp.p('<video width="640" height="480" controls="controls"
 >');
   if l_video_src_mp4 is not null
   then
      sys.htp.p('<source src="'||l_video_src_mp4||'" type="video/
 mp4" />');
   end if;
   if l_video_src_webm is not null
   then
      sys.htp.p('<source src="'||l_video_src_webm||'" type="video/
 webm" />');
   end if;
   if l_video_src_ogg is not null
   then
      sys.htp.p('<source src="'||l_video_src_ogg||'" type="video/
 ogg" />');
   end if;
   -- When the browser is not able
   -- to display one of the three sources, it will display
   -- the message below
   sys.htp.p('Your browser does not support the video tag.');
   sys.htp.p('</video>');
   --
   return l_result;
 end render_video;
```

8. In the **Callbacks** section, enter `render_video` in the **Render Function Name** text field.

9. In the **User Interfaces** section you can select for which user interface this plug-in is supported. So if you want to use this plug-in for a mobile page, then check the **jQuery Mobile Smartphone** checkbox.

10. Click on **Create Plug-in**. In the **Custom Attributes** section, Click on the **Add Attribute** button.

11. In the **Attribute** text field, enter 1. In the **Label** text field, enter `Webm type filename`. Click on **Create and Create Another**.

12. In the **Attribute** text field, enter 2. In the **Label** text field, enter `Ogg type filename`. Click on **Create and Create Another**.

13. In the **Attribute** text field, enter 3. In the **Label** text field, enter `Mp4 type filename`. Click on **Create and Create Another**.

14. In the **Attribute** text field, enter 4. In the **Label** text field, enter `Video`. Click on **Create**.

15. Click on the **Create Plug-in** button.

The plug-in is ready now. You can use this plug-in in your web page. Next, we will create the region:

1. In the **Application Builder**, click on the **Create Page** button.

2. Click on the **Blank Page** icon.

3. Enter a page number or leave the proposed page number. Click on **Next.**

4. In the **Name** text field, enter a name for the page, for example, `Video page`. Click on **Next**.

5. Select **Do Not Use Tabs**. Click on **Next**.

6. Click on **Finish**.

7. Click on **Edit Page**.

8. In the **Regions** section, click on the **Add Region** button (the **+** sign).

9. Click on the **HTML region** icon.

10. Click on the HTML icon.

11. In the **Title** text field, enter a title for the region, for example, `video`. Click on **Next**.

12. In the **HTML text** region source, you can enter text, something like `Check this video!`. Click on **Next**.

13. Click on the **Create Region** button.

The region is ready and now we can add the video plug-in to the region:

1. In the **Items** section, click on the **Add Item** icon.

2. Click on the **Plug-Ins** icon.

3. Select the **video** plug-in and click on **Next**.

4. In the **Item Name** text field, enter a name for the item, for example, `P2_VIDEO`. Click on **Next**.

5. Enter a label for this plug-in. Click on **Next**.

6. In the **Filename** text fields, enter the names of the video files.

7. Enter some text for the video caption. Click on **Next**.

8. Click on **Create Item**.

You now have a page with a HTML5 video. Click run to see it working.

## How it works...

The plug-in is rendered and results in the following HTML code:

```
<video width="640" height="480" controls="controls" >
  <source src="fruitbowl.mp4" type="video/mp4" />
  <source src="fruitbowl.webm" type="video/webm" />
  <source src="fruitbowl.ogv" type="video/ogg" />
  Your browser does not support the video tag.
</video>
```

The code starts with the `video` tag and this tag can have several attributes like `width` and `height`. Inside the `video` tag you can find the source. HTML5 can handle three different video types: MP4, WebM, and Ogg. Most browsers cannot handle all three types. If a browser cannot display a video file mentioned in the `source` tag, this tag is ignored. That is why, it is good practice to include all three of them in the `video` tag. If a browser cannot play the first one (MP4), it will try to play the second one (WebM). Otherwise, it will try to play the third option (Ogg). If the browser is not able to play one of the three video files at all, it will show the text that is put after the three `source` tags. In this case, you will see the message `Your browser does not support the video tag`.

The files can be referenced from a website, but you can also upload the images by going to **Shared Components | Images**. In that case, be sure to use the `#WORKSPACE_IMAGES#` prefix.

Unfortunately, despite the fact that HTML5 video should work on all browsers that support HTML5, it is not 100 percent guaranteed that this will always work. This recipe is tested on the four most important browsers (Internet Explorer 9 64 bit, Mozilla Firefox 19.0, Google Chrome, Apple Safari), tablets and mobile phones (Samsung Galaxy S2 with Google Chrome).

As the `video` tag is part of the HTML5 standard, it is also part of the DOM, which makes it possible to format the video with CSS.

# Creating HTML5 charts

With APEX you can include charts in your web page. In earlier versions of APEX, it was already possible to create charts but those charts were based on Flash. To support browsers that cannot handle Flash, an HTML5 chart can be used. When you create a Flash chart, APEX has a built-in fallback to a HTML5 chart, which means that when a browser is unable to display the Flash chart, it will show the HTML5 chart substitute.

However, you can also directly create HTML5 charts. In this recipe we will show how to create a HTML5 chart.

## Getting ready

Make sure you have access to the GM_COORDINATES table.

## How to do it...

Follow the given steps:

1. In **Application Builder**, click on the **Create Page** button.
2. Click on the **Chart** icon. Mind the **User Interface** radio button.

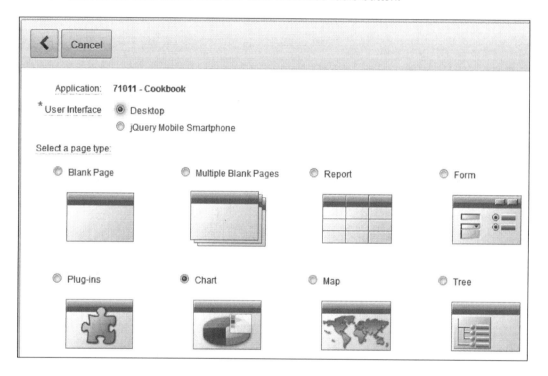

3. When the **User Interface** radio button in the previous step was set to **jQuery Mobile Smartphone**, you will now only see **HTML5 Chart**. Otherwise you will be able to choose between **Flash Chart** and **HTML5 Chart**. In that case, select **HTML5 Chart**.
4. Click on the **Column** icon.
5. Click on the **2D column** icon.
6. Enter a page number, page name, and region name or leave the default settings. Click on **Next**.
7. Select a tab set or leave the tab options to **Do not use tabs**. Click on **Next**.
8. In the **Chart Title** text field, enter a title for the chart. Click on **Next**.

9. In the text area, enter the following query and click on **Next**:

```
-- query to select the number of recorded
-- coordinates in one day
SELECT NULL LINK
     ,      trunc(date_time) date_time
     ,      count(trunc(date_time)) value
FROM    gm_coordinates
group by trunc(date_time)
[9672_13_11.txt]
```

10. Check the summary page and if everything is okay, then click on **Create**.

11. The page is ready now. Click on **Run Page** to see the result.

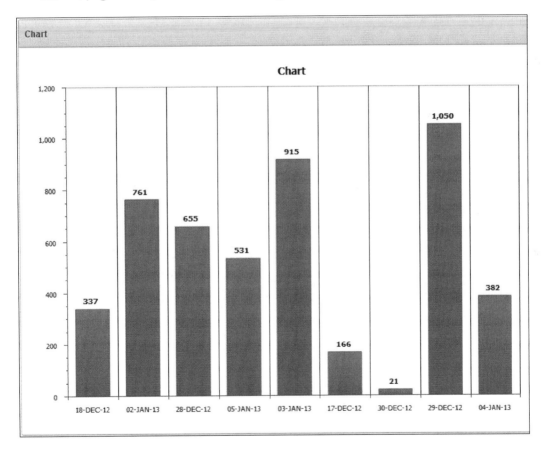

The graph shows the number of recorded latitude-longitude coordinates per day.

## How it works...

The HTML5 rendered charts make use of **Scaled Vector Graphics** (**SVG**), an XML-based file format for graphics.

SVG can also be included in HTML5 documents and the most popular browsers (Internet Explorer, Firefox, Chrome, Safari, and Opera) support SVG. Some of the advantages of SVG are as follows:

- Because it is vector-based, scaling of SVG objects doesn't show artifacts but smooth graphics

- SVG is XML-based which means that everything is described in text and that makes it visible for search engines

- SVG objects can be referenced in the Document Object Model, which makes it easy to apply CSS settings

The big difference between Flash charts and HTML5 charts is that with Flash, you can create 3D charts, whereas this is not possible with HTML5 charts. Below you can find an overview of all possible Flash and HTML5 charts:

| Flash/HTML5 | Type | Name |
| --- | --- | --- |
| Flash | Column | 3D column |
| Flash | Column | 3D range column |
| Flash | Column | 3D stacked column |
| Flash | Column | 3D stacked column(percent) |
| Flash | Column | 2D column |
| Flash | Column | 2D stacked column |
| Flash | Column | 2D stacked column (percent) |
| Flash | Horizontal bar | 3D bar chart |
| Flash | Horizontal bar | 3D range bar chart |
| Flash | Horizontal bar | 3D stacked bar chart |
| Flash | Horizontal bar | 3D stacked bar chart (percent) |
| Flash | Horizontal bar | 2D bar chart |
| Flash | Horizontal bar | 2D range bar chart |
| Flash | Horizontal bar | 2D stacked bar chart |
| Flash | Horizontal bar | 2D stacked bar chart (percent) |
| Flash | Pie & Doughnut | 3D pie |
| Flash | Pie & Doughnut | 2D pie |
| Flash | Pie & Doughnut | 2D doughnut |
| Flash | Scatter | Scatter |

| Flash/HTML5 | Type | Name |
|---|---|---|
| Flash | Line | Line |
| Flash | Candlestick | Candlestick |
| Flash | Gauges | Dial |
| Flash | Gauges | Dial percent |
| Flash | Gantt | Project gantt |
| Flash | Gantt | Resource gantt |
| HTML5 | Column | 2D column |
| HTML5 | Column | 2D range column |
| HTML5 | Column | 2D stacked column |
| HTML5 | Column | 2D stacked column (percent) |
| HTML5 | Horizontal bar | 2D bar chart |
| HTML5 | Horizontal bar | 2D bar range chart |
| HTML5 | Horizontal bar | 2D stacked bar chart |
| HTML5 | Horizontal bar | 2D stacked bar chart (percent) |
| HTML5 | Pie & Doughnut | 3D pie |
| HTML5 | Pie & Doughnut | 2D pie |
| HTML5 | Pie & Doughnut | 2D doughnut |
| HTML5 | Scatter | Scatter |
| HTML5 | Line | Line |
| HTML5 | Candlestick | Candlestick |
| HTML5 | Gauges | Dial |
| HTML5 | Gauges | Dial (percent) |

# 14
# Mobile

In this chapter, we will cover:

- ▶ Creating a smartphone application
- ▶ Creating a hybrid application
- ▶ Creating a list view report
- ▶ Creating a mobile form
- ▶ Using mobile item types
- ▶ Creating a mobile calendar
- ▶ Creating a date scroller with the Mobiscroll plug-in
- ▶ Uploading images using the camera on the device
- ▶ Using jQuery Mobile to fetch current GPS location
- ▶ Creating swipe events

## Introduction

When Oracle announced APEX 4.0, developers were anticipating it to deliver a lot of support for mobile applications. It was expected that developing web applications for smartphone devices would become easier. Even though the introduction of plug-ins and the possibility of using several JavaScript libraries helped a little bit in this matter, it wasn't until Application Express 4.2, that the possibilities really grew.

In this version of APEX, the JavaScript library jQuery Mobile has been embedded into the software itself. This benefits developers, because it is now possible to use the strength of jQuery Mobile directly from the APEX environment.

This chapter will include recipes to show how we can make the most of the features that jQuery Mobile has added to APEX, and how to build smartphone applications using built-in mechanics.

# Creating a smartphone application

In this recipe we will create a basic smartphone application that supports jQuery Mobile.

## Getting ready

The only thing needed is an APEX installation with at least Version 4.2 or higher.

## How to do it...

Creating a smartphone application is pretty straightforward, but there are things to keep in mind. The following steps will show how to create a simple application:

1. Log in to the APEX environment and navigate to **Application Builder**.

2. Click on the **Create** button.

3. Select **Database** and click on **Next**.

4. In the next screen enter an ID and a name for the application, then select **Start from scratch** from the **Create Options** listbox. Lastly, in the **User Interface** listbox select **jQuery Mobile Smartphone**.. After selecting that, click on **Next**.

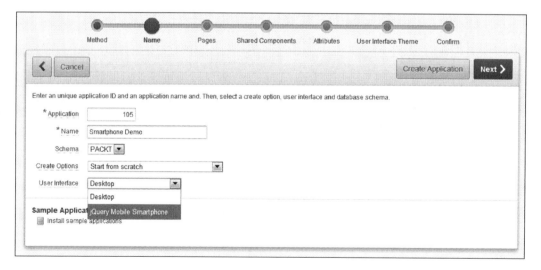

On the next page we find a selection of possible page types. Because we selected **jQuery Mobile Smartphone** as the application type, this list offers only page types that will work in a smartphone application. For instance the **List View and Form** is a special type that shows data in a list view, that is optimized for the small screen of a smartphone.

5.  For now, select **Blank** and name the page Home.

6.  Click on **Add Page** and then **Next** until we reach the **User Interface Theme** page.

    The contents of this page consist only of themes that are applicable for smartphones. Currently there is only one available.

7.  Select **jQuery Mobile Smartphone (Theme 50)** and click on **Next.**

8.  Click on **Create Application**.

And that's all that needs to be done to create a basic application that is optimized for smartphones.

## How it works...

As explained earlier in this chapter, APEX 4.2 has embedded the jQuery Mobile JavaScript library. This set of scripts holds numerous options for developers to create better and more complicated web applications.

When a jQuery Mobile Smartphone application is created in Application Express, the whole environment is optimized for this type of application.

More information on jQuery Mobile can be found at http://jquerymobile.com.

## There's more...

When looking at the contents of the new application, we can see that APEX has automatically created a Page 0 called **Global Page – jQuery Mobile Smartphone**. On this page are some elements that will be used throughout the entire application.

1.  Click on the title of Page 0.

    Notice the 2 regions and 2 buttons that are defined on this page

2.  Click on **Run Application**.

    Since Page 0 cannot be shown by itself, the application automatically goes to Page 1, as shown in the following screenshot:

Even though we never added anything to Page 1, we can still see a header bar with 2 buttons on it; a Home button (indicated by the little house icon) and a **Logout** button. These items and the header bar will always be shown on any page in the application.

Another thing that is noticeable, is that there is no Developer Toolbar at the bottom of the screen. Due to the limitations of a smartphone screen, this would not add value for a developer.

## See also

▸   Refer to the recipe *Creating a list view report* in this chapter for further information on how to make a page with a list view

# Creating a hybrid application

Sometimes, the application that is built needs to be available on different types of devices. One option is to create two different applications, but in APEX you can also create hybrid applications. Hybrid applications can show different pages dependent on the device. If you start the application on a smartphone, you get a different page from that when you start the same application on a desktop computer. We will demonstrate that in this recipe.

## How to do it...

In the following steps we will create the desktop application:

1. In the **Application Builder**, click on **Create**.

2. Click on the **Database** icon.

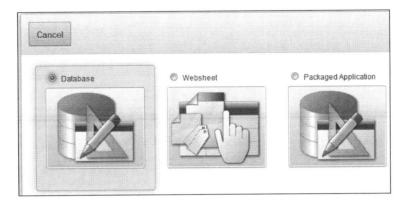

3. In the **Application** text field, enter an application ID or leave the default ID.

4. In the **Name** text field, enter a name for the application or leave the default name.

5. In the **User Interface** listbox, select **Desktop**.

6. Click on **Next**.

7. By default, a home page is added. You can add more pages if you like by doing this with the **Add page** button. Otherwise, click on **Next**.

8. Click on **Next**.

9. In the **Attributes** step, leave the default settings and click on **Next**.

10. Click on the **Theme 26** icon.

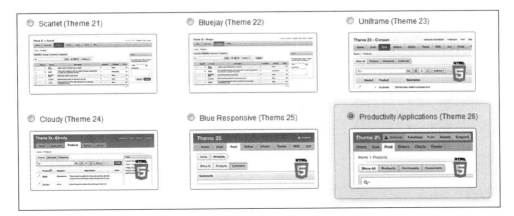

11. Click on **Create Application**.

    The desktop part of the application is ready. Now we will add the mobile part.

12. In the **Application Builder**, click on **Shared Components**.

13. In the **User Interface** section, click on **User Interface Attributes**.

14. At the bottom of the page, in the **User Interface** section, click on **Add New User Interface**.

15. In the **Type** listbox, select **jQuery Mobile Smartphone**.

16. Leave the other settings and click on **Next**.

17. Click on the **jQuery Mobile Smartphone (Theme 50)** icon.

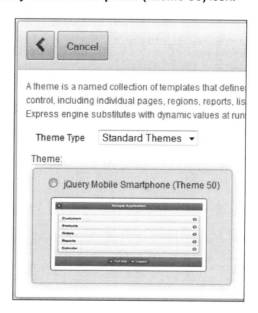

18. Click on **Create**.

The hybrid application is ready now. Try to run the application on different devices, such as a desktop, a laptop computer, or a mobile phone. You will see that you get different pages dependent on the device you are working on. Following is a screenshot taken from a Samsung Galaxy S2 with Android 4.1.2:

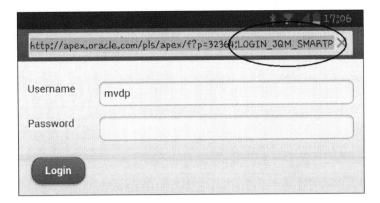

Following is a screenshot of what it would look on a desktop computer:

## How it works...

If you go to **Shared Components** and then **User Interface Attributes**, and scroll down to the bottom, you will see the two user interfaces that are available. Each user interface has its own home page and login page. Each user interface also has its own theme.

APEX can detect which device did the HTTP request. If the device is a mobile device, it will show the mobile home page. If not, APEX will show the home desktop page or login page.

Please note that APEX 4.2 considers tablets as desktop devices, not mobile devices. This means that if you start your newly created application on an Apple iPad, you will see the desktop page. We tested this on an Apple iPad and an Archos 101IT 10.1 Android tablet. In future versions of APEX, it is expected that next to Smartphone and Desktop, the Tablet Application Type will also be introduced.

# Creating a list view report

Reports are a common way of displaying information on a page in Application Express. Mostly a report will show a grid of rows and columns with information. On a smartphone screen, room to show information is limited. For this purpose, a list view is ideal. This recipe will explain how to create a list view report, based on a query from a table.

## Getting ready

We need a jQuery Mobile Smartphone application with an empty page to start this recipe. Also we need access to the EMP and DEPT tables.

## How to do it...

We will now create a list view report on a page in a smartphone application by following these steps:

1. In **Application Builder**, open the empty page where the list view will be created.

2. In tree view, right-click on **Regions** and click on **Create**.

3. Select **Report** and click on **Next**.

4. Select **List View** and click on **Next**.

5. Enter Employees in the **Title** and click on **Next**.

6. In **Region Source** enter the following query and click on **Next**:

```
select  emp.*
,       dept.dname
from    emp
,       dept
where   dept.deptno = emp.deptno
[9672_14_01.txt]
```

   In the following step, several options have to be set that will determine how the list will look. We will just use some of the basics to see how this works.

7. Check the items **Show List Divider** and **Inset List**.

   This will format the page to show groups of information. At step 10 we will select the column that will be the header of the group.

8. At **Text Column** select **ENAME**.

9. At **Supplemental Information Column** select **JOB**.

10. And at **List Divider Column** select **DNAME**.

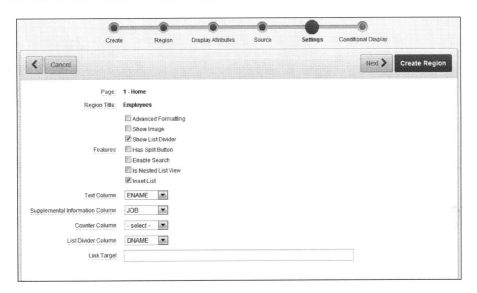

11. Click on **Create Region**.

We can now run the page to see the result. The best way to do this, is to take a smartphone and run the page in a browser as shown in the following screenshot:

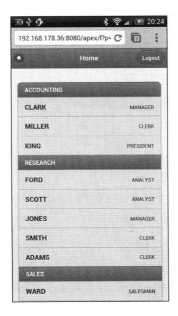

We can see that the list of employees is shown divided into groups of the same department as defined in steps 7 and 10. Next to the name of the employee is his or her current job.

## How it works...

List views are common practice when developing data-centric applications for smartphones. Even the operating systems of all current smartphones use list views to show data, for instance for showing phone settings.

Application Express is no different in this matter. Theme 50 supports a report template for list views, that offers a readable layout with several options to customize it declaratively from the Application Builder.

## There's more...

The list view that we built is a good start, but there are some more possibilities. First of all, it is possible to declare a search option for the region, without any programming.

1. In **Application Builder**, go to the page with the list view region, right-click on the region name and select **Edit Region Attributes**.

2. Check the **Enable Search** option.

3. In the **Search Column** attribute select **ENAME** to allow searching on the employee names.

4. In **Search Type** select **Server: Like & Ignore Case**.

   With this option, the application will search in server side. Furthermore it will disregard upper and lower case differences, and will find all occurrences of the search string even if there are characters before or after. Just like using percentage signs (%) in an SQL select statement.

5. In **Search Box Placeholder** enter `Search Name....`

   This is an **HTML5** option. It will show a text inside the search item, before the cursor is put inside it and the first character is typed.

6. Click on **Apply Changes** and run the page to see the result.

At the top of the page, a new item is created. When the name or a part of the name of an employee is typed, the list will be slimmed down to just the employees that fit the search string.

# Creating a mobile form

Next to showing data, the other most important feature of a database application, is inserting and editing data.

This recipe will show an example of a form that is optimized for use in a smartphone application.

## Getting ready

Before starting this recipe, you should have a jQuery Smartphone Application. The one we created in the previous recipe *Creating a list view report* is very suitable.

Also the EMP table should be available.

## How to do it...

Creating a mobile form is very similar to creating a form on a desktop application, so the first steps might look familiar, out of the rest of the following steps:

1. Navigate to **Application Builder** and open the application that we are going to put the form in.

2. Click on **Create Page**.

3. Select **Form** and click on **Next**.

4. Select **Form on a Table or View** and click on **Next**.

5. In **Table / View Name** select **EMP** and click on **Next**.

6. Make the **Page Number** field to 2 and enter Edit Employee as **Page Name** and **Region Title**.

7. Click on **Next**.

8. Select **Select Primary Key Column(s)** as **Primary Key Type** and select **EMPNO** as **Primary Key Column 1**.

9. Click on **Next**.

10. Select **Existing Sequence** and **EMP_SEQ** as **Sequence**.

11. Click on **Next**.

12. In the list of columns, shuttle all to the right and click on **Next**.

13. Leave all options on their default and click on **Next**.

14. Enter 1 for both the branching options and click on **Next**.

15. Click on **Create** to finish.

When we run the page, we can see a standard form with a list of items to represent the columns that are editable.

## There's more...

Assuming that we are using the application with the list view report that we created in the recipe *Creating a list view report*, we can now enhance the list view with a link to the form in this recipe.

1. Edit the page that holds the list view.

2. Right-click on the region name and select **Edit Region Attributes**.

3. In the item **Link Target** enter the following: f?p=&APP_ID.:2:&APP_SESSION.::&DEBUG.:RP,2:P2_EMPNO:&EMPNO.

   This URL contains the necessary information to navigate to Page 2 (the form page), clears the cache, and passes the primary key as a parameter

4. Click on **Apply Changes**.

When we run Page 1 now, we can see that a small icon was added for every employee in the list view. Pressing this icon navigates to the form, with the information for that employee available for edit as shown in the following screenshot:

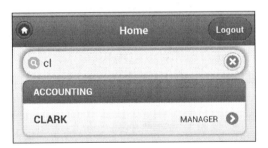

When we click on this icon, we are navigated to the page with the form where we can edit the data for the selected employee as shown in the following screenshot:

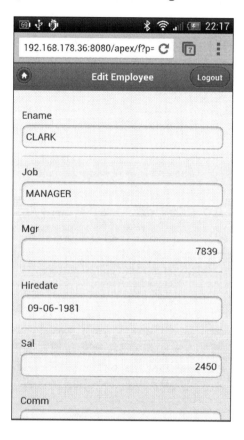

To enhance the user-friendliness of the application, it is possible to change some of the items, through the following steps:

1. Go to **Application Builder** and open Page 2.
2. Right-click on the item **P2_DEPTNO** and click on **Edit**.
3. Change the field **Display As** to **Select List**.
4. In the **List of values definition** enter the following query and click on **Apply Changes**:

```
select  dname  d
   ,       deptno  r
from    dept
[9672_14_02.txt]
```

When we run the page, we can see that the item has changed into a select list, that is automatically styled to fit the smartphone theme.

## See also

▸  The recipe *Using mobile item types* in this chapter explains more on some of the specific item types for smartphone applications

# Using mobile item types

HTML5 and CSS3 offer more possibilities regarding item types. Some of those item types are suitable for smartphone applications as well.

This recipe will explain how to use some of these item types.

## Getting ready

Make sure that a jQuery Mobile Smartphone application with a form is available. For this recipe we will assume that we use the application from the recipe *Creating a mobile form*, based on the EMP and DEPT tables.

## How to do it...

We will change one of the items on the form page, to become a slider item. This type of item is often used on smartphone applications, because it can easily be used with a touch screen.

The item shows a bar with different values, that can be changed by sliding along that bar.

1.  Open Page 2 of the application.
2.  Under the **Edit Employee** region, right-click on the **P2_COMM** item and click on **Edit**.
3.  In **Display As** change the value to **Slider**.
4.  Scroll down to **Settings**.
5.  Change **Minimum Value** to 0.
6.  Change **Maximum Value** to 1000.
7.  Change **Step Increment** to 100.
8.  Click on **Apply Changes**.

We have now created a slider item that will show a range of 0 to 1000 with 10 steps of 100. This can be seen when we run the page as shown in the following screenshot:

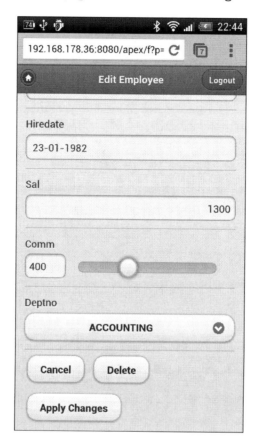

## There's more...

Another HTML5 item type that is available, is the Yes/No type. As its name suggests; it can only be used for fields that require one of two available values, like yes and no, or male and female.

1.  Alter the EMP table to add a column called Gender by running the following statement as the owner of the EMP table from the SQL Workshop:

    ```
    alter table EMP
    add gender varchar2(1);
    [9672_14_03.txt]
    ```

2.  Open Page 2 of the application.

3.  Right-click on the **Edit Employee** region and select **Create Page Item**.

4. Select **Yes/No** and click on **Next**.

5. Enter P2_GENDER as the **Item Name** and click on **Next** twice.

6. On the **Settings** page, change the item **Settings** to **Custom**.

   Four new items will appear.

7. Set **Yes Value** to F and **Yes Label** to Female.

8. Set **No Value** to M and **No Label** to Male.

9. Click on **Next**.

10. In **Source Type** select **Database Column**.

11. The **Database Column Name** automatically changes to **GENDER**. By default, APEX removes the part before the first underscore, and the underscore, so that only the part after the underscore is left. This is a suggestion. If you want to use another column name, change it manually.

12. Click on **Create Item**.

When we run the page, we can now see the item. With a slide, the selection can be changed from **Male** to **Female** and vice-versa as shown in the following screenshot:

## See also

▸   *Chapter 13, HTML5 and CSS3* offers recipes that shows more about HTML5 item types on a desktop browser

# Creating a mobile calendar

It was already possible to create a page of type calendar on a desktop application. Now, with the new jQuery mobile templates, it is also possible to create a calendar page for mobile devices. It should support native mobile device functionalities like swipe and tap-and-hold.

## Getting ready

Make sure you have an empty jQuery Mobile page page with the jQuery theme. You should check if you have access to the APP_EVENTS table.

## How to do it...

With the following steps we will add a Calendar region to a page in a smartphone application:

1. Go to the new empty jQuery Mobile page.

2. In the **Regions** section, click on the Add icon.

3. Click on **Calendar**.

4. Click on **Easy Calendar**.

5. Enter a title for the calendar and then click on **Next**.

6. In the next step, select the APP_EVENTS table in the **Table/View Name** listbox and then click on **Next**.

7. In the **Date Format** radio group, select **Date Only**.

8. In the **Primary Key Column** listbox, select **ID** and then click on **Next**.

9. In the **Link Target** listbox, select **Create new edit page** and then click on **Next**.

10. Click on **Next**.

11. Click on **Create**.

The calendar is ready. Take a mobile device and run the page. The difference with a calendar for desktop is that here you can also get a weekly view or a daily view. And what's even more fun, is that you can swipe over the calendar to step through the months. The day where the event is planned will show a blue dot. When you tap on that date, you will see the event below the calendar. Tap on the event to edit. When you tap-and-hold a day on the calendar, you will be redirected to a page where you can create a new calendar item. You can also tap on the create button to create a new event.

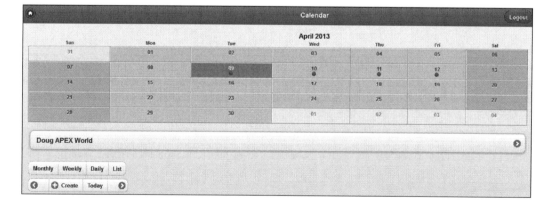

## How it works...

The wizard created two pages, one page for the calendar and one page for the details of the table used. The entire calendar functionality is built-in in the calendar template. It is the basic calendar template in the jQuery mobile theme. You can view the contents by navigating to **Shared Components | Templates | Basic Template**. If you click on the monthly calendar tab, you can see the month close format text area. You can see that APEX makes use of the jQuery functionalities that support swiping and tap-and-hold.

## There's more...

Testing on mobile devices can be annoying or time consuming. You have to type or edit the URL on the small keyboard. You could use a website such as `http://qrcode.kaywa.com` that generates QR codes for you as show in the following figure:

On the website, enter the URL of your APEX application and click on generate.

On your mobile device, download an app like Barcode Scanner by ZXing, that can read those QR codes. By scanning the code, your smartphone will automatically open the website, instead of the user having to type the complete URL.

You can also use a mobile device simulator on your desktop PC or laptop.

# Creating a date scroller with the Mobiscroll plug-in

When you tried to edit the events in the previous recipe, you might have encountered a small issue. On the Apple iOS devices, you get a nice date scroller when you tap on the date field. However, some Android devices don't show any date scroller but just the keyboard, and you have to type in the date yourself. Not very user-friendly. With the Mobiscroll plug-in you can get the same date scroller on Android devices. In this recipe we will show you how to do that.

## Getting ready

We will modify a page that was created in the previous recipe so you need to have completed the previous recipe.

Furthermore you need to download the Mobiscroll plug-in at `http://code.google.com/p/mobiscroll/downloads/list`. There you can find the latest version. We downloaded Version 2.3.1. Unzip the ZIP file and upload the `.css` and `.js` files through the following steps:

1. Go to **Shared Components** and in the **Files** section, click on **Cascading Style Sheets**.
2. Click on **Create**.
3. Click on **Choose file** and locate the `.css` file on your filesystem.
4. Click on **Upload**.
5. Go back to **Shared Components** and in the **Files** section, click on **Images**.
6. Click on **Create**.
7. Click on **Choose file** and locate the `.js` file on your filesystem.
8. Click on **Upload**.

## How to do it...

In the previous recipe, the Calendar wizard created two pages. Locate the Edit Calendar Entry page and click on it in the **Application Builder**.

1. In the **Page** section, click on **Edit**.

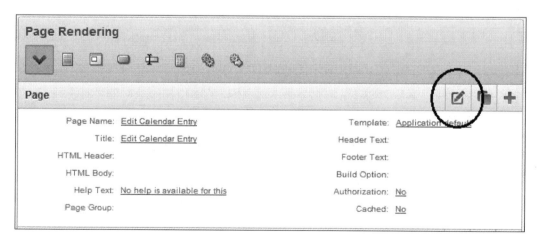

2. Click on the **JavaScript** tab.

3. In the **File URLs** text area, enter the following:

```
#WORKSPACE_IMAGES#mobiscroll-2.3.1.custom.min.js
```

4. In the **Execute when Page Loads** text area, enter the following:

```
$('#PX_EVENT_DATE').mobiscroll().date({
    invalid: { daysOfWeek: [0, 6], daysOfMonth: ['5/1',
'12/24', '12/25'] },
    theme: 'ios',
    display: 'modal',
    mode: 'scroller',
    dateOrder: 'mmD ddyy'
});
[9672_14_40.txt]
```

Where X in PX_EVENT_DATE is the page number you are working on, as replaced with **9**, the page number I am working on, as shown in the following screenshot:

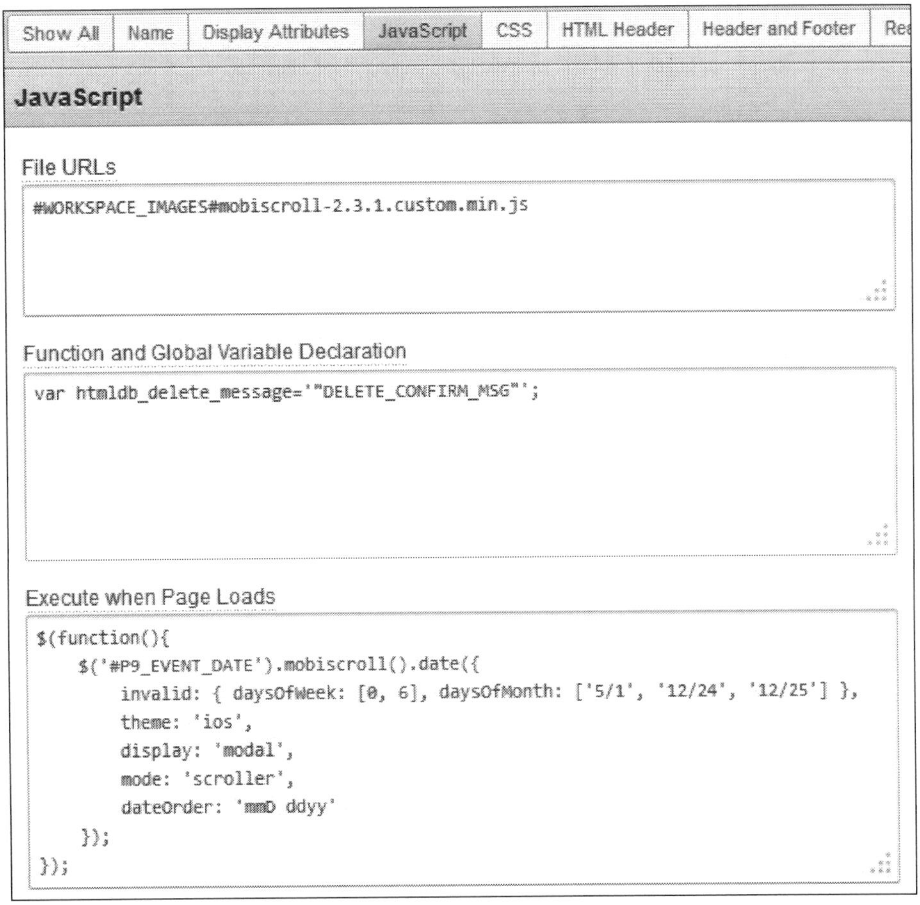

5. Click on the **CSS** tab.

6. In the **File URLs** text area, enter the following code:

   ```
   #WORKSPACE_IMAGES#mobiscroll-2.3.1.custom.min.css
   ```

7. Click on **Apply Changes**.

And that's it. Take your mobile device and go to the edit event page. Tap on the date field and check the date scroller, as shown in the following screenshot:

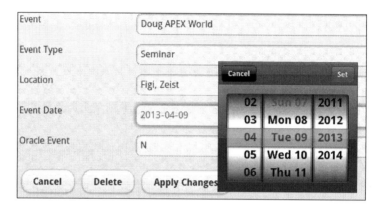

## How it works...

Mobiscroll uses a cascading style sheet to render the nice looking date scroller. The JavaScript library has all the functionality to handle the correct date settings. New in APEX 4.2 is that you can easily reference `.css` and `.js` files. Just enter the name of the files in the appropriate text areas in the page rendering section. Because we uploaded the files via the shared components, we use the `#WORKSPACE_IMAGES#` substitution string to reference the correct location, which is in fact the `WWV_FLOW_FILES` table.

Also new in APEX 4.2 is that you can enter just JavaScript code in the **Execute when Page loads** text area. No `<script>` tags and no `$function()`. In prior releases, you had to use the `$function()` built-in to make sure the piece of JavaScript code is executed after the entire page has loaded.

The date scroller is customizable. You can use different themes like jQuery Mobile (`theme: 'jqm'`) or Android ICS (`theme: 'android-ics'`). You can also choose to always display the date scroller instead of displaying it after the user taps on the date field. Use Inline (`display: 'inline'`) for that purpose.

## There's more...

You can use the Mobiscroll plug-in to display all kinds of scrollers, even with text and images. Please refer to the demo page of Mobiscroll (`http://demo.mobiscroll.com/`).

# Uploading images using the camera on the device

All smartphones have several kinds of hardware on board. One of the most common pieces of hardware is a camera.

In this recipe we are going to see how we can use the onboard camera of a smartphone to take a picture and automatically store it to the database.

## Getting ready

For this recipe we are going to need a jQuery Mobile Smartphone application. And also we need a table to store the data.

The table needs to hold some required columns. They can be created by using the following scripts:

```
CREATE TABLE  "APP_IMAGES"
   (
   "ID" number,
   "PICTURE" BLOB,
   "MIMETYPE" VARCHAR2(255),
   "FILENAME" VARCHAR2(255),
   "IMAGE_LAST_UPDATE" DATE
   ) ;
[9672_14_05.txt]
```

## How to do it...

When the table APP_IMAGES is available, we can start building our form to add data to it by the following steps:

1. Open the application in the **Application Builder**.
2. Click on **Create Page**.
3. Select **Form** and click on **Next**.
4. Select **Form on a table or view** and click on **Next**.
5. Select **APP_IMAGES** in **Table Name** and click on **Next**.
6. Enter Upload image as the **Page Name** and **Region Title**. In this recipe the page number will be 6.
7. Click on **Next**.

8. Set the **Primary Key Type** in **Select Primary Key Column(s)** and select **ID** in **Primary Key Column 1**.

9. Click on **Next**.

10. Select **Existing Sequence** and select a random sequence in the **Sequence** item. The **EMP_SEQ** sequence can be used, for instance.

11. Click on **Next**.

12. Select all columns and click on **Next**.

13. Click on **Next**.

14. Enter an existing page number to branch to, after cancel and submit, and click on **Next**.

15. Click on **Create**.

    The basics of this page have now been created. We could already run the page to see what happens, but we are still unable to save the image. For this we have to take some other steps.

16. Edit Page 6.

17. Right-click on the item **P6_PICTURE** and click on **Edit**.

18. Scroll down to the section named **Settings** and enter values in the following items, as shown in the following screenshot.

    **MIME Type Column** becomes MIMETYPE

    **Filename Column** becomes FILENAME

    **BLOB Last Updated Column** becomes IMAGE_LAST_UPDATE

    **Content Disposition** becomes **Inline**

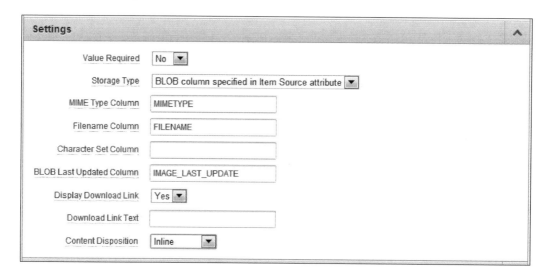

19. Click on **Apply Changes**.

    Now we can run the page on a smartphone to take a photo with the camera and upload it to the table. For this recipe we have used an HTC One X with the Google Chrome browser in Dutch. The screenshots and labels may differ on your device.

20. Take your smartphone and open a browser to navigate to Page 6 in the APEX application.

21. Tap on the button with the label **Select File..** or something similar.

22. If a popup opens, select **Camera** and take the picture, as shown in the following screenshot:

23. After the picture is taken, tap on **Create** to save it to the database as shown in the following screenshot:

The image is now saved in the BLOB item of the APP_IMAGES table. The other items are filled automatically with the right values. Select from the table to see the result, for instance in the SQL Workshop.

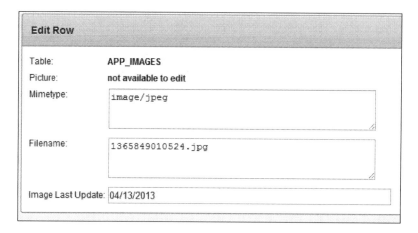

## How it works...

The software on modern smartphones is smart enough to interact with the hardware it is running on. Browsers can use commands in the operating systems to control certain hardware. What APEX does is no different. The browser understands that the command to upload a file can be interpreted to launch the camera application.

What APEX then does is an existing functionality to upload the image file into a `BLOB` column in the table. The other columns are used, so the database knows what kind of file is being uploaded.

## There's more...

We have now used a basic `BLOB` column to hold the image file. It's also possible to use `ORDImage` to automatically resize the picture, for instance to create a thumbnail to show on a report. That would be much friendlier to show on a smartphone screen.

The Oracle documentation at `http://docs.oracle.com/cd/E11882_01/appdev.112/e10776/ch_imgref.htm` has more information on this subject.

# Using jQuery Mobile to fetch current GPS location

Other than the features that can be used declaratively, APEX offers the possibility to call jQuery Mobile code directly. This recipe will show how to do that by creating a page with GPS coordinates for the longitude and latitude of the device on which the application is run.

## Getting ready

For this recipe, you will need a jQuery Mobile Smartphone application, like the one we created earlier in this chapter.

## How to do it...

First we have to have a page that can hold the items.

1. In the **Application Builder** go to the application and click on **Create Page**.
2. Select **Blank Page** and click on **Next**.
3. Enter a number for the new page and click on **Next**.
4. Name the page GPS and add one HTML Region by entering GPS at the item labeled as **1**.

5. Click on **Next**.

6. Click on **Finish**.

7. Click on **Edit Page**.

   We will now add two items to show the coordinates. We assume that the page number for the page we created in the previous steps of this recipe is **4**. Change if necessary.

8. Right-click on the GPS region and select **Create Page Item**.

9. Select **Text Field** and click on **Next**.

10. Enter P4_LATITUDE for the item **Name** and click on **Next** until we reach the last page of the wizard.

11. Click on **Create Item**.

12. Repeat steps 8 to 11 but replace the name of the item with P4_LONGITUDE.

    We now have two items, but we still need a way to fill them with data. For this we are going to add a piece of JavaScript to the page.

13. Right-click on the name of the page and select **Edit**.

14. In the text area labeled as **HTML Header** enter the following code:

```
<script>
navigator.geolocation.getCurrentPosition (function (pos)
{
    var P4_LATITUDE = pos.coords.latitude;
    var P4_LONGITUDE = pos.coords.longitude;
    $("#P4_LATITUDE").val (P4_LATITUDE);
    $("#P4_LONGITUDE").val (P4_LONGITUDE);
});
</script>
[9672_14_04.txt]
```

15. Click on **Apply Changes**.

16. Click on **Run** to see the result, as shown in the following screenshot (the browser might ask for permission to use location data. Accept to continue):

## How it works...

Oracle has integrated the libraries of jQuery Mobile into APEX itself. When we take a look inside the directory structure of APEX on the filesystem, we can see this for ourselves. In the directory `\\apex\images\libraries\` we can find several subdirectories, including one called `jquery-mobile`. Inside it are the contents of one or more versions of the library.

By doing it like this, we can directly call the contents of jQuery Mobile from our code. For instance calling the function `navigator.geolocation.getcurrentposition` like we did in this recipe.

## See also

▶   More information on jQuery Mobile can be found on the website
    `http://jquerymobile.com/`

# Creating swipe events

If you want to create applications for mobile devices, you also might want to support touchscreen specific events like swiping and tap-and-hold. In APEX, it is possible to create such touchscreen events. We will show how to create a swipe left and a swipe right event with dynamic actions in an employee information page.

## Getting ready

You need an existing jQuery Mobile Smartphone application to start with. Make sure you have access to the EMP and DEPT tables.

## How to do it...

First we will create a page.

1. In the **Application Builder**, go to the application you are working on and click on **Create Page**.

2. In the **User Interface** radio group, select **jQuery Mobile Smartphone**.

3. Click on **Blank Page**.

4. Enter a page number or leave it to the default value and click on **Next**.

5. Enter a name for the page, for example, Employee info and click on **Next**.

6. Click on **Finish**.

   The page is created, now we will create an HTML region

7. Click on **Edit Page**.

8. In the **Regions** section, click on the Add icon (the **+** sign).

9. Click on **HTML**.

10. Again, click on **HTML**.

11. Enter a title for the region, for example, Employee info and click on **Next**.

12. Click on **Next**.

13. Click on **Create Region**.

    The region is ready. Now we will create items for the region.

14. In the **ItemsRegions** section, click the Add icon (the **+** sign).

15. Click on the Textfield icon.

16. In the **Item Name** text field, enter PXX_EMPNO (where XX is the page number).

17. Click on **Next**.

18. Click on **Next**.

19. Click on **Next**.

20. Click on **Create Item**.

21. Repeat the item creation steps for ENAME, JOB, HIREDATE, SAL, and DEPARTMENT. Call the items PXX_ENAME, PXX_JOB, PXX_HIREDATE, PXX_SAL, and PXX_DEPARTMENT where XX is the page number).

You can also use the **Create multiple items using tabular form** link at the bottom of the **Create Item** page.

Now we have a page with a region and items. We will now create a page load dynamic action that populates the items with a query.

22. In the **Dynamic Actions** section, click on the Add icon (the **+** sign).

23. Enter a name for the dynamic action, for example, `page_load` and click on **Next**.

24. In the **Event** listbox, select **Page Load** and click on **Next**.

25. In the **Action** listbox, select **Execute PL/SQL Code**.

26. In the **PL/SQL Code** text area, enter the following code(replace XX with the page number):

```
declare
  cursor c_emp is
    select emp.empno
    ,       emp.ename
    ,       emp.job
    ,       emp.hiredate
    ,       emp.sal
    ,       dept.dname
    from    emp
    ,       dept
    where   dept.deptno = emp.deptno
    and     ((:PXX_EMPNO is null and emp.empno = (select min(empno)
from emp))
            or (:PXX_EMPNO is not null and emp.empno = :PXX_
EMPNO));
  --
  r_emp c_emp%rowtype;
begin
  open c_emp;
  fetch c_emp into r_emp;
  close c_emp;
  --
  :PXX_EMPNO       := r_emp.empno;
  :PXX_ENAME       := r_emp.ename;
  :PXX_job         := r_emp.job;
  :PXX_HIREDATE    := r_emp.hiredate;
  :PXX_SAL         := r_emp.sal;
  :PXX_DEPARTMENT  := r_emp.dname;
end;
[9672_14_50.txt]
```

27. In the **Page Items to Submit** text field, enter `PXX_EMPNO, PXX_ENAME, PXX_JOB, PXX_HIREDATE, PXX_SAL, PXX_DEPARTMENT` (where XX is the page number).

28. In the **Page Items to Return** text field, enter `PXX_EMPNO, PXX_ENAME, PXX_JOB, PXX_HIREDATE, PXX_SAL, PXX_DEPARTMENT` (where XX is the page number).

29. Click on **Create Dynamic Action**.

Now we will create the swipe dynamic actions

1. In the **Dynamic Actions** section, click on the Add icon.

2. Enter a name, for example, `swipe_left` and click on **Next**.

3. In the **Event** listbox, select **Swipe Left**.

4. In the **Selection Type** listbox, select **Region**.

5. In the **Region** listbox, select the **Employee info** region you just created.

6. Click on **Next**.

7. In the **Action** listbox, select **Set Value**.

8. Uncheck the **Fire On Page Load** checkbox.

9. In the **Set Type** listbox, select **SQL Statement**.

10. In the **SQL Statement** text area, enter the following query (where XX is the page number):

```
select  emp.empno
    ,       emp.ename
    ,       emp.job
    ,       emp.hiredate
    ,       emp.sal
    ,       dept.dname
from    emp
    ,       dept
where   dept.deptno = emp.deptno
and     emp.empno = (select min(empno)
                        from emp
                        where empno > nvl(:PXX_EMPNO,0));
```
[9672_14_51.txt]

11. In the **Page Items to Submit** text field, enter PXX_EMPNO (where XX is the page number) and click on **Next**.

12. In the **Selection Type** listbox, select **Item(s)**.

13. In the **Item(s)** shuttle, transfer all columns to the right.

14. Click on **Create Dynamic Action**.

15. In the **Dynamic Actions** section, click on the Add icon (the **+** sign).

16. Enter a name for the swipe action, for example, `swipe_right` and click on **Next**.

17. In the **Event** listbox, select **Swipe Right**.

18. In the **Selection Type** listbox, select **Region**.

19. In the **Region** listbox, select **Employee info** region.

20. Click on **Next**.

21. In the **Action** listbox, select **Set Value**.

22. Uncheck the **Fire On Page Load** checkbox.

23. In the **Set Type** listbox, select **SQL Statement**.

24. In the **SQL Statement** text area, enter the following code (where XX is the page number):

```
select  emp.empno
   ,        emp.ename
   ,        emp.job
   ,        emp.hiredate
   ,        emp.sal
   ,        dept.dname
from    emp
   ,        dept
where   dept.deptno = emp.deptno
and     emp.empno = (select max(empno)
                            from emp
                            where empno < nvl(:PXX_EMPNO,0));
```
[9672_14_52.txt]

25. In the **Page Items To Submit** text field, enter PXX_EMPNO.

26. Click on **Next**.

27. In the **Selection Type** listbox, select **Item(s)**.

28. In the **Item(s)** shuttle, transfer all items to the right.

29. Click on **Create Dynamic Action**.

The page is now ready. Run the page and try to step through the employees by swiping to the left, and to the right on your mobile device.

When swiping to the right, the page should show the next employee. The swipe action to the left should show the previous employee.

## How it works...

The swipe actions are supported by jQuery Mobile. APEX supports it by enabling it in the dynamic actions.

When swiping left or right is detected, the dynamic action of type `Setvalue` executes the query and populates the items.

 When you specify a SQL statement as `setvalue` action, the affected items should be mentioned in the same order as the SQL query.

In the SQL statement you can reference page items, but these page items should then be specified in the **Page Items to Submit** text field.

## There's more...

APEX supports more mobile device specific events like Orientation change (when you turn the device), Tap and hold (Tap on an item and hold for a second) and touch events to support drag-and-drop. Refer to the APEX manual to see the details.

Native to applications for mobile devices are page transitions. These are effects that appear when switching from one page to another.

To change the page transition for an application, perform the following steps:

1. Go to **Shared Components** for the application.
2. Click on **Themes**.
3. On the right-hand side of the screen, click on **Edit Theme**.
4. Click on **jQuery Mobile Smartphone**.

5. Scroll down to **Transition Defaults** or click on the tab page with that name.

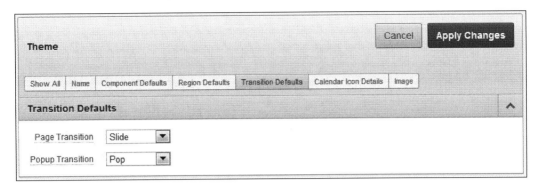

6. Change the listbox for **Page Transition** and **Popup Transition** to a different value.

7. Click on **Apply Changes**.

Now we can run the application to see the effect.

# Index

**Thank you for buying**
# Oracle APEX Cookbook
### *Second Edition*

# About Packt Publishing

Packt, pronounced 'packed', published its first book "*Mastering phpMyAdmin for Effective MySQL Management*" in April 2004 and subsequently continued to specialize in publishing highly focused books on specific technologies and solutions.

Our books and publications share the experiences of your fellow IT professionals in adapting and customizing today's systems, applications, and frameworks. Our solution-based books give you the knowledge and power to customize the software and technologies you're using to get the job done. Packt books are more specific and less general than the IT books you have seen in the past. Our unique business model allows us to bring you more focused information, giving you more of what you need to know, and less of what you don't.

Packt is a modern, yet unique publishing company, which focuses on producing quality, cutting-edge books for communities of developers, administrators, and newbies alike. For more information, please visit our website: www.PacktPub.com.

# About Packt Enterprise

In 2010, Packt launched two new brands, Packt Enterprise and Packt Open Source, in order to continue its focus on specialization. This book is part of the Packt Enterprise brand, home to books published on enterprise software – software created by major vendors, including (but not limited to) IBM, Microsoft and Oracle, often for use in other corporations. Its titles will offer information relevant to a range of users of this software, including administrators, developers, architects, and end users.

# Writing for Packt

We welcome all inquiries from people who are interested in authoring. Book proposals should be sent to author@packtpub.com. If your book idea is still at an early stage and you would like to discuss it first before writing a formal book proposal, contact us; one of our commissioning editors will get in touch with you.

We're not just looking for published authors; if you have strong technical skills but no writing experience, our experienced editors can help you develop a writing career, or simply get some additional reward for your expertise.

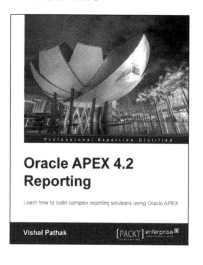

Oracle APEX 4.2
Reporting

Learn how to build complex reporting solutions using Oracle APEX

Vishal Pathak        [PACKT] enterprise 🟥

# Oracle APEX 4.2 Reporting

ISBN: 978-1-84968-498-9        Paperback: 428 pages

Learn how to build complex reporting solutions using Oracle APEX

1. Provides an introduction to the APEX architecture and is a step-by-step guide to setting up the APEX environment on WebLogic

2. Integrations of the reports with the most popular reporting technologies and generation of exotic and typical reports alike

3. Packed with complex APEX applications to help you learn newer ways of fulfilling reporting requirements in APEX

Oracle APEX Best
Practices

Accentuate Oracle APEX development with proven best practices

Learco Brizzi
Iloon Ellen-Wolff      Alex Nuijten     [PACKT] enterprise 🟥

# Oracle APEX Best Practices

ISBN: 978-1-84968-400-2        Paperback: 298 pages

Accentuate Oracle APEX development with proven best practices

1. This book will get you started with Oracle APEX for developing real-world applications that perform and maximize the full potential of Oracle APEX

2. You will also learn to take advantage of advanced SQL and PL/SQL along the way

3. Combines the knowledge of Oracle Apex Experts -- Alex Nuijten, Iloon Ellen-Wollf, and Learco Brizzi

Please check **www.PacktPub.com** for information on our titles

Made in the USA
Middletown, DE
20 April 2017